C000151454

SEX LIVES
OF THE
RICH & FAMOUS

Andrea Love

PRION

First published in Great Britain in 1998 by Carlton Books
This edition published 2004 by

Prion
an imprint of the
Carlton Publishing Group
20 Mortimer Street
London W1T 3JW

Text copyright © Andrea Love 1998
The right of Andrea Love to be identified as the author of
this work has been asserted by her in accordance with the
Copyright, Designs and Patents Act 1998

All rights reserved
This book is sold subject to the condition that it may not be
reproduced, stored in a retrieval system or transmitted in any
form or by any means, electronic, mechanical, photocopying,
recording or otherwise without the Publisher's prior consent

A catalogue record for this book is available from the British Library

ISBN 1 85375 548 6

Printed in Great Britain
by Mackays

CONTENTS

☆ ☆

INTRODUCTION

✩ ✩

Where should we begin? Adam and Eve have a fair claim for consideration, they were right there at the launching, but were they guilty of a sexual exploit?

We are talking affairs and orgies, assignation, seduction and fornication, oomph, lust, desire, erotic, carnal knowledge, bonking, rumpy-pumpy, sensuous, amorous, and voluptuous, provocative sex, but most of all illicit sex!

Artists and actresses, politicians and pop-stars, composers and courtesans, down the centuries so many of these notables possessed that extra vigour. Conquerors and kings, presidents and princesses, headline names whose pulsating, vibrating, excessive energy was spent behind closed doors. Bedroom doors.

The drive providing fame and fortune by day, turned to passion and desire by night. Home was not where they arrived to unwind and relax. They could always find the time, forever prepared to run the risks, and there was never a shortage of erotic and exotic willing partners.

Their sexual urges were phenomenal. The daring, wicked immorality of their illicit romances furnished so much excitement, to players and audience alike, feminine wiles and masculine lechery employed by beautiful women and powerful men. Lord Chesterfield, in one of his famous letters, had this to say:

> *The pleasure is momentary,*
> *the position ridiculous*
> *and the expense damnable.*

Lady Patricia Campbell followed up with this advice:

> *It doesn't matter what you do in the bedroom,*
> *as long as you don't do it in the street and frighten the horses!*

And Hollywood's actor-director and comedian Woody Allen commented:

> *Is sex dirty? Only if it's done right!*

CHAPTER 1

STARS OF STAGE, SCREEN AND SPORT

☆ ☆

Marilyn Monroe

There can be no better place to begin our research than Hollywood, where so many distinguished celebrities arrived during the twentieth century to set up home, earn millions of dollars in the film industry and turn this stretch of Californian countryside into a notorious and fascinating sexual playground. By far the most famous sex symbol to come out of Tinseltown was the voluptuous blonde bombshell Marilyn Monroe. The discreet affairs Marilyn enjoyed during the 1950s and 1960s were snapped up and exposed by today's media. Among her lovers were President Jack Kennedy and his brother Bobby and even the scientist Albert Einstein.

Marilyn was first married at sixteen, and her dreams were already dominated by sex; in one particular recurring scene, she posed and performed a striptease inside a beautiful church watched by the preacher, an organist and a silent but admiring congregation. Such a sexual appetite probably helped her career; "this woman has extraordinary flesh impact," was the Twentieth Century Fox studio's response when she took her first screen test. Marilyn confessed "I think about sex constantly" and described her own love life as "selectively promiscuous."

Marilyn would learn to hate Hollywood – she called the place "an overcrowded brothel" – and that is undoubtedly how she handled the success ladder. Her first patron was producer Joe Shenck. Nearly fifty years her senior, he unkindly recalled, "She was good on her knees – and while she was at it I could fondle those wonderful tits." When her first big film contract was signed and sealed, the woman born Norma Jean Mortenson released her famous sigh and told former flatmate Shelley Winters, "That's the last cock I'll have to suck."

"I don't know if I do it right"

But the man who brought early fame was agent Johnny Hyde. Her best acting roles were evidently the ecstatic orgasms she faked with him, and roles as kept women in *All About Eve* and *Asphalt Jungle* were the result. Marilyn had listed a number of men she planned – or hoped – to seduce. Whether she realized there were two Einsteins we will never know. Albert Senior, the physicist famed for his theory of relativity, would be over sixty when she reached puberty. How was she to know, an Einstein is an Einstein and Albert Junior was also a famous scientist. Shelley later came across a photograph of Einstein signed, "With respect and love and thanks ... Albert." Author Norman Mailer summarized, "She was pleasant in bed, receptive rather than innovative," and she apparently told Marlon Brando, "I don't know if I do it right." One of the first books on Marilyn's life listed Frank Sinatra among her lovers; apparently she would pose suggestively in the nude before huge mirrors while he sang in the background, and she treasured an emerald necklace he sent her.

The making of *Gentlemen Prefer Blondes*, and *How to Marry a Millionaire* six years later, established Marilyn as a sex goddess, and in 1953 she married a real macho man, baseball's Joe Di Maggio, "strong, silent and possessive, but well-endowed and a great lover" she reported. When they divorced, she had a full-length cut-out of Di Maggio installed in a box-room and would go in there, giggling and posturing naked in

BLEACHED OUT

Perhaps her most famous remark came when Marilyn was asked what she wore in bed. "Chanel No 5" was the reply. She was always conscious of her body – when surgeons removing a troublesome appendix bared her stomach, they found a note taped to her skin: "Just a small scar please – and thank you with all my heart ... Marilyn." Both doctors and nurses later reported she was "not blonde all over" but soon afterwards, as the story got round Hollywood, Marilyn started matching her pubic hair with a bleach. When that area became inflamed and infected for all the wrong reasons, it halted her sexual activity for a while.

front of it. Then she wed a complete opposite, intellectual playwright Arthur Miller –
and through this period she suffered two
miscarriages.

There were rumours at the time, but we
now know positively, of her famous affair
with President Kennedy, which began in
1961. Frank Sinatra introduced Marilyn to
buddy and fellow actor Peter Lawford, who
just happened to be the president's brother-
in-law and who provided the entrée to the
White House. "Imagine me as the First
Lady," she jested, claiming she was smug-
gled aboard the presidential jet for the initial high-speed, high-altitude coupling.

THE MAID'S STORY

According to long-serving maid Lena Pepitone, her boss was total-ly uninhibited, belching and farting constantly, and never wearing underwear. In the final months of her life, lonely and depressed, she would trawl the Los Angeles bars. Lena reported Marilyn's handsome chauffeur and her masseur were happy to put in a little overtime to cheer up their employer.

They enjoyed secret assignations at Lawford's beach house in Santa
Monica, and more publicly in suites at the Beverly Hills Hotel. They were
seated together at a charity function where the president slid his hand under
her dress and discovered she most certainly went without panties. Famously,
she sang "Happy Birthday" huskily at his forty-fifth birthday party, a fund-
raising bash at Madison Square Garden, but Jack tired of her and handed
Marilyn over to the Government's Attorney General, brother Bobby. Their
consummation was very much at ground-level, in the back seat of a car on a
beach in California.

Marlon Brando became a lover and a good friend, and to this day he refus-
es to discuss their time together. At thirty-five and anxious about her status,
she had high hopes and a highly publicized affair with French heartthrob
Yves Montand, her co-star in *Let's Make Love*, but he refused to leave his wife
Simone Signoret. Cary Grant, co-star in *Monkey Business*, said of her sexual
impact, "It's nice to know I am happily married." A screenplay was discussed
pairing Marilyn with bosomy Jane Russell as sisters, with Mae West playing
their mother. But the veteran actress said, "I don't play mothers." When she
tried to take her revenge on the Hollywood Brothel – turning up late or not
at all and behaving outrageously on set – she was fired from her last film,
Something's Got To Give. Sleeping pills and barbiturates became her companions and left on her own one Saturday night, she took an overdose. "I don't
seem able to fulfil anyone's total needs," she wrote.

Enrico Caruso

Italy has produced more than its share of hot-blooded lovers and similar quantities of opera singers, and until Pavarotti hit the high notes in recent years, none was more popular than Enrico Caruso. He was the first singer to appreciate the opportunities created by the phonograph – the forerunner of today's LPs, CDs and tape-recordings – and it made him very wealthy.

He escaped the slums of Naples – where he was brought up with no fewer than twenty brothers and sisters – because he volunteered to sing in the church choir. His voice was so melodic it frequently brought ladies in the congregation to tears. Recognizing what this could do in the right setting, a male member of the church hired young Enrico to serenade his loved one. Others followed suit, and Enrico was not slow in identifying opportunities for himself. A podgy little man with a bulbous figure and a ridiculous waxed moustache, his lilting melodies enchanted women by the hundred in Italy, England and America.

Early in his career he was forced to flee from an operatic company when the theatre manager, whose daughter had agreed to marry Caruso, discovered he was regularly bedding a ballerina who was also the opera director's mistress. Both men were eager to get their hands on the popular rising star. He took the ballerina with him but, always attracted to older women, Caruso was soon in love with a dark and sexy co-star, Ada Giachetti, and they set up home together.

She was ten years older, and gave up her own career to take care of Enrico and their two illegitimate sons. He flirted outrageously with his numerous female admirers who wrote constantly suggesting liaisons, and the couple were driven wild by their own jealousies, accusing each other of finding other lovers. After a dozen years of passion, Ada ran off with their chauffeur and Enrico embarked on a torrid affair with her younger sister. The former lovers

THE DEATH OF CARUSO

• • • • • • • • • • • • • • • • • •

Enrico well knew the value of his voice, in terms of finance and romance, yet he was addicted to cigarettes. He would smoke fifty or sixty a day – his favourite was a particular brand of Arab tobacco produced in Cairo. As an antidote, he wore a home-made necklace of anchovies, stringing together slivers of the pickled and salted fish to wear around his throat. Though he carried on singing throughout his life, a lung infection claimed him in the end and he died from pleurisy aged forty-eight.

• • • • • • • • • • • • • • • • • •

remained at loggerheads – she accused Caruso of stealing all her jewellery and he was forced to settle out-of-court, granting her a monthly allowance.

The Monkey House Scandal

A succession of mistresses in America and Europe kept Caruso very busy and extremely fit, but his greatest fame was achieved in 1906, not on stage but in court. Walking through Central Park in New York, he was arrested and accused of pinching a strange woman's bottom. The case became known as the Monkey House Scandal, and the city's newspapers accused the opera star – who always maintained his innocence – of being "an Italian pervert whose aim is to seduce innocent American ladies".

The victim was thirty-year-old Hannah Graham, who refused to go into the witness box. The police officer who made the arrest had a history of filing false charges, and admitted in court he was not only a personal friend of the victim, he had also been best-man at her wedding. Then a mystery woman gave evidence from behind a white veil stating Caruso had fondled her breasts at the Metropolitan Opera House, and a police commissioner's testimony referred to a file showing Caruso was a frequent molester of women. He was convicted, fined and went into hiding. However, his eventual return to the New York stage was a triumph.

PIQUED PUCCINI

Caruso's most celebrated part in opera was playing Rudolfo in Puccini's *La Boheme*, and the composer became jealous of the singer's beautiful voice. The young Neopolitan, known for his sweet nature on and off-stage, eventually sang all the leading tenor roles from every opera, in Milan, London and New York. But when Tosca made its premier in the year 1900, Puccini had deliberately excluded any role for a tenor in his magnificent new opera. Caruso pointedly included an aria from Tosca in his very first recording.

Apart from eighteen months when his voice broke down, Enrico Caruso was feted for twenty-five years, but many affairs ended when his partners complained of being "worn out by his constant energy." At the age of forty-five, entirely out of character, Enrico surprised everyone by marrying twenty-five-year-old prim and proper Dorothy Benjamin, the daughter of an old, established New England family who instantly disinherited her. They were a devoted couple and before he died, she bore him a daughter.

Elvis Presley

The sexual potency of his performances – whether on stage, on film or on record – made the poor, black-haired boy from Mississippi into the most popular singer of the twentieth century, and in his prime, he was far and away the biggest money-earner in show business. Newspaper columnist Hedda Hopper described the former lorry driver as "a woeful menace to teenage girls", while preachers up and down America made character assassinations they had previously reserved for the Devil himself. Elvis used his voice, his guitar, and most of all his hips to drive his female fans wild. Doctors described their collective behaviour as "erotomania", and they drove themselves into a frenzy masturbating in public, in the auditorium.

The first hundred girls ...

A record producer who went on to sign up Sir Swivel Hips had often told colleagues, "If we could find a white boy with a negro's voice and a negro's style with lyrics, I promise you we could all make a fortune." When the teenage Elvis, fresh out of high school, sent him a $4 trial-record – originally a birthday present for his mother – it was a dream come true. Before he reached twenty-one, Elvis had banked his first million dollars and bonked his first hundred girls.

The background to his singing style was Gospel Church meetings. Throughout his life he remained a devout Christian and rarely missed Sunday services wherever he went. "If what they say is true about my singing, I'd be some kind of sex maniac and rightfully locked away in an institution," Elvis admitted. His career rocketed in the late 1950s, and he set up home in a huge mansion he called Graceland, outside

FAKING FLORIDA

In 1955, Elvis Presley's stage-act had already attracted so much media attention that Florida's state attorney entertained a police request that he be ordered to "perform without moving", and slapped the singer with a restriction order. Colonel Tom Parker considered cancelling all his scheduled concert appearances in Florida, but Elvis went out, sang, and stood still, while his shrewd manager milked the court order for all the considerable publicity it was worth.

Memphis, Tennessee. Then he went into the Army for his two-year National Service and was posted to Germany, where he met the young girl who would become his wife and later a very sexy film star.

Priscilla was only fourteen, the daughter of an officer in his unit, and Elvis persuaded her father to send her to Memphis when he was demobbed. She completed her formal education then went to finishing school, all the time being groomed to take her place at the singer's side. They were married when she reached twenty-one. They were going to bed together long before that, but Priscilla conceived on honeymoon and exactly nine months later Lisa Marie was born. That was the formal side of his sex life. For several years Elvis had stayed away from the concert tours, previously an ever-ready source of bed-mates, but then Hollywood beckoned, offering a new and very fertile hunting ground – and 'Cilla nearly always stayed at home.

MIRRORS & MOVIE CAMERAS

In his twenties, Elvis would take two or three women to bed in a day. This ole Southern boy had a two-way mirror in his bedroom, watching others having sex to help turn him on, and he video-taped his own performance for later viewing, or watched the live-action in a ceiling mirror above his bed. Later in life his drug-habit dampened his sex drive, and frequently frustrated the women who had arrived with only one thing in mind. But the Memphis Mafia soon learned how to deal with the complaints from these unviolated ladies they had so recently recruited.

The Memphis Mafia

Out in California, hundreds of young women leaped into his bed. Most were unknowns, waitresses and receptionists, secretaries and shop assistants, but there were a scattering of hopeful starlets and a sprinkling of leading actresses. Tuesday Weld, a pouting nymphet, was just developing her career when her name was linked with Elvis. Juliet Prowse was in the same mould, and Ann Margret had only just arrived on the west coast, an export from Europe. These alleged affairs were kept quiet at the time – the Memphis Mafia were adroitly covering his tracks. Elvis could never go out, could never do his own romancing, so the bodyguards picked his partners and there were hundreds more who turned them down, thinking their approach was a wind-up. If only these women had known. Just before he married, Elvis told his parents he had slept with a thousand women, and promised to be faithful. He had no chance.

But 'Cilla wasn't daft. She knew what was going on, and felt suffocated by her home life at Graceland. She fell for the man who taught her judo and six years after their wedding, she divorced Elvis with a modest $2 million settlement. He increasingly turned to drugs, but soon a local girl moved in, Linda Thompson, the tall and very shapely reigning Miss Tennessee. She was a virgin – very important for Elvis – and devoted, and only left him when he started to prefer three-in-a-bed sessions with Linda playing a minor role.

Another local lass and beauty queen followed Linda, nineteen-year-old Ginger Alden, who held the rather minor title of "Miss Memphis Traffic Safety of 1976." She followed the pattern of willowy women with long legs and firm buttocks. Older women held no attraction for Elvis, and big feet were a total turn-off. The drugs – all manner of drugs, but mostly pills – got to him in the end, and he resorted to getting his kicks from watching a pair of prostitutes performing together, as long as they were pretty, slim and had small feet. Grossly overweight, he died aged forty-two from a heart attack.

Bette Davis

When she set her eyes on a man she wanted in her bed, Bette Davis made sure of the conquest. After her screen career, which always came first, sex and plenty of it was the most important aspect of her existence. The conduct of her private life was outrageous. She had at least five abortions during and in-between her four marriages, dozens of affairs, and at the height of her fame she loved to pick-up home-coming servicemen for quick and casual sex. She won two treasured Oscars in her early days in films, but her famed bitchiness meant she had many enemies in Hollywood. Perhaps they were the reason she was later nominated for another seven Academy Awards in a period of only nine years, but won none of them.

> ## A BIOLOGICAL NEED
>
> ● ● ● ● ● ● ● ● ● ● ● ● ● ● ● ● ●
>
> Bette's sexual psychology intrigued one of her lovers, director Vincent Sherman. "She obviously needed sexual release but there wasn't a great deal of foreplay or afterplay," he confided. "I don't think she liked feeling vulnerable or submissive during sex, I think she resented it and deeply distrusted men. Sex was a biological need for her and when it wasn't there, all the nervous energy you saw in her was because her sex drive had no outlet."
>
> ● ● ● ● ● ● ● ● ● ● ● ● ● ● ● ● ●

Davis's most enduring role was probably playing opposite Joan Crawford, her screen sister, in *Whatever Happened to Baby Jane*. There was no love lost between the two great stars, and their mutual distrust and distaste for each other was apparent as they made the film. The reasons for their feud went back nearly thirty years. Joan was engaged to Franchot Tone and later married the highly-sexed actor, who was known as "Jack the Ripper" in his university days because of all the panties he ripped off young women in the back seat of his car. Tone and Bette Davis made the film *Dangerous*, which won her the first Oscar playing an ageing alcoholic star, and she was determined to have him. Producer Harry Joe Brown walked into her dressing room and caught the couple in the throes of making love; they hadn't even bothered to lock themselves in. The producer apologized, the actor laughed and Bette, returning to the action, merely said, "Close the door as you go out."

The young actress could look truly stunning in the middle of an affair, and she loved to get laid by her leading men, occasionally turning her charms on the studio's more senior operators. Many years earlier, Bette had auditioned for a young director, William Wyler, and the wardrobe mistress sent her on stage in a tight-fitting, low-cut cocktail dress. The director said loud enough for everyone to hear, "What do you think of these dames who show their tits and think they can get the job?"

Sexual sparks

He turned her down for that part, but they were to work together on *Jezebel*, which brought the second Oscar, and she fell in love. Their affair brought the best out of her acting. "I adored Willie, he was the only male strong enough to control me," she later admitted, "the sexual sparks were there from the very beginning but on stage, I could really hate him." Her next film brought her up against Errol Flynn, and she surprised everyone by spurning every advance he made. She had no respect for his rumoured bisexuality or his unprofessional approach to acting. She was married, but both husband and director-lover were away, and Bette Davis needed regular and frequent sexual exercise. At a party she met studio and airline owner Howard Hughes, and went to bed with him on their first date.

Hughes often suffered "first-time nerves", and was shy and fumbling, even impotent, until Bette got to work on him. He was so grateful that the next time he decked out his bedroom with dozens of gardenias. They covered the bed and for years the actress swore she could always smell their scent whenever she made love. She became more brazen, and took Hughes to her home in Coldwater Canyon. In New York, her husband Ham Nelson heard about Bette's latest affair. He returned home secretly, ran a microphone under the bed and, from the basement, recorded the lovers having sex. The tape earned him a $70,000 pay-off from Hughes, and a divorce from his wife.

A NARROW ESCAPE

Bette had a narrow escape when her lover at the time, well known in Hollywood and married like herself, failed to turn up at a hotel they had booked in false names in Acapulco. The actress went instead to stay at the Mexican house of a well-known Californian hostess, the Contessa di Frasso, who was still wed to an Italian nobleman, and was known to be friendly with the dictator Benito Mussolini and the gangster Bugsy Siegel. She was being watched by the F.B.I., who switched their surveillance to Bette Davis when she showed up. She never knew and fortunately, she was unaccompanied.

Sustenance from the Canteen

In 1942, with America locked in war with Germany and Japan, Bette Davis helped launch the Hollywood Canteen, a servicemen's club on Cahuenga Boulevard where soldiers, sailors and airmen on leave could drink and dance and mingle with the stars who called in each night. An affair with Gig Young as they made *Old Acquaintance* was cut short when he was drafted into the Navy, but the Canteen was always there when frustration threatened. Bette took to calling in five or six nights a week, blatantly taking her pick from the hordes of men surrounding her. Actor Jack Carson asked one soldier, "What's the attraction?" and the man replied, "I hear she screws like a mink."

Her second husband became an alcoholic, and died when he fell and fractured his skull. Not long after she married William Sherry, he was propositioned by Joan Crawford, still trying to get her own back for the Franchot Tone incident. He was an out-of-work artist and a suspected gold-digger, and at the age of thirty-nine Bette had her first child. Three years later they were divorced. When she began working on *All About Eve*, she met Gary Merrill. "I had feelings of almost uncontrollable lust," he said later, "I walked around with an erection for three days." He was married and their liaisons were supposed to be secret, but her child's nanny revealed, "He would come over late and I'd hear the bed going up and down all night."

> ## A ROLL IN THE HAY
>
> • • • • • • • • • • • • • • • • •
>
> Bette was always nervous of playing in comedy, and in June Bride she was uncomfortable with the male star Robert Montgomery. She publicly accused him of "copping a feel under the hay" as they rode on a farm wagon for one scene. It turned out to be fleas; he wasn't lusting after her, merely scratching.
>
> • • • • • • • • • • • • • • • • •

As soon as he obtained a divorce, Bette made him husband No 4. They adopted a son and daughter, but were divorced after ten years of marriage.

The actress then labelled sex as "God's joke on humanity". Four years passed before another man came into her life – "a homosexual who just needed a real woman to point the way," she told friends. He was twenty-seven, Bette fifty-six, and they soon broke up. She then met actor Richard Tate, but they too shared a thirty-year age difference. He admits introducing her to cannabis and the first time they went to bed, they virtually stayed there for "three days and four nights." Bette Davis remained sexually active into her sixties, and died at the age of eighty-one.

Jack Johnson

World boxing's first black heavyweight champion was blamed for race riots right across America in the early 1900s. As he flattened white men inside the ring and floored the white women who flocked to his fights and his bedside, police claimed the riots induced by Jack Johnson led to nineteen deaths in seven years. He was a magnificent prize-fighter, invincible in his prime, and arguably the most hated sports personality who ever performed in the United States.

Johnson was only twelve when he ran away from home in Galveston, Texas. His early teens were spent in New Orleans, Philadelphia, New York and Chicago, and when he discovered a natural ability with his fists, he decided to develop that and earn a living at country fairs and side-shows, taking on all-comers for five and ten dollars a time. A natural scrapper, he began his professional career at seventeen, losing only seven times in 113 bouts. Jack's first and only black wife was Mary Austin, a girl he met at school, but she hated boxing. He set up home with a stunning black girl, Clara Kerr, who robbed him of all his money and possessions when she ran off with one of his friends, but he never forgot her. Many years later, he heard she was accused of killing her husband, and paid for her lawyers. When she was acquitted on gounds of self-defence, he bought her a bar.

Dominating the boxing ring at home, he taunted racist whites in segregated America, and worst of all flaunted the white women who took his arm. Magazines carried his pictures, silk-suited and sipping champagne through his personal gold flute, or driving

A STIFF SENTENCE

Jack Johnson's behaviour – or alleged behaviour – with the willing white ladies of America so upset their menfolk that there was a concerted effort to nail him. Police had to resort to the Mann Act, imposed to prevent white slavery, that said transporting a woman across state boundaries for immoral purposes was a federal crime. The vengeful Belle Schreiber testified, on oath, that the black boxer had driven her from one state to another on several occasions. "This was for unlawful sexual intercourse, for prostitution, for unnatural sexual acts and all kinds of immoral purposes," said Belle, without adding any descriptions of the alleged crimes. Out on bail, he was forced to flee to Europe. When he returned five years later, after losing his title to a 25th-round knock-out, Johnson was gaoled for twelve months in Leavenworth Prison, where he became athletics coach.

his huge sports car. But he managed to stay fit for the ring while living the life of a socialite. Newspapers eagerly reported his affairs with beautiful white women. In Chicago, where he made his home, Jack appeared on stage – first in cabaret, then taking the part of Othello in Shakespeare's play.

Hattie McLay was an Irish girl living in New York who was by his side when he won the coveted heavyweight title. Jack Johnson was thirty and had to go all the way to Sydney, Australia, to meet the holder Tommy Burns. However, Hattie started sleeping with Jack's manager, then hit the bottle. Jack fell for a whore, Belle Schreiber, who worked in Chicago's famed and classy cat-house, the Everleigh Club. She cost $50 a time until she moved in to live with him, and accompanied Jack to San Francisco where he was due for a big fight. Hattie read about the boxing promotion and arrived in the hope of a reconciliation. The women fought over their champion, who offered to keep the peace and sleep with each in turn every night.

PSYCHO BABBLE

As Johnson infuriated white America, psychologists and writers theorized that men "felt threatened by the negro's gigantic penis, the object of their own women's fantasies." The target of their jealousy played his part in full, appearing in public at training sessions, with sparring partners, and at big fight weigh-ins with bandages stuffed down the front of his skintight trunks. He looked enormous.

Out of the frying pan ...

Reporters, never far from this natural source of news, heard about the arrangement and lay in wait with their photographers. Jack needed to get back to his training quarters so after his double act, he used to slide down a rope from Belle's room at the rear of the hotel. According to a story which appeared years later, the hotel owner's daughter intercepted the famous boxer and his even more famous private parts, and grabbed him right there as he descended the rope. "She got frantic, she wanted the feel then the sight of my manhood and I was forced to satisfy her."

Three times a night was no preparation for a fight, even for a world champion, and when he refused the girl the next night, she told her furious father Johnson had raped her. He paid off the man to avoid the bad publicity, duly won the fight and was soon in love again, this time with Etta Duryea, a blonde who became his first white wife. When news broke of his forthcoming marriage to a white woman, a senator from Georgia railed in Washington, "This is an outrage, a degrading and infamous outrage." Wealthy and well-connected, she became a social outcast when they married in Pittsburgh. Three years later, in 1912, she committed suicide.

Lucille Cameron, a nineteen-year-old white lass from St Paul, was his next wife and Johnson was threatened, more than once, "if you ever return south, a public lynching will surely be the outcome." Then he was arrested on a trumped-up morality charge.

European exile

The couple spent five years in exile in Europe, where he continued fighting and carried on courting the white women who found him so fascinating. Paris was very much his scene, and a fling with leading actress Gaby Deslys was followed by an affair with Mistinguett, a dancer with the Folies Bergere. In Germany the woman who would be executed as a spy, Mata Hari, became a short-term lover, then back home in Hollywood, screen star Lupe Velez fell for his charms. Divorce from Lucille was followed by yet another white-wedding, and another blonde, Irene Pineau.

Life ended for Jack Johnson at the ripe old age of sixty-eight, and he was buried in Chicago beside the grave of Etta Duryea, who had shot herself thirty years earlier.

Clara Bow

The first of Hollywood's famous screen goddesses, from the age of twenty Clara Bow developed a lifestyle to match her studio image. But the leading lady never tried too hard to conceal her insatiable appetite for strong men and long-lasting sex. These were the carefree 1920s, and Clara went slightly too far when she reportedly took the University of Southern California's football team to bed. Not all at once of course, but the Trojans, as they were known, would go back to her home for after-match parties which turned into orgies inside and naked touch-football games on the lawns outside. When their form dropped off, coach Howard Jones ordered the team to stay away from Clara's home in Bedford Drive, Beverly Hills, "individually and collectively".

Even before the Depression hit America, father Robert had difficulty finding jobs and mother Sarah, from whom Clara inherited her good looks and sex appeal, put food on the table by entertaining gentlemen at home in Brooklyn, New York. Daughter was locked in the cupboard on these occasions, but she was growing up fast. At seventeen she entered a magazine beauty competition. She won, and the first prize was a screen test in the rapidly developing movie business out in Los Angeles and a small part in the film *Beyond The Rainbow*. Clara landed a contract in the biggest studio of them all, Paramount, worth a breath-taking $7,500 a week. Five years later, she was Hollywood's leading box-office idol.

Clara starred in some amazingly-titled films, like *Rough House Rosie*, *Call Her Savage*, *Mantrap* and *Dangerous Curves*, but it was her performance opposite Gary Cooper in a film simply called *It*, that earned her the label she would carry for the rest of her days, the "It girl". She was a looker with won-

---

BAD PUBLICITY

The Roaring Twenties had seen Clara emerge as Hollywood's leading female star, but in 1931 Paramount Studios had to suspend her films after a blaze of bad publicity. She accused her secretary Daisy de Voe of falsifying signatures on cheques and embezzling $15,000. At trial, the judge would not allow Daisy's lawyers to introduce evidence of Clara's wild sex life, so before she went to gaol for a year, Daisy sold her story to a New York newspaper. Among the stories of their screen-favourite's frolics at home, readers learned she had stripped off and publicly performed for friends with her dog Duke, a Great Dane.

derfully promising eyes, but talking movies arrived at the height of her fame, and a squeaky Brooklyn twang coupled with her scandalous love-life brought early retirement by the time she reached thirty.

Double the sex for a better night's sleep

Clara was a chronic insomniac, but she soon learned how to avoid becoming bored in bed and discovered she actually adored the exercise. Two different men in two different beds in two entirely different houses was not a rare escapade. One of her first Hollywood lovers and the director of some of her earliest movies, Victor Fleming, suspected Clara did not go straight home when she left him. The older and vastly experienced director, who thought he was teaching his brilliant pupil a few sexual wiles, had her followed and discovered she often called on younger stunt-men and film extras for another bout of sex before returning home. There were times when she picked up men on the street if she saw one she fancied and happened to be in the mood, which was most of the time.

Broadway producer Harold Richman did the same thing. He bragged about his romance with Clara, "The only woman I have ever had who could keep up with me in bed," and she publicly retorted, "Keep up? I leave him way behind." Playing in New York was no different. On the way home from Harold's bed, detectives told him she frequently called on another lover.

SUICIDAL SAVAGE

Bob Savage was a hopeful journalist and would-be poet, the son of an East Coast millionaire, and he had a brief and wild fling with the star while ignoring her reckless love-life. When she refused to marry him, Savage slashed his wrists and left the blood pouring over her signed photograph. He was saved, but when Clara heard about the suicide attempt, she told a press conference, "He's got to be kidding, real men use pistols."

She worked just as hard as she played, turning out six or seven films nearly every year. A New York film critic praised her role in *Mantrap* saying, "She could flirt with a grizzly bear," and Clara carried this screen-image into real life, frequently indulging in three-in-a-bed sessions.

Gilbert Roland, co-star in *The Plastic Age*, singer Eddie Cantona and actors Bela Lugosi and John Gilbert were among her early conquests. Gary Cooper later said their reported romance was a publicity stunt for the *It* film, but Clara's version was somewhat different. She talked of Gary joining her in the bath with her two dogs and gave a very vivid description, and high marks, for both his equipment and performance. Paramount had failed to insert a morality clause in her contract so they added a "contingency bonus" to all her films and hung on to the money, hoping to ensure her good behaviour. "It don't make sense," said Clara. "If a man does it he's a stud. If a girl does it she's a slut."

A Texas doctor, William Pearson, took out her appendix in an emergency operation as she filmed *Three Weekends*, then left home and moved in with his patient. But the wronged wife filed for divorce, sued Clara for alienation of affections, and the studio had to buy her off with $56,000 of Clara's bonus-money. The star had at least one abortion, but finally she married actor Rex Bell who made a series of westerns, and they had two sons. They parted, but Clara had salted enough of her earnings away to live comfortably until she died aged sixty.

Gary Cooper

There were times in the 1920s, '30s and '40s when it seemed every woman in California was hell bent on achieving a common ambition. They all wanted to lay Gary Cooper, the soft-voiced, hard-muscled actor who was probably the most famous screen cowboy of all time. At the height of her fame on Broadway and in the London theatre, the husky-voiced beauty Tallulah Bankhead was asked why she was going to Hollywood and she replied, "first for the money, second to make movies, and lastly to f**k that divine Gary Cooper."

He was not a shy man, but when he was starting out in films, Gary Cooper's approach to a new relationship was invariably as the reticent and restrained partner who had to be persuaded by the woman he had targeted.

OUT IN THE OPEN AIR

Gary Cooper made the film It in 1927 with Clara Bow. During filming and in the midst of a wild affair, she apparently told Hedda Hopper, the Hollywood gossip columnist, "That man is hung like a horse and you know what, he can go all night long." She also admitted they both preferred to make love in the open air, driving up into the hills by day or on to the beach beside the Pacific at night.

"It worked every time," said director Howard Hawks. "You would see him having this reluctant conversation with a girl, hanging his head, looking at his feet and pawing the ground like a nervous stallion. And you knew, you just knew, they were on their way." No matter how big or how small the part, every woman who came on to the set to work with Gary Cooper was fair game and married or single, they were usually just as eager to get started.

His father went out to America from England in the 1880s, and though he was a successful lawyer, bought a ranch in Montana where Gary grew up. Those days working with the ranch hands set him up for a career which began as a stuntman, falling off horses, and led to two Oscars, for *Sergeant York* and *High Noon* – rated by film historians as the finest western ever made – and to nominations for *The Virginian* and *The Plainsman*. He was constantly at work and at play, and after they made *Farewell to Arms*, Helen Hayes said, "I was ready to leave my husband and my home if only he had said the word."

Something else

Gary Cooper was signed up to Paramount Studios, who had sexual wildcat Clara Bow on their books. They partied on and off set making *It* in 1927, then he moved on to the Mexican spitfire Lupe Velez when they were set to play opposite each other in *Wolf Song*. Miss Velez said later, "I couldn't wait, neither could he. We were introduced, spoke a few words and that same evening we went straight at it. He was something else in bed." They might have whispered behind closed doors, but outside their furious rows were a renowned source of hot gossip for columnists and led to Gary having a nervous breakdown.

The studio sent him abroad to recover. In Rome he met a beautiful but older American woman who had married into Italian nobility. The Contessa Dorothy di Frasso decided the screen cowboy was patently in need of some good, old-fashioned European culture. He repaid her kindness so well that she accompanied him to Hollywood when it was time to go back to work.

Then he found a wife outside the world of acting, and married an East Coast socialite Veronica "Rocky" Balfe. He conceded, "I am happy to leave that other life, the playboy role, it's in the past," but his bride insisted the word "obey" be omitted from their wedding vows. It suited both parties. Gary Cooper was a still a playboy at heart and from the start the couple lived their own lives, even to the extent of staying in different hotels when they holidayed together.

Before they were paired on set, Marlene Dietrich, the smouldering German actress with the ultra-sexy voice, came under Gary's spell. Despite the recent marriage, Marlene's own man John Gilbert was convinced she had fallen in love with Cooper and hit the bottle with a vengeance. The news he had dreaded was announced from Paramount, that the two were going to make *Desire* together, and John Gilbert drank himself steadily

ENTRANCING INGRID

He co-starred with Ingrid Bergman in *Saratoga Trunk*, and though their steamy affair was suspected in Los Angeles, the studio's publicity department managed to keep it a secret from the public. The Swedish-born actress, with her clean good looks and natural charm, had been packaged as the perfect woman and when filming finished, studio chiefs were so worried – anticipating a double-divorce – that they held up the box office release for two years. Years later she confessed, "I was no different to every other woman who played opposite Gary, we all fell in love with him."

into oblivion that night. His body was found the next morning.

During the years of the Second World War, Cooper briefly turned to politics, campaigning for the Republican Thomas Dewey. Back in Tinsel Town he was soon in the middle of another affair with rising young star Patricia Neal. It lasted for more than a year but faded before he could obtain a legal separation from Rocky, a Catholic who had given him a daughter, Maria, and to whom divorce was out of the question. There were more brief flings before the couple were reunited, and Gary Cooper was forced to acknowledge his advancing years. Film critics panned his role as Audrey Hepburn's paramour in *Love in the Afternoon*; she was in her early twenties and he was fifty-six. The reviews drove him off to a private clinic for a facelift, but three years later he died, from cancer of the spine.

Janis Joplin

The singer who came to fame with a San Francisco rock group called Big Brother and the Holding Company once tried to pacify an unruly audience, "My music ain't supposed to make you wanna riot, it's supposed to make you wanna f**k!" Janis Joplin was America's wild woman of the 1960s pop-scene. Men reacted to her performance the way women reacted to Elvis Presley, but her demands were too much for most of the men in her own life. On a 72-hour rail journey across America, she complained "I've only had fifty of the men riding on this train, maybe I should make it a round trip and have a few more."

Another time, as she left the stage at a Californian rock concert, Janis said, "Why is it if I'm such a big star, I can't even get laid." That was not remotely true, but the men she laid rarely stayed around her for long. This was certainly a hangover from the days when she found herself alone and without the price of a meal or a joint, in San Francisco in 1961. She tried prostitution, but even at five dollars a time, she could not find enough clients and later recalled this episode in her life. "I would have f**ked anything, sucked anything, taken anything, and when I had the money I did. I swallowed it, shot it up, smoked it, licked it, you name it."

Janis returned home and started to build her reputation around the southern states, then blasted to stardom with Big Brother. According to her, the rock band, which was obviously going places, sent an agent with strict orders to get her into bed and put her under contract. Janis forever boasted, "I got f**ked into Big Brother, they wanted me that bad as their lead singer." It was a good deal all round. She and the band were a revelation at the original Monterey Pop Festival, and their album *Cheap Thrills* pushed them to the top of the charts.

Janis was a true artist. As a teenager she could write, she could paint and she quick-

THE UGLIEST MAN

At High School the girls held a competition for The Ugliest Man on Campus and cruelly, someone nominated Janis. That scarred her forever, and as she toured America she would grab good-looking teenage boys grateful for the chance to bed a famous rock star. Janis conceded, "I'm too ugly to get the men I really want." But they may have been put off by her forthright approach, "Let's go backstage and get it on."

ly became an accomplished musician, then discovered she had a natural blues voice and people wanted to listen. So began her career, singing for free drinks in the cafes and bars near her home in Port Arthur, Texas; it was her introduction to drugs as well as booze. She dressed like a beatnik and rapidly became a promiscuous good-time girl, ready for anything, anytime.

Men or women, one or two...

Her own sex were fair game as well, and Janis delighted in making love to women friends and others on the music scene. Not all of them were lesbians, many were bisexual like herself, and it seemed a natural extension to these exertions to invite a man along for boisterous threesomes. She was wary of casual pick-ups to the extent she always suspected they might try to exploit her financially, but in an effort to keep faith with her men and her women, the people who knew her, worked with her and admired her talents, Janis confessed she frequently faked her orgasms. Then she fell in love.

The man was just as big a star as herself, singer-turned-actor Kris Kristopherson. But Janis was doomed; a threesome developed of which she wanted no part. One of her female lovers caught his eye and when Janis demanded a showdown, Kris went off with the other lady. Country Joe McDonald came along just in time, the last of her affairs which amounted to anything, although it lasted less than six months.

All her adult life, virtually from her high school days, Janis was into drugs, all kinds of drugs, and told her friends, "I don't expect to see thirty, and I really don't care." The first nine months of 1970 saw her furiously at work, touring and recording and constantly in need of drugs, satisfying her addiction and maintaining the energy for her music. In the midst of making her third album that year, Janis went back to her suite at the Landmark Hotel in Hollywood. No one knows why, but she injected an unusually large shot of heroin and died alone, of an overdose. She was twenty-seven.

SOUTHERN COMFORT

Janis Joplin made no secret of her liking for bourbon. Southern Comfort was her favourite, and when she met a marketing executive from the Kentucky distillery, induced him to make her a present of a fur coat; "for all the free publicity I've given to your product," she challenged. She won, too.

John Barrymore

John was born into an acting dynasty. The Barrymores dominated the American stage at the turn of the century, and the man who was called the Great Profile was given an early start to the profligate life-style he maintained to the grave. He started drinking at fourteen, and became an alcoholic the following year when he lost his virginity, seduced by his step-mother. John Barrymore's life was full of excesses, in his early fifties, in yet another attempt to dry-out, he went cruising with members of his family who had made sure every bottle of booze was removed before the yacht put to sea. But he managed to stay drunk for the entire course of the voyage by secretly siphoning off alcohol from the engine's cooling system.

At home and abroad he was attracted by prostitutes, "There are times when I can't be bothered with the pursuit at the beginning of an affair and all that emotional torment at the end." In India, he named a Calcutta brothel "The Pelvic Palace", and though he didn't stay every night, he rented a room there for a month. He maintained the girls were all devotees of the Kama Sutra and happily showed him every one of the 39 positions for enjoying sex. The actor claimed he also performed a ceremony to give a new name to their God of Love, dubbing him The Worshipful Master Dingle Dangle. Later on the same trip, he patronized a whorehouse in Madras and became so enthralled by the establishment and all its inmates that he reserved the lot exclusively for himself for seven days. On this occasion he did stay every night; he was never one for sightseeing.

He was the brother of the equally famous performers Ethel and Lionel Barrymore, and both parents were on the stage, Maurice and Georgiana. They could have afforded to send young John to study painting in Paris, but he needed money, easy and quick money, to begin enjoying life, and

THE LAST CONFESSION

John Barrymore maintained the character of a rogue even on his deathbed. In hospital he told doctors he thought it was time for the priest and when the man arrived to administer the last rites, he asked, "Anything to confess, my son ?" The reply was "Yes, to having carnal thoughts." Not entirely surprised – the man's dry humour was legendary – the priest responded, "About whom?" The actor raised a hand and pointed at the nurse in the room, "About her, just a few minutes ago."

joined a New York newspaper as a cartoonist. Not yet twenty-one, he was fired for getting drunk in the office. He turned to acting where his early appearances as a comedian earned a salary but later, serious roles brought the fame, especially Shakespeare's *Hamlet* and *Richard III* in London.

The earth moves

Critical acclaim followed the parts he played in Hollywood, in great films like *Dr Jekyll and Mr Hyde*, *Moby Dick*, *Grand Hotel*, and, very much in character, *Beloved Rogue*, but the name that stuck came from the 1940 movie *The Great Profile*. His flamboyance and outrageous behaviour kept his name in the headlines, often for the wrong reasons. He was in San Francisco in 1905 when the great earthquake struck but managed to sleep through the commotion. "Well, not sleep, I was kinda busy in the bedroom and we didn't realize what was going on outside," he confessed, without naming the lady.

In later years a lovers' scandal forced him into hiding to avoid the bad publicity. He was sleeping with a very sexy teenage showgirl, Evelyn Nesbit, whose parents, knowing of her own fast-growing reputation, discovered the affair and decided another of her lovers was infinitely preferable. They persuaded her to marry Harry Thaw, a jealous and crazy millionaire, but when he learned Evelyn was still going to bed with a well-known architect, the husband murdered the man in front of several witnesses. As reporters delved into the background of the murder case, Barrymore's name emerged and he disappeared abroad until after the trial.

These teenage lovelies attracted the man almost as much as the prostitutes. He had a brief affair with actress Mary Astor, who was only seventeen and visiting the actor in his Hollywood hotel suite, with mother along as chaperone. But, as Barrymore told his drinking pals, he would settle the older woman down with a drink on the balcony to enjoy the sun, and slip her daughter into the bedroom for a quickie.

However, Tallulah Bankhead, who was hardly the shy and retiring type, astonished

YOU WOULDN'T WANT TO OWN ONE ...

He often went on great drinking bouts with his stage chums Gene Fowler, Ben Hecht and W.C. Fields, the great comedian who once wrote to his wife, "I am in receipt of your complaint 68,427." No one is entirely sure who said it, but both Fields and Barrymore are identified with a famous gag about women: "They're like elephants, you like watching them but you wouldn't want to own one."

him when she turned down an after-lunch tryst in his dressing room, and then maintained that stance as they played Broadway together. In between romances John married four wives, the last one Elaine Barrie, who made some very racy films including one entitled *How to Undress In Front of Your Husband*. "That little filly turned me into a racehorse again," said the actor.

His daughter Diana Barrymore was also an actress. She became an alcoholic and committed suicide at the age of thirty-nine. She wrote an autobiography *Too Much Too Soon*, filmed in 1958, by which time father had long since died at the age of 60. John Barrymore had averaged $75,000 a picture and earned close on $4 million in his lifetime, yet when he died he owed $75,000.

Sarah Bernhardt

SARAH'S SPOUSE

Though she admitted taking "thousands of lovers", Sarah Bernhardt had only one husband, a handsome Greek playboy and, for a short time, a roving diplomat for Athens. Aristides Damala was ten years her junior and for the one year of their marriage maintained a series of well-publicized affairs, so she dumped him. But seven years later, as he lay dying from a long-lasting drug habit, Sarah nursed him constantly to the end.

"I have been one of the great lovers of the nineteenth century," said the actress Sarah Bernhardt. That was neither an idle nor conceited boast, she was merely speaking the truth: the kings, princes and emperors of at least seven European countries may have been rather more than mere admirers. As a teenager, her ambition was to become a nun. But her mother, an unmarried courtesan who largely ignored her as a child, watched the girl recover from tuberculosis and turn into a ravishing beauty, and, using her influence with the latest lover, the Duke de Mornay, persuaded her daughter to train for the stage at the Conservatoire in Paris.

Her stage career began at the Comedie-Francaise, but a natural ability and her wonderful voice took her into more serious roles. Interviewed when she was playing Queen Maria, Sarah said, "My mother's career meant our house was always full of men. I disliked men and that form of slavery, lucrative though it was, had no appeal to me." So Sarah, as a lover, became a gifted, gregarious and busy amateur. She was still in her teens when she got over her initial dislike of the opposite sex, especially the aristocratic ones. First there was Count Keratry, then Henri, the Prince de Ligne whom she bore a son, Maurice.

In her twenties she was courted and revered all over Europe by talented men who admired her skill on stage. Dramatists Oscar Wilde and Victor Hugo wined and dined her, the illustrator Gustave Doré wooed her, and the poet-novelist Emile Zola adored her. They all came to see her perform and drifted into and out of her life off-stage, competing for her affections with a succession of Europe's Monarchy.

At home there was Prince Napoleon, nephew of Bonaparte, then further afield King Alphonso of Spain and King Umberto of Italy, who feted her publicly at palace functions in Madrid and Rome ... and earned gossip about what happened when the lights went out.

Across the English Channel, she appeared publicly on the arm of the Prince of Wales who went on to become King Edward VII. Before they even met, the Emperor Franz Joseph of Austria sent Miss Bernhardt lots of letters and extravagant gifts from Vienna. The Archduke Frederick of Germany invited her to recoup from a long illness at his family schloss, and King Christian of Denmark took her sailing around the islands of Zeeland.

Older, more outrageous, and more adored

At thirty-six, Bernhardt formed her own troupe and toured the world, forever achieving public forgiveness from her adoring fans for her outrageous love-life. Many of Sarah's lovers were her leading men wherever she played, in London and Paris at first, then in Berlin, New York and San Francisco. At the age of sixty-six, she began an affair in America with Lou Tellegen who had only just turned thirty. "The most glorious time of my life was the four years I toured with Sarah Bernhardt," he wrote later as he recorded his life story.

MY DESTINY

Soon after her seventieth birthday surgeons amputated Sarah's right leg, but her life remained the theatre, with parts written specifically for her, restricted to a wheelchair on stage. When asked if she would now give up love, this amazing woman responded, "Only when I draw my last breath. What remains of my energy and my vitality lies entirely to their subservience to my destiny as a woman."

She was undoubtedly eccentric as well as talented, and her fame took on another dimension when she revealed her wish to be buried in a rosewood coffin lined in red satin. This was made for her as a teenager when tuberculosis was threatening to end her life prematurely, but she kept the wooden box and the actress conceded she often slept in it. However, a book published by a jealous rival, actress Marie Colombier, may have been closer to the truth. She wrote, "Sarah demanded her intimate friends should keep her company in the narrow box which made some of them hesitate; this funereal furniture killed their desire."

For a woman who doctors said would not see her twenty-first birthday – the tuberculosis constantly plagued her throughout life – Sarah Bernhardt was truly an amazing woman. She was almost painfully thin – an early critic praised her as "a nicely polished skeleton" – yet she had extraordinary energy and was still acting and directing until shortly before her death at the age of seventy-eight.

Errol Flynn

Soldier, sailor, pirate, prince, ranch-hand or Robin Hood, the man was born to play swashbuckling roles, and Errol Flynn kept that act going in his off-stage roles for nearly twenty five years as rogue, reveller, hell-raiser and womanizer. Flynn was only fifty when he died from a heart attack, casting doubt on his oft-repeated statement that he had spent 12,000 nights making love. That would account for exactly two-thirds of his entire life.

He had a double obsession, a huge sexual appetite, which he had plenty of opportunities to satisfy both within the movie industry and outside it, among the force of willing women who flocked to his side, coupled with a fear of castration. He explained this to a magazine writer before he died. "Before I ever got into the film business, I had a serious argument with a rickshaw driver. He was an Indian working in the Pacific Islands who pulled out a knife and slashed straight at my trousers. The blade ripped the trousers, tore my skin and only just missed the vital parts." To prove the story, Errol Flynn could show a deep scar in his groin.

The man's entry into the film world was very unusual, to say the least. His parents were Irish-American who went to Tasmania, where he was born. Although his fame was achieved in the States, Flynn maintained a lifelong love-affair with the South Seas, with Australia and China and what were then known as Malaya, Siam and the East Indies.

> **JAILBAIT**
>
> • • • • • • • • • • • • • • • • • •
>
> Fellow actor and bosom pal David Niven, in many ways a similar screen character, used to tell a story of how Errol Flynn would make a detour when they were out together, and stop the car outside a girls' school as the pupils were leaving for home. "The trouble is, you know and I know that's pure jailbait out there, San Quentin jail, but dreaming about them isn't against the law," he would say.
>
> • • • • • • • • • • • • • • • • • •

He skippered yachts chartered by rich holidaymakers, led jungle safaris and hunting groups, and was on his way to New Guinea when he met a film producer intent on making a film on the mutineer Fletcher Christian. Charles Chauvel saw in Flynn the natural material for the lead part. His appearance in the rather corny feature *In The Wake of the Bounty* was seen by studio chiefs at Warner Brothers, who immediately put him under contract.

Lust without boundaries

That was late in the 1930s, and the next decade saw him in epics like *The Adventures of Robin Hood*, *Captain Blood* and *The Charge of the Light Brigade*. He didn't hang around the Hollywood scene or, for that matter, the homes he set up with a succession of actress wives, Lily Damita, Patrice Wymore and Nora Eddington. He also spent little time with the four children they gave him. Flynn loved to sail and was constantly on the move around the world. During a spell of bachelorhood, he installed a one-way mirror at home to watch house-guests enjoying themselves, and admitted that he found watching other couples making love was a tremendous turn-on. This went a stage further in Puerta Vallata and Acapulco, where he watched Mexican hookers have intercourse with actors on stage and occasionally performing with animals. More than once in his career, rumours circulated Hollywood that Errol Flynn was bisexual; young men were said to have committed suicide after he broke off their relationships.

But his reputation was confirmed in a highly publicized trial in 1942 when he was prosecuted for raping two teenage girls, Peggy Satterlee, sixteen, and Betty Hansen, seventeen. The first girl claimed she was forced to accommodate the actor twice, aboard his yacht Sirocco, and the second told the judge that Flynn had stripped her in a bedroom at his house, and blushingly added, "He then put his private parts into my private parts."

But the jury accepted this was not the

> ## ORIENTAL EXPERIMENTS
> • • • • • • • • • • • • • • • • • •
> Experimenting with drugs began before Flynn arrived in Los Angeles. Morphine and opium were readily available in China, and as he learned the sexual techniques of the Orient, he put them to good use. But cocaine was his favourite, then and later in life, and its potency was proved, enhancing the man's performance as he applied a pinch of coke to the end of his appendage – a dangerous technique that, ironically, can result in chemical castration.
> • • • • • • • • • • • • • • • • • •

first time police chiefs had conspired with L.A. lawyers trying to extract huge bribes from studio bosses to keep their valuable assets out of any unwelcome limelight. Charges against both girls, one for an illegal abortion and the other for oral sex, had been dropped when they agreed to give evidence against Flynn, who was acquitted. Seven years later he was similarly charged and acquitted of raping a very pretty nineteen-year-old French girl aiming for Hollywood stardom. The case did neither of them any good.

The bad publicity and his premature ageing, the results of over-indulgence on too many fronts and of spending too much time in bright sunlight at sea, brought an early halt to his movie-making, even though he was still only in his forties, but not to his love-life. In the year he died, in 1959, Errol Flynn was planning to marry for a fourth time. His bride was a teenager just out of school, seventeen-year-old blonde Beverly Aadland. They met as she tried for a screen part in Hollywood, and in a matter of weeks the day was set for the wedding. The dress was made, invitations sent out and her proud but worried mother made all the arrangements for an open-air reception. The day before, the groom sent word that he couldn't get there. The girl never saw or heard from Flynn again.

Babe Ruth

Babe Ruth was, and still is, the best-known name in baseball and when his career ended in 1935, Yankee Stadium in New York was dubbed, "The House that Ruth Built," he had filled the ground with adoring fans so often. When Babe Ruth died thirteen years later, police estimated more than a hundred thousand of them paraded past his funeral bier at the stadium. He had a rare talent. He was a record-breaking pitcher and batter, and his love life was legendary. There were women waiting in every town when he went on tour, and his team-mates rarely saw their star attraction until he turned up at the ground then disappeared again as soon as the game was over.

Every woman in the joint ...

One team manager's nerves became so frayed with his last-minute arrivals in the dressing room that he appointed watchdogs from among the other players to go carousing with his top man. The first one reported back, "He is the noisiest f**k in the union. I was next door and all night long the man was grunting and groaning, whooping and hollering. How does he keep it going for so long?" One word describes his sex life: insatiable. Ruth was a regular customer at a whorehouse in St Louis. He arrived there early one afternoon, produced a fistful of money and instructed the madam to close down. "I am taking over the joint until I've had every woman you got here just now," Babe told her.

True to his word, and to the ladies' great amusement, he took each one in turn right through the evening, the night and the next morning. Before leaving for the game, he had a huge breakfast, consisting mainly of an 18-egg omelette – one for every woman he had bedded there. The man had a massive

PARTY PARTY

Babe Ruth was a great party-goer and party-giver. In a Detroit hotel on the eve of a big game, he rented four adjoining rooms, had the partitions removed and asked the management to send up a piano. Then he wandered around the hotel and outside on the side-walk inviting women to join him and his team-mates at a party upstairs. Half-way through the revelries Babe announced, "All right ladies, anyone who doesn't want to f**k can leave right now."

appetite for women and for food. He could not go without a regular diet of lots of red meat – great platefuls of steaks or chops for breakfast, the same again for dinner and hot dogs by the dozen all day long. They provided the energy intake for the main business of the day and the night.

He was born George Herman Ruth to a poverty-stricken Baltimore family who later became exasperated with his teenage exploits and sent him to St Mary's Industrial School, which almost certainly saved him from the juvenile courts. At school, the left-handed pitcher was spotted by talent scouts and he was signed by the Baltimore Orioles, then playing in a minor league. He was only nineteen when he married Helen, a dark, attractive girl from Texas, and that same year, in his first senior season, he was sold to the Boston Red Sox where he developed his battings skills. Five years later they sold him for a world record fee of $125,000, to the New York Yankees, his reckless social life already well established.

BLACKMAIL

Dolores Dixon was 18, a shop girl in Manhattan who caught his eye one day in 1922. They went to bed and she became pregnant. Dolores claimed as he had promised to marry her, he had committed statutory rape. The married baseball star had a choice, to face either a paternity suite or a breach-of-promise claim. Either way the girl wanted $50,000. "It's straightforward blackmail," said Babe, and settled out of court before the case came to trial.

Helen saw very little of her husband during their fourteen years of marriage. When Yankees manager Miller Huggins turned to her for help, hoping to tame their unruly man, she admitted, "Nothing I say ever had any effect; he loves women, all kinds of women, as much as he loves baseball." In 1925 Huggins, who was paying Ruth the massive wage of $80,000 a season, slapped a fine on him, "For misconduct off the ball field," to which Babe Ruth later responded, "I was lucky he didn't find out about the rest." Despite his busy and wild private life, the man led the American League in home runs for twelve years. He set several baseball records which remained in place for decades.

He separated from Helen and married divorcee Claire Hodgson, a photographic model and some-time actress. The lady had style. Babe Ruth adored her, and she changed every aspect of his life, especially the partying. She imposed a strict diet, cut down on his drinking and gambling, forced him to have early nights before the big games, and often turned up at away venues when the team took to the road. "He was a beast, so were most of his women, but all that happened before he met me," said Claire, and they remained happily married for almost twenty years until he died of throat cancer.

Singers and Swingers

A quartet of superb singers each had interesting and varied love-lives and some wild and wonderful stories to tell. Three were American jazz singers, masters or rather mistresses of the blues. First there was Bessie Smith, who was so enraged with a chorus girl "for messing with my man" that she beat her up and threw her out of a railway carriage. Billy Holiday was only ten when she was sent to reform school, her crime being to get herself raped by a middle-aged neighbour. Then there was Josephine Baker who was adored in cabaret by New Yorkers and Parisians alike, and whose sexual penchant was to make love standing up. All her lovers needed to be tall, like herself. Lastly was the enchanting little songbird from France, Edith Piaf, who had three-somes in bed with her half-sister.

Don't mess with Bess

Bessie had a very quick temper, and often an argument would soon turn into a full-bloodied fight. The big black singer from Tennessee was a lusty, busty lady who was careless with money. In at the very beginning of record production, she earned only $125 for each song she recorded and signed an agreement which earned her no royalties from sales. Bessie's first husband died within months of their marriage, then she wed her manager Jack Gee. Both had lovers, supposedly kept secret from their partners, in a touring cabaret show.

Battling Bessie

When a suspicious Bessie confronted the chorus girl on a stationary train, punched her and threw her on to the tracks, Jack

BOOZING BESSIE

Bessie Smith was a notorious boozer. Her capability for drink was boosted when she took a particular lover during the days of prohibition: Richard Morgan was a bootlegger who went on to became another manager-husband. Bessie ended her active lesbian love-life and became a voyeur, frequently attending kinky sex shows in Chicago and Detroit. She was forty-three when she died in a car accident.

climbed down to rescue the girl. The singer's temper was still high and she leaned from a carriage window and emptied Gee's own gun at him as he fled across the station. The train left without either him or the girl. Bessie was arrested and charged for attacking another girl. Her own lover, a young dancer Algy Pitts, was given a thousand dollars to pay Bessie's bail. But he left town with the money, and Bessie languished in gaol.

Long before singer and manager finally parted company, Bessie found she preferred to take women to bed and the chorus line and backing singers for her cabaret show always included more than one lesbian partner. That led to a different form of lovers' fights, and there were sexual affairs of every hue wherever the group performed. Hotel bills often included amounts to cover broken furniture.

Sex, drugs and jazz

Billie Holiday's start in life was anything but easy. Her mother was only thirteen when Billie was born in Baltimore. Her father played guitar in several bands, and was more often out of work. When Billie was raped and sent to reform school, her tutors were the wrong kind of teachers, and lesbian lovers gave her early and practical lessons on sex. On release, she became a prostitute and performed for clients who paid for sex with young teenagers, but Billie's main job was as a "gopher" for the brothel where she worked. The advantage was the introduction this gave her to the world of jazz. There was always music playing in the whorehouse, and Billie's early experience came from these lonely sing-alongs.

She acquired a reputation as a voracious lover. Nearly all her lovers were musicians, and Billie often said "good and regular lovin' puts the passion in my voice." If her audience was not appreciative, Billie, who never wore undies, would hoist her skirts and give them a flash in response, sometimes turning and bending to give them a

LADY DAY

Billie Holiday gained her first name from childhood. Eleanora turned into a tom-boy and father called her Bill. But in the world of music she was known as Lady Day, which originated from her days in the whorehouse. She occasionally sang for waiting customers, but refused to pick up their tips in the traditional manner, lowering her body to recover the coins with her vagina. The other girls started calling her Lady Holiday. The great tenor saxophone player Lester Young shortened her surname and after their recording partnership was established, the singer was always Lady Day.

rear view as well. They loved her for it. A long-term man in her life was a drummer known as Big Sid, "And that's not because he's so god-damned tall" Bessie would explain. The other men in her life were often club-owners where she performed, but Billie was wild. She went to opium parlours, snorted cocaine and finally developed heroin addiction and died, penniless, at the age of forty-four.

Only royalty need apply ... if they're tall enough

Josephine Baker's life was full of variety. Her family lived in one room in St Louis, but she left home aged thirteen. Bessie Smith provided her with a first job as her personal maid. Within four years she had graduated to chorus girl and when she went to Paris, she became the first black member of the Folies Bergere. They turned her into a singer as well as a dancer. She went on stage wearing only a belt of bananas and danced to a backdrop of mirrors, a novel act even for the Folies.

One of her early admirers was a wealthy Arab she called "The Sheikh", but he was short and fat and Josephine liked to take her lovers standing up with her back to the wall. "He can't get his thing much higher than my knees," she explained. Apart from her height, she was strikingly attractive. Though she didn't know her father, he was believed to have been a wealthy Spaniard, prevented by his family from marrying her mother Carrie. Her looks captivated a long line of admirers, and a brief exchange of telegrams began a short and amazing love affair with Crown Prince Adolph, heir to the throne of Sweden. Like many others he went backstage to meet the singer at the Folies. Although he was married he invited her to visit Sweden and next morning she sent a message saying "When?" To her surprise the reply came at once, "Tonight!" For such a renowned patron, the Folies had to bow and give her time off, and Josephine joined him in a sumptuous, private railway carriage as the train left Paris to chug through northern Europe to Stockholm. The prince took her to the deserted, royal summer palace where they stayed secretly for a month.

In the Second World War the Germans occupying Paris knew that Josephine Baker, formerly married to a Jewish businessman, was working for the French Resistance. She was the source supplying one of the earliest German code-books to allied intelligence, and the Nazis decided she should die. Hermann Goering himself invited her to dinner and under threat from Goering's gun, she was forced to eat cyanide-laced fish. She rushed to the bathroom where a plan for her escape was in place, slid down a laundry chute to waiting friends, and was rushed to a stomach pump. Miss Baker was close to death for a month. After the war she was honoured by France with the Croix de Guerre.

The singer had many lovers and husbands, but could not carry children full term, so she turned to adoption and eventually brought up a family of 11 youngsters, all from different countries, in her country chateau. She died of a heart attack at sixty-eight shortly after a triumphant tour of her home country, still a great jazz singer.

From menage à trois *to warmth from the stars*

The final member of our ladies quartet is Edith Piaf. She could sing jazz, "le Be-bop", but passionate love songs were her forte. The tiny Frenchwoman was not attractive, painfully thin and under five feet tall, but she was able to claim, "I've got small, sagging breasts, a low-slung arse with little, droopy buttocks. But I can still get men and that's where I get to know about my men, they can't cheat in bed." She didn't wait for men to pursue her, either. When Piaf fancied a man she went after him: she sat through a score of performances of a Paris play, besotted with the rugged American actor John Garfield. Finally she had him, but it turned out to be a one-night-stand.

Her love-life began when she was very young. She was born Edith Giovanna Gassion and both mother and father, travelling circus performers, deserted her and she was raised with her half-sister Momone by a grandmother who ran a Paris bordello. She entertained several men there as a young teenager and went on the streets herself aged fourteen, explaining later, "I wanted to keep all the money."

In between clients she used to sing on the street and this set her towards

THE SPARROW & THE BOXER

There were many famous men among Edith Piaf's lovers, and one was the world's middleweight boxing champion Marcel Cerdan. The fight at Madison Square Garden when he stripped American Tony Zale of the crown is still regarded as one of the finest championship bouts of all time. In 1949, Edith was performing in New York while Marcel was home in France with his wife and three children. She missed him terribly, and persuaded the fighter to fly out and join her. He died when the plane crashed on route. Piaf was under sedation for weeks, to stop her from committing suicide.

stardom, for one of her first clients was a theatrical impressario who took her to bed but also recognized the quality of her voice. He changed her name, bought her a new wardrobe, groomed the girl and put her into cabaret to learn the business.

In those early days there was often only just enough money for one bed in a dinghy hotel room, and Edith would end up there with Momone and a young lover named Louis Dupont. No one had any objections, not even the hotel keeper whose bill was frequently settled with a contra-deal. But once off the streets and singing inside, her fame spread quickly. A host of famous names came to hear Edith Piaf and some, like heart-throb actor Yves Montand and singer Charles Aznavour, stayed on after the show was over. She lived by the creed, "A night without a man is like a day without sunshine."

Like many artists before her, the constant sexual activity gave her singing the drive and passion for which she became renowned, and the rest of her life was lived at the same pace, working hard, drinking hard and playing around with drugs. Momone defined her beloved sister, "Jealous and possessive, she constantly ate her heart out. She was wild in bed, screaming and howling, and afterwards she often locked her guys in the room until she was ready again. In many ways I guess she was unbearable." In between scores of lovers, Piaf also had two husbands before she died at forty-seven, worn out and mourned the world over.

Clark Gable

If he had never made another film, this man's portrayal of Rhett Butler, southern gentleman, sexual rake and all-round rotter in *Gone With The Wind*, would have provided ever-lasting fame. But in the 23 years he was under contract to MGM Studios, Clark Gable made 60 films, and another dozen either side of that. He remained a leading star in films during all those years, yet he won just a single Oscar. Despite the charm, the macho style, his notorious good looks and undoubted sexual magnetism, his rating as a lover among the many ladies in Hollywood he took to bed was pretty poor.

A lousy lay

Married five times, he was romantically linked – at least by the gossip columnists – with nearly all his co-stars. Grace Kelly went skinny-dipping with him in Africa, and Jean Harlow admitted she was bitterly disappointed with his performance. He had a raging affair with Joan Crawford who commented, "he had more sheer animal magic than anyone else in the world." Ava Gardner's opinion was more open, "I believe every woman who worked with Clark Gable must have felt sexual urges beyond belief." Marilyn Monroe confessed, "just looking at him gives me goose-bumps all over." But the woman who was to become the love of his life and his third wife, actress Carole Lombard, said, "I adore Clark, but he's a lousy lay." Ironically for this male sex symbol, the title of the film which won Clark Gable his coveted film award was *It Happened One Night*, playing the part of a newspaper reporter.

Gable's father roamed the mid-west oil fields for employment and the family went with him. Clark found work by his side until he decided to become an actor, working

A DESPERATE COUPLE

For three years Clark Gable and the beautiful Carole Lombard were blissfully happy, but desperate to have children. They took top medical advice, studied temperatures and monthly cycles, checked sperm-counts, and tried everything. As a close friend commented, "If someone had told Carole you were sure to get pregnant doing it hanging from a train window, they would have done it hanging from a train window."

first back-stage as a call-boy, then in a circus, and again under canvas in a travelling theatrical company on the west coast. He had minor roles in silent movies and took extra parts when talkies came along, but Hollywood was slow to recognize his potential and he went back to the theatre. Marriage to actress Josephine Dillon saved the day. She became his voice coach and when he made two sound movies at the age of 30, as a gangster in *The Finger Points* and *Night Nurse*, MGM snapped him up.

Squeaky clean macho man

From then on he was always the romantic hero, whether he was playing a cowboy or playboy, a philanderer or adventurer, but he rarely appeared bare-chested. Gable was obsessed with cleanliness as well as his immaculate clothes, and besides showering every two or three hours through the day, he also shaved his chest and armpits. He was a very popular figure around the studios, hanging out with the cameramen and technicians rather than the stars, taking them fishing and shooting, and though his succession of wives filled most of those years, he was never a one-woman man.

His second wife was a Texas divorcee, millionairess Rea Langham, thirteen years his senior. The actor always maintained, "The older woman has seen more, heard more, done more and knows more. I'll take the older woman every time." After her came Miss Lombard. She was small and blonde, witty and bubbly and they called each other Ma and Pa. Marriage changed both of them, though he kept straying with a variety of actresses. She preserved her sense of humour, once telling a reporter, "Yes, my husband has refused to leave his footprints outside Grauman's Chinese Theatre. He'll do it only if they let him leave his cock-print as well."

After her untimely death three years into the marriage, with the war years behind him, Clark Gable really hit the amorous trail. He was not averse to bedding high-price call-girls: "I can always pay them to go away." He once surprised the studio publicity men when he asked, "Do you know what the ladies in this line-up of yours have in common?" He was holding a photo-

> ### WAR HERO
>
> The macho image on screen was fulfilled in real life during World War II. Gable volunteered for the U.S. Army Air Corps, rose to the rank of major, and was awarded the Air Medal for "exceptionally meritorious achievements during five bomber missions."

graph of some of MGM's biggest names and though he was promiscuous, Gable was never boastful about his sexual conquests. "I've had them all, every one, on and off screen," he announced.

His fourth wife, for a brief period, was Lady Sylvia Ashley, and lastly Lombard-look-alike Kay Spreckles, who persuaded the actor to buy a ranch and took him into semi-retirement. This time he reversed direction, taking his private life on to screen. His last role was as an elderly cowboy in *The Misfits*, playing opposite Marilyn Monroe. Two weeks after they finished filming, he died of a heart attack.

Grace Kelly

Ice-cool and aloof, an exotic and untouchable beauty queen. This was the public impression Grace Kelly maintained, but Hollywood knew differently. Even when she became a real-life princess, the passionate, sex-loving side of her nature came out for an occasional airing. To her friends and Tinsel Town colleagues, the ultra-glamorous, blonde actress never attempted to hide this side of her make-up. Relating the stories of her many screen-star romances she posed the question, "When you're in a tent in Africa with someone like Clark Gable, what else is there to do?" The screen's biggest male heart-throb was 27 years her senior. The overture to their first coupling was stripping off beside Lake Victoria in Africa, where they were filming *Mogambo*, then swimming and fornicating at the lakeside.

Her sex message on screen was very subtle, but in real life Grace was very open and very determined where men were concerned, particularly potential lovers. A decade or more before the so-called permissive society took over, she was never afraid to make the first move. Before leaving home as an 18-year-old for drama school in New York, she made the decision to lose her virginity, surrendering herself to the husband of a close friend who was out for the day. During that first term she bedded her drama tutor in his flat one winter afternoon. Before they had even kissed she disappeared, stripped and lay naked on his bed, taking 30-year-old Don Richardson totally by surprise. "She was happy and busy in bed," he recalled years later, "but she always knew when she'd had enough. We were young and healthy and after, say, four times, that was fine for her. She was perfectly normal, she had her orgasms and she enjoyed them."

BEG YOUR PARDON

● ● ● ● ● ● ● ● ● ● ● ● ● ● ● ● ●

Filming on the Alfred Hitchcock thriller *To Catch A Thief* came to an end on the great man's birthday, August 13th. Grace and the rest of the cast were convulsed as champagne and a huge cake were brought on to the set and the director's prim and proper, plum-voiced English secretary announced, "Come into the other room and have a piece of Mr Hitchcake's cock."

● ● ● ● ● ● ● ● ● ● ● ● ● ● ● ● ●

From soap ads to Hollywood via Persian princes

She was destined for a permanent place among Royalty. Brief but wild flings with the Shah of Persia and Prince Aly Khan may have prepared her for later life. The Shah met her at a reception just after high-powered talks with President Truman, and she was dazzled. They went out together six nights in a row and he gave her three beautiful pieces of jewellery, which she later presented to her bridesmaids the day she became Her Serene Highness, wife of Prince Rainier III of Monaco.

Grace paid her way at drama school by working as a model, advertising cigarettes, soap, beer and insect sprays. She was inexperienced but quickly in demand, and soon able to command fees of up to $2,000 a session. She kept up the affair with Richardson, but had a string of men in her young life. The drama tutor walked out when he discovered her latest suitor was Aly Khan. The technique of the Islamic heir was no secret – there were always presents for his partners and the same gold bracelet always marked the eventual coupling. Grace playfully posed for the tutor, naked apart from a small gold crucifix and the bracelet, which the tutor instantly recognized.

> ### LIKE FATHER LIKE ...
> ● ● ● ● ● ● ● ● ● ● ● ● ● ● ● ● ● ●
> While her looks were inherited from her Teutonic mother, Grace Kelly's sexual genes came straight from her father, an Olympic gold medal oarsman. A successful property developer in Philadelphia and a stern Catholic, he had mistresses all over town. He once had a department store gift-wrap 27 identical make-up cases to be delivered to different women whose names and addresses he supplied.
> ● ● ● ● ● ● ● ● ● ● ● ● ● ● ● ● ● ●

Actor Alex d'Arcy was nearer forty when he took the model-cum-actress who was still just in her teens. "I had known her about ten days and put my hand on her knee in the back of a taxi," he revealed. "I was startled at her reaction, she leaped into my arms and spent the night with me. She was a very, very, very sexy girl, quite the opposite of how she seemed, shy and demure in public but a tigress in bed. Touch her once and she would go through the ceiling."

A sexual buccaneer

Off she went to Hollywood and after Clark Gable, the rising star kept up the traditions of many who had gone before, and got laid by a succession of leading men who played opposite her. Her ambiguity, on-and-off stage, fascinated director Alfred Hitchcock who cast her in *Dial M for Murder*. Ray Milland was the star and probably the first into her bed. "But on that picture, Grace f**ked everyone," said Hitchcock, "she even f**ked little Freddie Knott who wrote the screenplay." Miss Kelly became reckless, a sexual buccaneer who "knew how to lead men on and was prepared to f**k everything in sight," said a fellow-actress.

William Holden in *The Bridges of Toko-Ri* was another lover who was truly smitten and wanted to marry her, but needed a divorce first. Bing Crosby came under the same spell as they made *The Country Girl*, which also starred William Holden. He gave way to the great crooner, who had his freedom, could openly court the young woman half his age and who actually proposed to Grace. But Bing was too easy-going, too bland, and the early sparks in bed did not last for long.

The closest she came to marriage until she went to Monaco was with Manhattan couturier Oleg Cassinni, who squired many Hollywood beauties including Gene Tierney, Pier Angeli and Anita Ekberg. Strangely, she held him at bay for six months, sensing he loved the pursuit even more than the act. The eventual marriage to Prince Rainier, in 1956, produced what might be considered the Wedding of the Century. However, soon enough the public and the private Princess played different roles, spending much of her time alone – or at least away from her husband – in Paris.

Right up to the day of her untimely death in 1982 in a tragic car accident on the road to Monte Carlo, her biographer Robert Lacey has revealed a sequence of very quiet and very secret affairs. The hyperactive sex life she craved and enjoyed as a young woman could not be equalled, but Princess Grace was willing to try.

Lillie Langtry

No woman throughout history has ever used her glamour, her wiles in bed, and the fame these attributes lent to her name, to better effect than Lillie Langtry. Her lovers spattered the social scene in London at the back end of the last century. The artist's model who became a very modest actress was the world's first pin-up. Sex for this red-haired clergyman's daughter was more of an occupation than a pleasure, and she used this to good effect, banking a fortune in cash and receiving many gifts showered on her by aristocrats and industrial millionaires from Europe and America, ranging from diamonds and pearls to houses and racehorses.

Lillie's most famous lover was undoubtedly the Prince of Wales, the eldest son of Queen Victoria, who became King Edward VII. At first their affair scandalized London, but once it was accepted, they were often invited as a couple to official functions and celebrations. She made no secret of her expectations and the prince was heard to complain publicly, "Madam, I have spent enough on you to buy a battleship," to which Lillie retorted "... and enough in me to sink one!"

Her ready humour made the woman even more attractive to men. As her life progressed, Lillie would prove to be an astute businesswoman, maintaining a successful racing stable at Newmarket, owning and managing her own theatre and backing a number of successful business ventures. She came from a French family who settled in Jersey, in the Channel Islands, and was born Emilie Charlotte le Breton. Her father was the Dean of Jersey, and by the time she was 21 her looks were captivating the young swains from England and France who holidayed on the island and stopped off on their yachts to replenish supplies. One of these was moderately wealthy Edward Langtry, who married her and installed her in his London home. But Edward was a fop, a playboy and drunkard and reputedly impotent, certainly no match for his vivacious bride, who soon saw her opportunities to make the most of the London scene.

She soon learned her beauty had a definite value and that scandal was accompanied by very welcome publicity. Lillie became an artist's model, and her image was the first to be reproduced on postcards, replacing the popular cartoons. Those postcards soon found their way on to the walls of sixth form and university dormitories, pinned to ships' bulkheads and barrack doors. A mass of red hair reached almost to her shoulders, she was tall and slender, and when she appeared in an advertisement for Pears soap, she chose to be paid pound for pound – £132 to match her exact weight.

Lillie conquers all

She rejoiced in the title of "The Jersey Lily" when she became the first society lady to appear on stage, and though she was inexperienced as an actress, she made her debut in a leading role, at the Haymarket Theatre as Kate Hardcastle in *She Stoops to Conquer*. She went on to play Shakespeare and tour America, where the infamous Judge Roy Bean became an admirer if not a suitor. He opened a saloon in Langtry, Texas, named it the Jersey Lily and left her his revolver in his will. But her ambitions did not lie in the theatre, not on stage at any rate. By now her husband had exhausted his fortune and was an inmate of an asylum where he eventually died. But long before, Lillie had become the toast of London.

Mark Twain in America, and George Bernard Shaw and Oscar Wilde at home all wrote of her in books and plays, while Gilbert and Sullivan dedicated lines in an opera to her. At a theatrical party the French writer Victor Hugo proposed a toast, "I can only celebrate your beauty by wishing I was thirty years younger," said with a twinkle in his eye. But her fame was really created by her long and open affair with the Queen's son who was himself married, and they would meet in London at the homes of friends to spend the afternoon in bed. He would arrange for both to be invited for weekends to country house-parties, where the hostess never failed to place them in adjoining bedrooms. However the Prince of Wales was conscious of his rank and when Lillie, just once, overstepped the mark with a party trick, the affair ended. When he finally acceded to the throne, Lillie became a great friend of his wife, Queen Alexandra.

Among her many titled partners, Crown Prince Rudolf was prominent for a time. He was heir to the Austro-Hungarian Empire but later died beside another mistress in a double-suicide. Lillie followed him with Prince Louis of Battenberg, a nephew of her former lover King Edward, and he fathered her only child, a daughter named Jeanne-Marie. Then a second marriage gave Lillie a title of her own, when she wed Hugo de Bathe who became a baronet in 1907. She was 54 but still an active and attractive socialite. Ten years later, her looks finally fading, she decided to retire from London life altogether. Lillie didn't want any pity from her former friends and lovers. and she went to live alone in Monaco, where she died at 74.

Charlie Chaplin

The Cheeky Chappie, comedy king of the silent screen and the product of several orphanages and workhouses in London where he was born and brought up, Charlie Chaplin was the first actor in Hollywood to make a million dollars in one year. He possessed a tremendous sexual drive throughout his life, fathering the last of several children when he was in his seventies, and not all of them were born to his four wives. Three of his brides were still teenagers when they went to the altar with Chaplin. He was always attracted to young girls, and titillated by a few who had not even reached their teens.

He was a workaholic who went from acting to writing screenplays, then was a director and producer, before finally composing songs and award-winning musical scores for films. His endless search for perfection and the long hours he put in at the studio, preparing sets and rehearsing his stars then cutting and editing the tremendous footage he always shot were as much to do with the break-up of his early marriages as his constant philandering. Though he had a personal magnetism for women, he also had an unusual reputation. Several partners admitted they wanted to fondle and feel this amazingly large appendage they had heard so much about. Chaplin called it "The eighth wonder of the world."

His schooling in South London was sparse, and interrupted after his father deserted the family and his mother went mad. She was a music hall artist at the turn of the century, and taught her son to sing and dance. The lad got his first job lathering chins in a barber's shop for customers who wanted a shave, then worked sweeping out a music hall after shows, where he also got to play walk-on parts in comedy routines. That set him up, and at 17 he joined the Fred Karno troupe touring Britain and Europe and finally, America, where he arrived at the age of 24. The great slapstick

SIR CHARLIE

Fame and fortune earned in America, Charlie Chaplin was forced to flee his adopted country in 1952 at the height of Senator McCarthy's Communist witch-hunt among the film-makers in Hollywood. He made his home in Switzerland, returning twenty years later to collect an honorary Academy Award and again the following year, 1973, to pick up his Oscar for writing the musical score for the film *Limelight*. In Britain, the country of his birth, he was honoured by the Queen in 1975 and became Sir Charles Chaplin.

comedian and film-maker Mack Sennett spotted Chaplin's comic talent and signed him up to make the now-famous, silent one-reelers for $150 a week. Already the actor had seen the opportunities and taken advantage of the girls employed in the business.

The money gets bigger, the girls get younger

Later, when Chaplin started to take a part in making his films, epics like *The Kid*, *The Gold Rush*, *City Lights* and *Modern Times* rolled out. He made a total of eighty films. In one year, in the 1930s, he turned out eight productions which, remarkably at that time, paid him more than $1,000,000. However, he always found time for the ladies and early on in his career acknowledged a penchant for deflowering young virgins. One of these became his first wife, Mildred Harris, who was only 14 when Chaplin tested her for a film part. Two years later at mother's insistence – for her daughter was pregnant – they were married, but no child was born and in another two years they were divorced.

His second marriage had trouble written all over it ten years before it happened. Chaplin was captivated by Lita Grey when she was only six years old, and mother frequently brought her child-prodigy to the studios to audition and spend a little more time dancing and twirling for the director, whose appendage became even more unusually large at the sight. He started grooming her for stardom at the age of 12. Studio bosses were so worried, they installed a permanent chaperone for the girl. At 15 he claimed her virginity in the bathroom at his Hollywood home and not surprisingly, for Chaplin loathed contraceptives, she became pregnant soon afterwards. He suggested abortion, then offered her $20,000 to marry someone else, but when he was threatened with a paternity suit, he married the girl.

Two years and two children later came divorce, and Lita decided to get her own back for the humiliations she had suffered

A SUPREME ART

"Never take sex for granted," he advised friends and sons alike. "Lovemaking is a supreme art that can never be learned at once and needs constant practice." To prepare himself for his own bouts in bed, Charlie loved to watch others at play. Actor John Barrymore, who was no slouch when it came to this particular form of practice, was a neighbour and Chaplin installed a high-powered telescope to watch what went on in his bedroom. Barrymore was aware of this, and left the curtains drawn back for the delighted voyeur.

from the man twice her age. Her 40-page divorce petition was sold to the public at one dollar a copy, and revealed he had five regular mistresses as well as countless one-night stands during their marriage, and he constantly urged her to perform fellatio, copulate in public and join in his favourite, menage-a-trois. The stunning Paulette Goddard was wife No 3, married aboard his yacht *Panacea*. Though he bribed the skipper to tear the relevant page out of the ship's log, he later revealed they had wed. Initially actress Joan Barry failed in her quest, pursuing him endlessly – breaking into his house cost her a month in gaol. However, she did file a paternity suit, and though a blood test failed to prove he was the father, the judge ordered him to pay maintenance.

He was a slave to sex. Visits to brothels in Los Angeles and in Mexico when he filmed on location came in between affairs with socialites, actresses and dancers like Clare Sheridan, Pola Negri, Marion Davies and the leggy Peggy Hopkins Joyce. She was a star of the *Ziegfeld Follies* who almost made Chaplin her sixth millionaire-husband. Finally came beautiful, black-haired Oona O'Neill. She was only 18 when she went up the aisle with 54-year-old Chaplin in 1943, and gave him eight children. "If I had known someone like Oona earlier in my life, I would never have had any trouble with women" Chaplin admitted. He died on Christmas Day at Vevey, in their home above Lake Geneva, at the age of 88.

Jean Harlow

The description "platinum blonde" did not exist until it was applied to this actress, one of Hollywood's first sex symbols, by the eccentric millionaire Howard Hughes, who directed and produced her first major film. Soon afterwards thousands of young women followed her style; Jean Harlow began a nation-wide craze for dyed blonde hair. Hughes also directed her early career, and after making the discovery that she preferred to go bra-less – in fact, she preferred to go without any underwear at all – had the wardrobe mistress at his studios design ultra low-cut dresses, form-fitting in white satin, for the new star. She was a sensation on screen in the early 1930s, and wearing one of these gowns she delivered a line repeated over and over by women all around the world, on and off-screen, "Do you mind if I slip into something more comfortable?" Ten words, as much of a trade mark for Jean as her famous hair and of course, no other actress had dared to appear in public without a brassiere. In those early days she took a tip from a wise old cameraman and used to rub ice on her nipples to make them stand out, particularly erotic and even risqué then, for close-in shots.

Biographers and interviewers had divided opinions on whether she was naturally lusty and promiscuous, disliked sex and treated it as a career currency, or was a merely a typical, healthy girl with an above-average appetite. With her looks, the number of leading actors who pursued her, and the

> ## HOLLYWOOD HEARTTHROBS
>
> • • • • • • • • • • • • • • • •
>
> A string of great Hollywood names were on her escort-list almost as soon as she arrived in Tinsel Town. Spencer Tracy and Clark Gable were among the first, William Powell was the very last. Gossip columnists expected them to marry, and they may even have been engaged when she collapsed and died suddenly. After he left the chapel of rest shortly before she was buried, a single white gardenia was found in her hand with a note saying, "Good night dearest darling." It was later revealed that Powell had reserved the lot next to her grave.
>
> • • • • • • • • • • • • • • • •

Hollywood publicity machine working overtime, all sorts of stories were bound to circulate. She came from Kansas City, born Harlean Carpentier. When her mother remarried to an Italian-born gangster Marino Bello, the family moved to Los Angeles. Her step-father had spotted Jean's potential. She was not averse to entering films, and with his connections and a good agent, a number of minor screen parts soon followed. She proved to be a natural comedienne. But Howard Hughes recognized her real talent; after casting her in *Hell's Angels*, far and away the most expensive film production at that time, she was made. Within two years, Jean Harlow became Hollywood's biggest money-earner. She crammed a lot of living into her 26 years, and a lot of lovers, but in real life, tragedy was never far away.

First sex in a line of failures

Her introduction to sex was not a wonderful experience, though it did provide a means to a desired end. She was at boarding school, and at 16 hated being away from home, and when the son of a wealthy banker proposed, that provided the near-perfect exit from school. She eloped with Charles McGrew, who was just 21. News of their marriage infuriated both sets of parents who immediately separated the couple and the following year, without ever meeting again, they were divorced. In later years she reminisced, "We made love, sure, it wasn't very good. I was expecting so much but as I recall, it was a pretty messy business."

The next marriage was an even greater disaster, to Paul Bern the number two man at MGM Studios and more than twice her age. Half of Hollywood was fantasising about Jean Harlow, yet, at 21, she made the strange decision to wed a short, thin-lipped, under-developed man who, according to a number of actresses with screen ambitions, had the penis of a small boy. She expected him to listen to her problems, imagined or otherwise, and sort them out, while he hoped this sex queen would raise his performance level. He even told a friend, "Every man I know gets an erection just talking about her." Two months after the wedding ceremony, Paul Bern committed suicide. A maid later sold the story of the scene 24 hours preceding his death. Apparently, Bern surprised Jean, rushing into the bedroom wearing nothing but an enormous rubber phallus and huge water-filled testicles. He pranced around the room squirting liquid from the end while his wife reeled about helpless with laughter. Bern later put a pistol to his head and his suicide note read, "Unfortunately, this is the only way to make good the frightful wrong I have done you and to wipe out my abject humiliation."

That set her off on a series of wild one-night stands, with extras and stuntmen, bar pick-ups, store salesmen she chatted-up who couldn't believe their luck – friends couldn't believe their stories either. Her remorse lasted a year until she married again, this time to MGM's leading cameraman Hal Rosson, but that only lasted eight months. She badly wanted a baby and was devastated when doctors told her she was sterile. Her death was the final tragedy. She was filming *Saratoga* when her kidneys failed and she broke down, suffering from uremic poisoning. Her mother, by now a devout Christian Scientist, refused to allow any medical treatment until it was too late.

Jimi Hendrix

Jimi Hendrix's untimely death at the age of 27 came at the end of the swinging '60s, the years which finally liberated western women, and the guitarist and rock-singer took full advantage of the women who shamelessly flocked to his side – and his bed. This was the decade when women began burning their bras and making the first move, and many either publicly enjoyed or simulated orgasms while watching their pop idols perform, stimulated by the antics of the men on stage.

Jimi gave a new meaning to the words multiple orgasm, holding his guitar low down in his crotch and grinding away with hips and thighs, Elvis-style, as he belted out the decibels. Up to ninety per cent of his audiences were women, who erupted as he finished a song, wildly smashing his instrument to bits.

He made no secret of his huge appetite for sex and soon after his arrival on the music scene in America, he became famous not only for his antics on and off-stage but for the size of his member, which a black backing singer claimed, "is damn near as big as his guitar". Jimi called the instrument his "electric lady" and the other instrument his "personal plectrum". He was a star in the rock business for less than six years but during that time, in the late 1960s, he became a sex symbol, especially for white women. On tour the road managers would frequently select girls from among the willing groupies, three at a time, to join their boss in his hotel suite. He would take them all to bed together and, so legend has it, he regarded their climax as a matter of personal honour and rarely failed to satisfy them at some time during the day or later that evening. Jimi called these groupies "Band Aids", but he was never unkind or rude to the girls he made love to. He never belittled his loyal fans.

The 1960s was full of big names, pop groups and solo stars were constantly being

EXPLOSIVE

• • • • • • • • • • • • • • • • • •

Jimi was well aware of the effect his performance had on his female audience – the cost of broken guitars was more than matched by the publicity this attracted. At a pop festival in Monterey in 1967, he went one stage further. At the culmination of a particularly explosive performance, Jimi quickly poured lighter fluid over his guitar and caused a near-riot as he set light to the instrument up there on stage under the floodlights.

• • • • • • • • • • • • • • • • • •

discovered on both sides of the Atlantic, and Jimi Hendrix was a long time getting to the forefront in the music business. He was born and brought up in Seattle, and gained more than good looks from his mother, a wild-living, hard-drinking, full-blooded Indian woman. He pushed aside his musical talents after learning to play good guitar before he went to high school. He joined the army, but was forced out of his parachute unit with an injured leg and back. Chas Chandler, who had left The Animals group to become a pop impresario, persuaded Jimi he had it in him to make a career on his own, after four years playing in backing groups for stars like Ike and Tina Turner, Wilson Pickett and Little Richard.

The voodoo genius of music and the erotic

Chandler had watched Jimi perform and observed him privately at play, and knew instinctively that the man had a strong animal attraction for women. He was undoubtedly highly talented on guitar, and his voice wasn't bad, but Chas Chandler saw real potential with his strange looks and easy, undeveloped style. He took him to England, where the Beatles and Rolling Stones dominated a powerful pop scene, and introduced him to two local musicians. When they perfected their very individual stage act and went on tour as The Jimi Hendrix Experience, they stormed to success in England. Back home in America, Chandler booked them to open proceedings at a series of rock concerts given by The Monkees, who had persevered with a boy-next-door, clean-cut image. Jimi's openly erotic exhibition on stage drew bag-loads of bad publicity for the main act and his group was fired, the rest of their appearances cancelled.

That was just what Chandler had aimed for, and from then on his man was a big star in his own right. He had hordes of women. In England there was one special lady, red-headed Kathy Etchingham, who put up with his infidelities and said, "Jimi takes women like most people smoke cigarettes." In America the tall, black beauty Devon Wilson joined him from Quincy Jones's side, and became rather more than his personal assistant. She too was voracious and promiscuous, claiming to have had an affair with Mick Jagger, and when she wasn't filling Jimi's needs herself, she pimped on his behalf. They shared more than sex – though Hendrix was never addicted to alcohol or drugs, she stayed around when he got drunk, went on his LSD trips, and diverted to pills and heroin now and again.

PLASTER CASTERS

• • • • • • • • • • • • • • • • •

Two teenage groupies came up with an invention which would not only get them into bed with the biggest names, it would also provide their own fame on the music scene. They called themselves the "Plaster Casters" and intrigued by the idea, several singers and musicians allowed one girl to get them erect, while the other slapped wet plaster on the proud appendage. It took one minute for the plaster to set – no easy matter for the prototype but the girls became very adept – and later they would make a model from the mould they had created.

The girls' story of their session with Jimi Hendrix is hilarious. "He had got just about the biggest rig I ever saw, and we got a beautiful mould. He had no trouble keeping it hard for the entire minute but the plaster dried in his pubic hair and he got stuck. We couldn't help it; the real reason he couldn't get his rig out was that it wouldn't get soft. But he was a real sport, when we showed him the impression he put it back inside to make sure it was a perfect fit."

• • • • • • • • • • • • • • • • •

But the woman who was closest to him, and was there on the night he died, was the striking German, Monika Dannemann, who claimed they were going to be married. At first it was thought Jimi had died of a drugs overdose, but the post mortem showed he had taken too many sleeping pills, probably by mistake as he had been on a heavy drinking binge, and suffocated, choking as he vomited in his sleep. That was in September 1970, two months before his twenty-eighth birthday. Inevitably he became a cult figure, achieving far greater fame and respect after his death.

Joan Crawford

She was born Lucille Lesueur, danced on Broadway as Billie Cassin, and later in life was also known, somewhat contrarily, as First Queen of the Movies and Box Office Poison. MGM Studios took the dancer from New York to Los Angeles, sent her to acting school, put her on a strict diet and called in a top dentist to give her that perfect smile. She finally settled on the name Joan Crawford, the result of a corny fan-magazine contest, and went on to complete fifty years of film-making. But off-screen she could be a bitch; she drew up a stringent daily, weekly and monthly time-table for Husband No 3, minor actor Philip Terry, allotting him the occasional hour in the late afternoon for sex which she called, "Time With Philip."

That was certainly unusual, for Joan never regarded sex as a chore. Douglas Fairbanks Jnr. and Franchot Tone were among her husbands, Spencer Tracy and Clark Gable among her lovers, and she was yet another actress who described Gable, the wonderfully virile man on screen, as "lousy where it really counts." She was so determined to turn him on and improve his performance that Gable later acknowledged he invented all manner of excuses to avoid the sex-traps Joan Crawford laid for him. She eventually gave up, but they remained friends for nearly thirty years. Rock Hudson was certainly a companion, though she may not have got him into bed.

MOMMIE DEAREST

The actress badly wanted children and a complete family, and tried several times to conceive but miscarried. In 1939 she turned to adoption – a daughter was named Joan Crawford Jnr – and five years later, a son Philip Terry Jnr after her current husband. Divorced, she had both renamed Christina and Christopher, and given the surname Crawford. Three years later she adopted two more. Cathy and Cynthia were tiny babies who she always referred to as "the twins", but the girls were born four weeks apart, came from two different families and didn't look remotely alike.

Hors d'oeuvres are served at home

She was twice publicly blamed for breaking up a marriage, both times named as a correspondent in divorce suits. A dramatic actress in front of camera, she knew how to shock in the flesh, quite literally. Always flamboyant and occasionally eccentric, her dinner-dates never knew what to expect when they called, and she often appeared in see-through lingerie when she answered the door personally, making her intentions for the first part of the evening perfectly clear. That routine was sometimes varied. On her one and only date with awe-struck new star Kirk Douglas, as soon as they got home, she slipped out of her dress while he was still closing the front door, stripped him and took him right there in the hall.

She enraged her first mother-in-law Mary Pickford who told Joan, "If you make me a grandmother, I promise I'll kill you." She had an abortion then miscarried, and the marriage with Douglas Fairbanks broke up. The next marriage ended somewhat differently; she came home early from the studios and found Franchot Tone in bed with a young actress. Her third marriage just drifted. She wed Terry a month after meeting him. They were never suited, but the smaller bedrooms were filling up and at long last Joan was able to play happy families.

As she revealed in her 1962 autobiography, *A Portrait of Joan*, she suffered both parental indifference and physical abuse as a child, and then forced her own children to endure similar treatment. At 49, after three actor-husbands, she wed a commercial giant Alfred Steele, who was the president of Pepsi-Cola. He made Joan a co-director and they flew around the world promoting his drinks company. But she refused to completely relinquish her status as a star and a

THE CASTING COUCH

Stories about Joan Crawford's early stage years are difficult to prove but are spiced with circumstantial evidence which points to them being true. The publicity men at MGM Studios kept the media lid on tales about her home-life and the ill-treatment of her four children, but the woman took action herself to cover-up the days when she made sex films, back in the twenties, particular an explicit, silent one-reeler called *The Casting Couch*.

Confidantes said twenty years later, at the height of her Hollywood fame, she hired a private detective to track down and destroy every copy. It cost her $100,000, but the agent reported one collector refused to sell nude photographs he had collected of the actress taken from film clips. His house burned to the ground some weeks later and nothing was saved, not even the sleeping owner of the pictures who died in the fire.

Hollywood legend – the following year, when she was cast in *Torch Song*, Miss Crawford called on the film's director Charles Walters. She always maintained a trim figure, and walked into his home wearing only a housecoat which she threw open announcing, "I thought you would want to see what you have to work with."

Alfred died of a heart attack after the customary four years of marriage when she was only 53 and still very active, and soon to play in perhaps her most famous role, opposite Bette Davis in *Whatever Happened to Baby Jane?* Joan Crawford was one of the most shrewd and glamorous actresses ever produced by Hollywood.

FOUR WEDDINGS

She had four husbands, and after the weddings they had to move in with her. Each one lasted four years and when they moved out, Miss Crawford did two things: she changed the name of her Hollywood estate ,and she changed all the toilet seats in the house. Though she admitted this was quirky behaviour, she never revealed what made her do it.

James Dean

Heterosexual homosexual or bisexual? The argument has raged on ever since James Dean died in the car he loved to drive at over a hundred miles an hour. In truth, the excesses in his life may have been a substitute for sex, which to him seemed more what was expected, especially from a young man with his sultry looks who happened to be a film star, rather than the enjoyable pursuit of a normal male in his twenties. Fame came easily for such a talented actor, even though he made only three films of note: *Rebel Without a Cause*, *East of Eden* and *Giant*, and the manner of his death, so tragic at the age of 24, has only added to the legend in the years that have since passed.

The young star personified the broody, restless and confused youth of the 1950s. Millions of young Americans saw themselves up there on screen when they went to the cinema to see his films. But his portrayals were far more attractive to older women, who desperately wanted to mother him. James Dean was only nine when his mother died, and that little-boy-lost frailty was a natural part of his image. In turn, he was always attracted to older women, but suffered for a while after publicly revealing his technique: "they all want to mother me so I sit there quietly, put my head in their lap and boom, it works every time."

He was brought up on a farm in Indiana by an aunt and uncle. The girls at school were understandably slow to appreciate his future qualities as a sex symbol. They recall a shy youth who almost stuttered and wore glasses to counter his short sight. Through high school he had only two interests, very fast cars and drama. Then off he went for two years to an acting school in New York, where he was named "Most Promising Newcomer" in 1954. By then he had already spent many months in Hollywood trying to gain attention – this was a period when he tried a homosexual life-style. "It paid the rent and bought the food," is a

PECCADILLOES

Following the deaths of famous stars, it is much easier to invent or embellish the rumours and stories of their life-styles – the truth of James Dean's sexual peccadilloes could only be established by those who were there at the time. They are hardly likely to testify in public! One story held that he liked to be burned, enjoying the pain caused by a glowing cigarette, and his coterie were alleged to have called him "The Human Ashtray". There was never any substance to this story.

quote attributed to him, and an indication that he was forced to hustle in California, not necessarily that he preferred men to women or enjoyed both.

Back in New York he resumed a more conventional love-life, moving in with actress Elizabeth Sheridan, but that affair foundered when, following the award, his career rocketed. He could dance, was a fair artist and took sculpture classes. He loved to drift around New York's clubs and play drums in the small combos, he had a tilt at writing poetry, and then a novel. James Dean had many natural gifts, and best of all was the genius he exposed on screen when Hollywood finally beckoned. But his character was always flawed, never happier than when he was behind the wheel of a very fast car.

Fast cars, great sex

Singer Eartha Kitt shared his passion for speed. They were never lovers, she was always a genuine just-good-friend, and she would ride pillion on Dean's motor cycle. The actor said that among the younger girls he took to bed, an ultra-fast spin by either bike or car acted as an aphrodisiac for each of them, "and a prelude to some really great sex". Out in Hollywood he had a long on-off relationship with a highly-charged young actress, Barbara Glenn, but even when they were very much together, both enjoyed affairs on the side. He moved on to another neurotic partner, the reserved Italian actress Pier Angeli, cleaned up his act and appearance, and contemplated marriage with her. But the young man was not a Catholic, and she married crooner Vic Damone.

> **PORNOGRAPHY**
>
> • • • • • • • • • • • • • • • • •
>
> Not only were many of the stories false, there was a highly porno-graphic picture of a young man, alleged to be James Dean and look-ing remarkably like him, sitting in the lower branches of a tree with a huge erection. That was evidence enough for many of his former lady-loves who testified it could not pos-sibly be him, "not unless the pic-ture was re-touched," they said.
>
> • • • • • • • • • • • • • • • • •

On September 30th 1955, he was driving a silver-painted Porsche Spyder on his way from Los Angeles to a race in Salinas. The Porsche was crushed and he died instantly in a prang with another car that began a death-cult unequalled in the next forty years. Youngsters who had bought chewing-gum wrappers he had thrown away sold them on at huge profits, they paid fifty cents to sit behind the wheel of his wrecked car, and a tacky magazine which published *James Dean's Words From the Other Side* sold a quarter of a million copies. In the words of one famous actor, "Had he lived, he could never have sustained his personal publicity."

Isadora Duncan

The renowned, original barefoot dancer occasionally carried her lack of stage-attire to wild extremes. A Chicago preacher famously accused her of appearing in public, "With not enough clothes to pad a crutch." In later life, her fame as a randy actress who could not care less about her image endeared her to fans in Europe and America. Yet she remained a virgin until she was 25, and when she decided to abandon chastity, Isadora once again went to extremes. The deed was done by Hungarian actor Oskar Beregi who bedded her round the clock all through a weekend in Budapest. When she returned to the stage for Monday's performance, she was noticeably exhausted, dragging her feet through her dance-routine celebrated for its grace and elegance.

She failed to learn her lesson; in fact, Isadora took this marathon copulation several stages further in Berlin the following year, and spent the best part of two weeks on her back – it would be incorrect to say "in bed" – with theatrical designer Gordon Craig. The bed in his apartment was too small for really satisfying sex and by now the dancer knew what to expect, so they threw his blankets on the floor and conducted their frantic and extended orgy there, while her distraught manager cancelled shows saying she was ill, toured police stations and hotels and called her recent lovers, all to no avail. Although he thought she had been kidnapped, Isadora was determined to make up for lost time. She had one very good reason to remember this Berlin bonking session, a daughter named Deidre was the result.

BIZARRE ACCIDENT

Cars and communists were to prove Isadora's downfall. Her two children and their nurse died in a bizarre accident when her car, parked beside the Seine in Paris, rolled backwards down the bank and into the river, and they were all drowned. She later married a Russian and, returning to America after the 1917 Revolution, espoused favourable but unpopular views of the new regime, even deliberately adopting a red scarf as part of her new stage costume.

Isadora was different. Her style was unique and not based on ballet or any recognisable classic form of dance, but it was her wardrobe – or rather the lack of one – that shot her to stardom at the age of 20. All her costumes went up in flames when her New York hotel burned down. Forced to improvize, the dancer became the first to appear in see-through outfits. This was such a sensation that it became her hallmark. Her re-tailored wardrobe contained body-hugging costumes, diaphanous dresses, and an array of streamers that she sometimes used in place of any formal clothing, dancing virtually naked.

A man in every city

The dancer rarely remained faithful to any one man for long. Her career took her to numerous cities, and once she relinquished her precious virginity, there was a lover in every one. Then she met a family of fans when she was introduced to four sons of the sewing machine magnate Isaac Singer, who had a total of 23 children. She moved in with the eldest and quickly added a grandson to the brood. Isadora stayed with Paris Singer for nearly seven years, her first companion from outside the world of theatre. When they broke up, she went back to her own industry and set up home with Walter Rummel, who wrote musical scores for Broadway shows. He joined her touring troupe and showed her that infidelity was a two-sided business, so she dumped him in Athens.

Russia had dropped off her itinerary during the bloody years of the revolution, but in 1922 she returned to Moscow, always a favourite venue for her, and stayed long enough to marry for the first time at the age of 44. Sex had always been a form of relaxation for Isadora, and her choice of men was usually based on a single attribute, their athleticism in bed. Husband No. 1 had just become Russia's poet laureate. Sergei Yesenin, only 27, was already addicted to vodka among other things. His tantrums and outrageous life-style cost her a fortune, paying off irate hotel owners and managers for the furniture he smashed as they toured, and as a passionate Bolshevik he enraged America when she took him home. A year later she sent him back to Moscow.

Isadora's looks were fading along with her agility and her popularity when her death marked the final tragedy of her 49 years. She was living in the South of France, when posing for cameramen in a high-powered sports car – an open-topped Italian Bugatti – she stood up waving from the passenger seat, as the driver revved the engine and roared away with squealing tyres. Both ends of a long scarf Isadora was wearing caught in the spokes of a rear wheel, and she died instantly as her neck was broken.

Conductors of Music and Romance

Duke Ellington and Leopold Stokowski had two aspects of life in common: their love of music and their passion for women, lots of women. They were both masters of the keyboard, and though they were at either end of the music scene, achieved their fame with baton in hand. The two men acquired a certain infamy in America through their frenetic love-lives, lasting very nearly half a century. But they came to their careers by very different routes. Duke Ellington learned to play the piano by memorising and copying key patterns from the ragtime song-rolls at home in Washington D.C., on his parents' pianola machine; Stokowski took the classical path, graduating from piano to organ through various music academies in London, Oxford, Paris and Berlin.

The "King of Swing" – married only to music

Duke Ellington was a smart dresser and a poser while a teenager, which was how he acquired his nick-name, and he had just formed his first band when he married a sweetheart from his schooldays at the age of 19. Though they were eventually separated, Edna Thompson remained his wife for 48 years, but the Duke, who was soon to be elevated in the musical ranks to become the "King of Swing", used his married status as a foil. He found it easier to dissuade the many women he loved and lived with from marriage by claiming that he could never divorce Edna and marry any one of them. All through his life there were actresses and singers, dancers and society ladies, who

FOUR KISSES

Duke Ellington greeted every woman to whom he was introduced in exactly the same way, especially those he already knew intimately when they were accompanied by their husbands. He kissed each one four times. It became his hallmark, and when a close friend asked why he did this, the band-leader explained, "It really represents one for each cheek!" He transported swing music on to another plane and told a biographer, "Music is my real mistress, she plays second fiddle to no one else."

patronized the clubs and concert halls where he fronted his swing-bands, to keep the Duke sexually satiated. Famously, he was asked by a club-owner one night to make his choice from the chorus line-up and replied, "I'll take the three on this end."

He was suave and charming and took big-band music on to another plane, arranging and recording some of the great swing classics. Gorgeous Creole girl Beatrice Ellis was a dancer from the Cotton Club in New York's Harlem. She went to bed with the Duke, and carried on doing so for nearly forty years. She once pulled a gun on him, trying to extract a promise that he would marry her, but the man courageously refused. Singer Fernanda de Castro Monte was another mistress who tried the same gun-toting ploy, again to no avail. During their years together they were known as the Duke and Duchess. On one occasion, as her man went away on yet another tour, she went to the station to see him off. With the band hanging out of the windows hooting and hollering, Fernanda opened her fur coat to give Duke a special platform farewell, and something to remember while he was away. She was stark naked underneath.

In a word: insatiable

Leopold Stokowski, born in London to a Polish emigrant cabinet maker, was able to learn his music courtesy of a wealthy sponsor. As a conductor, he was the first to record orchestral music, and the first to allow electrified instruments into the concert hall. He had so many affairs, especially with his young students at Philadelphia's music college, that the city's Curtis Institute became known as the "Coitus Institute". His fame arrived when, without any experience, he took the baton in front of the Cincinnati Symphony Orchestra. For the next thirty years, as resident conductor of the Philadelphia Symphony Orchestra, he popularized classical music around the world.

CREATIVE SEX

Leopold Stokowski had amazing stamina at work and play. He toured the world as a conductor well into his seventies and later continued to make guest appearances. He was the inspiration for the musical score of Disney's film *Fantasia*, wrote a book *Music for All of Us*, founded orchestras all over America and was the prime mover of low-price concerts in New York. He maintained that constant sexual activity provided his musical creativity and among scores of mistresses, his greatest conquest was film actress Greta Garbo. She described their first mating, "I felt the electricity going right through me, from head to toe," and they lived together for ten blissful months in an Italian mountain-top villa overlooking the Mediterranean. He died at the age of 95.

His first wife was a concert pianist who stayed a dozen years before she tired of his infidelity and divorced him. That allowed the conductor to conduct his love-life more openly. Married or single, young or old, he had no great preference as long as they were willing and available. Then he met the much younger Evangeline Johnson, millionaire heiress to a pharmaceutical fortune, and three weeks later she became his second wife. She was a liberated and leading member of New York society and accepted his wanderings from their wedding vows but when the affairs with well-known actresses started hitting the headlines, she quit and divorced him.

The next and last Mrs Stokowski was another fabulously wealthy woman, the blonde and beautiful Gloria Vanderbilt, who was only 23 but clearly enchanted by the baton-waving of Leopold. They wed in Reno, Nevada, where her own divorce had just come through and she had already inherited millions of dollars, with more to arrive from the family fortune. She could not cope with the demands of a husband forty years her senior and sought psychiatric help, but the best advice her doctors could give was "turn a blind eye", and that she did while Stokowski carried on having affairs into his 80s, when they finally divorced.

Lola Montez

A series of famous lovers tried and failed to keep up with the sexual demands that this dancer and actress made on their stamina. The composer Franz Liszt was one of many who left his satiated and sleeping mistress, wrote a farewell note, dressed and crept from their hotel bedroom in Paris. As he paid the bill, he handed a further amount to the manager explaining, "This should cover the cost of the furniture she will break when she wakes up and discovers I have left." Her fiery Irish temper was by now famous – the woman had publicly horse-whipped a lover who enraged her – but Lola's striking beauty, her rash promiscuity, and her wild personality constantly drew high-born and wealthy men to her side.

Her introduction to sex was bizarre. She was 18 and still at boarding school when her parents replied to a newspaper advertisement and arranged a marriage to a 60-year-old judge in India. She was distraught, but she was saved by one of her mother's many lovers, an English army officer who seduced the girl when she came home on holiday. They wed, then four years later went their separate ways. He cited adultery, and a special Act of Parliament was passed in a blaze of publicity in London, granting Lieutenant Thomas James a judicial separation. In its way, that forced Lola's hand, led her to a lucrative career, and years later, forced her to flee England because she had never divorced and was charged with bigamy. Her stage routine became famous in Europe and America, where she joined the Californian gold rush, and her Spider Dance, an extension of classical Spanish dancing she had failed to master, started riots among her male audiences.

This was the middle of the last century. Liberation for women was a hard struggle, and ladies like Lola, parading their sex with their talent, were at the forefront of the

BIGAMOUS DESERTER

George Heald was the well-heeled cavalry officer in the British Army who bigamously married Lola, deserting his regiment as well as his friends and family when they fled London to live in America. He suffered dreadfully at her hands. In one of her tempestuous outbreaks, she stabbed him. Later, with his fortune dwindling, he became an alcoholic. By the time they separated, the syphilis she had contracted during her early sexual escapades was starting to dog her with periodic outbreaks of illness, claiming Lola's looks and eventually her life.

fight. She would strut to the footlights, lift each one of many coloured pet-ticoats, shake imaginary spiders free and crush them underfoot. Flashing her legs and underwear, she was condemned by society, but there was no other act like it in the world. The dancer turned courtesan, and men were willing to pay high prices for her favours. She even charged a dollar for a ten-minute chat. Sex came at a far greater price, and it cost certain lovers their lives as well as their fortunes.

Courting sex and death in Paris and California

Paris was a natural base for the dancer where, after an exhausted Liszt desert-ed her, she bedded writer Alexander Dumas – the father but, as far as we know, not the son. She moved on to a wealthy publisher and another Alexander, Monsieur Dujarier, who turned to drink when Lola finally spurned him. Provoked by an employee, he challenged the man to a duel. Dujarier lost the duel – and his life!

A fiasco in Germany and the revolutions breaking out not only in France but all over Europe inclined Lola to start her life afresh in America where she married again, to Patrick Hull the editor of a San Francisco newspaper. But he had the marriage annulled a few weeks later when he learned she had contin-ued an affair with a psychiatrist within a week of the wedding ceremony. The psychiatrist died very soon afterward in a mysterious hunting accident.

Out in California, she met out-of-work actor Noel Follin who became her manager as well as her lover and persuaded Lola to accompany him to Australia. She toured the cities and mining camps and was wildly pop-ular again, and wealthy, but sailing back to America, the couple had a furious argument and Follin grabbed all their money – mostly in gold coins – and jumped overboard in mid-Pacific. Yet another outbreak of syphilis took the last of her looks and all of her hair, and

THINK OF BEDROOMS

Marie Dolores Eliza Rosanna Gilbert was born in Limerick and adopted her stage name after training in Seville. The writer Aldous Huxley wrote, "When you met Lola Montez, her reputation made you automatically think of bedrooms." King Louis of Bavaria was infatuated when she danced in Munich; she moved into his palace and was made Countess of Landsfield. She began to wield so much unwelcome influence that demonstrators forced her to flee once more, and the king had to abdicate. Some hundred years after she died, the title Ballet Lola Montez was adopted by three sep-arate, international companies.

the be-wigged Lola turned to Christianity and works of charity. She spent the last years of her life lecturing on fashion and feminine beauty and then, in New York, striving valiantly to show the city's prostitutes a different way of life. Lola knew what she was talking about.

Kirk Douglas

A tough life in the early days of childhood was almost a prerequisite for success in Hollywood for America's biggest stars in the 1930s, 40s and 50s. But surely, no one had it tougher – or made it bigger – than Issur Danielovitch, who became Izzy Demsky and finally, Kirk Douglas. His parents were both Russian Jewish emigrants who could neither read nor write and brought up Kirk and his six sisters speaking a mixture of Yiddish and English, so their start at school was fraught with problems. Father earned his living as a ragman in Amsterdam in upper New York, a junk-dealer whose most precious possessions were his horse and cart.

Izzy was not a good student. His autobiography *The Ragman's Son*, reveals he was told "you are not college material," but Izzy knew a college education was essential to fulfil his dreams of becoming an actor. The English teacher Louise Livingstone discovered he liked to recite poetry, and introduced him to the romantic verses of Byron, Shelley and Keats, gaving the enthusiastic schoolboy extra tuition. She told him, "To be a great actor you must be a great person, you must be educated and trained." The caring widow, who was nearly thirty years

> ## SINATRA'S GUN
>
> *The Ragman's Son* reveals his failures with some of the great beauties of his time. After Lauren Bacall, there was Tallulah Bankhead at a studio party, who told the new arrival in Hollywood, "Don't look at me like that, young man." Ava Gardner walked into his room at two in the morning. "He's got a gun," she admitted, referring to husband Frank Sinatra – they were all staying in the same hotel. Kirk was tempted, but he persuaded Ava to return upstairs, and nothing happened. He was ready for the gorgeous Lana Turner when they starred in *The Bad and The Beautiful* but they couldn't shake off her jealous suitor, Fernando Lamas, and nothing happened.

older, did more than educate Izzy, she seduced him, and proceeded to give her 14-year-old favourite his sexual tuition at her home after his private lessons.

It was his first experience and the romance which began in the teacher's bedroom lasted right through college and high school, through his first roles on Broadway, then on into Hollywood. She urged him to save every penny he could earn on a morning paper-round and week-end jobs in a grocery store, and to send off for college and drama school entries. Though he had others lovers in those early days, he stayed in touch and wrote regularly to Louise who penned a book of poetry, marking each stage of their long relationship. As his fame and fortune arrived, Kirk Douglas paid for her care and nursing in her final days.

The actor writes at length of his bitter experiences as a young Jewish boy growing up in 1930s' America, of the anti-Semitism he suffered at high school and then during his search for a good-paying summer job. He tried the lakeside resort hotels close to the Canadian border, but Izzy Demsky was refused again and again. The first time he said "Don Demsky" he became the bell-hop at the Orchard House, a "restricted" hotel, which meant "No Jews". The attractive lady proprietor confided she couldn't stand Jews, and could spot them a mile off, as they smelled peculiar. But she took a fancy

CLINICAL CRAWFORD

His first starring role in *Champion* brought a congratulatory telegram from Joan Crawford, who Kirk Douglas admits had been the object of his early sexual fantasies. He phoned to thank her and landed a date, without realising the predatory actress was setting him up for a seduction scene. He describes what happened when they returned from the restaurant, "We went back to her house and never got past the foyer. The door closed and she slipped out of her dress; she had a beautiful, trim body and there we were on the rug...the lovemaking was professional, clinical and lacking in warmth. I got out fast."

to the young bellhop, and led him to her bed on the last night of the season. "Hate can become such an aphrodisiac, I had a tremendous erection," Kirk admits.

Revenge taken hot

They fornicated, and as she moaned and groaned he waited until it was too late for her to stop. Then he told her, "That is a circumcized Jewish cock inside you. Do you think you'll get contaminated, maybe even die? I am a Jew, you are being f**ked by a Jew." She had her orgasm then lay silently on her bed while he dressed, left the room and left the hotel. But the anti-Semitism continued through university and a variety of vacation jobs in other hotels, at a steel mill, and wrestling at fun-fairs. The name Kirk Douglas came at drama school in New York, suggested by fellow actors at the Tamarack Playhouse, when he graduated aged 22, in the year 1939.

Kirk was used to being poor, and to pay his way as he learned the business of acting, he became a waiter and managed to survive on the tips he collected, eating the unfinished meals he took back to the kitchen. He was already a ladies-man, and drama school provided a never-ending string of affairs. He failed in an attempt to seduce Lauren Bacall but met the girl who would become his first wife, Diana Dill. His first role on Broadway gave him four lines, as a singing telegram boy, then America entered the war and Kirk joined the navy.

Though he went back to New York after the war, Kirk Douglas was on his way to Hollywood in a matter of months. Diana gave him two sons, but the marriage broke up. Returning to his bachelor days, he first escorted glamorous Rita Hayworth, herself recently divorced from Prince Aly Khan, then the talented Patricia Neal who was trying to salvage an affair with Gary Cooper. A long affair with the beautiful Gene Tierney followed, and she insisted that when he came calling, he climb through her bedroom window. Marlene Dietrich provided "affectionate sex" he says, nursing him through pneumonia after filming on location in Wyoming. "She seemed to love you much more if you were not well."

Then Kirk met Pier Angeli as they made a circus-movie *The Story of Three Loves*. "I was completely bowled over by her. I was intoxicated by the trapeze, by the altitude and by Pier," he says. By the time filming ended they agreed to get engaged – she was 19, he was 35. Her obsessive, domineering mother obstructed his every romantic move however and the innocent, virginal Italian actress was also playing games. Before they parted – Pier eventually committed suicide – Kirk had met German-born Anne Buydens, the woman who would become his second wife and life-long partner.

Hermione Gingold

She was called, on more than one occasion, The Funniest Woman in the World, and wrote a delightful autobiography *How to Grow Old Disgracefully*, dedicated to her many friends, "without whose help it would have been written in half the time". At 81, still performing on Broadway, this English comedy actress began an affair with a young man aged 26, and was moved to say, "The trouble with men is that there are not enough of them." This was Hermione Gingold, a lady who, nearing seventeen and passionately kissed for the first time by her first boyfriend, was convinced the result would be a baby. She confessed her guilt to mother, whose lecture on the facts of life had gone no further than the injunction never to sit on a strange lavatory seat, and was relieved to learn the truth.

She was undoubtedly one of Britain's greatest unorthodox characters. Reviewer and critic Sheridan Morley wrote, "Hermione Gingold is an original, a one hundred per cent, solid gold eccentric." Threats to write her memoirs, to name names, and to tell all her stories unnerved her former husbands and lovers and several friends, but the woman stayed faithful to her own image. "After one is dead, people write such terrible things about one," she told her friend Lady Anne Eyre. "Of course, in my case they will all be true, but I would write them myself and get the record straight."

Michael Joseph, writer turned publisher, was her first husband and there soon followed two sons, Leslie and Stephen. Then she miscarried soon afterwards, and decided she could not sleep with her husband any more, "I was afraid of having another baby." This was soon after the 1914–18 war, and they were both in their early twenties, but even in showbusiness, Victorian values were still in vogue. "Michael and I simply had no idea where to get advice on

> ## PINK SHOES
> • • • • • • • • • • • • • • • • •
> Confronted by an admirer who asked, "It's Hermione Gingold, isn't it?" she replied, "Who? I've never heard of her, she must be very ugly." Shopping with a friend, she said, "I think I'll buy these pink shoes, they'll draw attention away from my face."
> • • • • • • • • • • • • • • • • •

how to stop babies coming," she admitted. As the marriage began to fail, she started an affair with Eric Maschwitz, who wrote *A Nightingale Sang in Berkeley Square*, and later became director of light entertainment at the BBC.

But very soon she discovered his infidelities with a cousin, a couple of actresses she knew and her best friend. Then Hermione decided to have a few affairs herself.

Learning, teaching and performing

Nude swimming with Peter in Lake Maggiore, blue film shows with Anthony on the Cote d'Azur, a long affair with Leslie, a student of Indian philosophy, and acting in London for £3 a week were all part of extending her life experience and career in the 1930s. Horror actor Vincent Price used to come round to her flat for singing lessons, "and he proved to be a very able pupil," she said wickedly.

SHOPPING LIST

● ● ● ● ● ● ● ● ● ● ● ● ● ● ● ● ●

Her sarcastic one-liners were legendary. Asked by a playwright what she thought of his script, she told him, "My dear boy, in future I advise you to write nothing more ambitious than a shopping list." When a TV chat-show host queried, "Hermione, is your husband still living?" in a voice once described as powdered glass in deep syrup, she said, "It's a matter of opinion."

● ● ● ● ● ● ● ● ● ● ● ● ● ● ● ● ●

Then came war years again, 1939 to 45, and the terror of living in bomb-blasted London. "It was the most immoral time of my life," she confessed. "If I felt I needed an excuse, I had the one of not knowing which day or night was going to be my last. So the loan of my body to a handsome young American who was going to France, with no one to tell his fears to or make love to, seemed the least I could offer. It was my contribution to the war effort, and I needed them as much as they needed me." After the war, when she settled in America, the United Nations gave her a special medal "for furthering Anglo-American relations."

The lady was adored in cabaret and stage revues by the American GIs and typical of the then-risqué verses she penned especially for them was *Thanks Yanks!*: "That very nice boy, from old Illinois, who led an attack on my flanks. The least I could say, was 'thanks'." Many offers to play on Broadway led Hermione to settle in New York, and though she never married again, she was rarely without a man by her side, at least at night. "I use men as they use me," said the lady, "I hope I've made a lot of men happy and what I did, I did with dignity. Fortunately, AIDS wasn't with us then – quite a few of my lovers have been bisexual." At the age of seventy-four she was simultaneously engaged to two men, a long-suffering lover she called Beaudoin and actor

Peter Bull, and gave both the heave-ho. But Hermione was not ready to give up, not yet, and the last love of her life was an Indian named Little Big Boy, just 55 years younger. They stayed together five years, "then after I turned eighty five, I discovered sex was not so important any more which surprised me; up till then I had always been a sex maniac," she wrote. In her ninetieth year Hermione Gingold died, and her autobiography was published shortly afterwards.

PARTY AT THE PALACE

She was the mistress of repartee. As a guest at Buckingham Palace, at a Royal Garden Party, Prince Philip came over and asked "What are you doing here?" Her immediate retort brought a smile from the Queen's husband, "I was about to ask you the same thing."

Douglas Fairbanks, Jnr.

He was born with an astounding pedigree for an actor, and the drop-dead handsome looks he developed with a natural, suave charm were too much. Then the action-packed war years of the 1940s turned the fledgling film star into a real-life hero. When that conflict ended, the established sex-symbols out in Hollywood, chaps like Errol Flynn, Gary Cooper and Clarke Gable, were forced to recognize they had missed an important rung on life's lusty ladder.

Douglas Fairbanks Jnr. was certainly a chip off the old block, for father Douglas had been the uncrowned King of Hollywood back in the silent days of films in the 1920s. A gallant, swashbuckling idol and star of the original *Three Musketeers*, *Robin Hood* and *Thief of Baghdad* – all later remade into lavish, Technicolor productions – father passed on his good looks and his talent, honed and refined for the son by stepmother and leading-lady Mary Pickford. But naturally, for the necessary introduction to sex, the youngster had to make his own way. Youngster he truly was; the tender thirteen-year-old, who easily looked three or four years older, was seduced by his school tutor's girlfriend of twenty-two, deep in the bushes on the Bois de Boulogne in the middle of Paris ... and he fainted!

The actor wrote his humorous memoirs in two parts, *Salad Days* and *A Hell of a War*. In the second he relates this happy experience: "I never suspected that variety could also be the spice of carnal gamesmanship, and then I became delightfully dizzy and I just plain passed out." When he came round the girl offered to continue with these extra tutorials but mother soon complained that he was working too hard, being tired and pale with dark circles under his eyes, and ordered a respite.

NO HANKY PANKY

• • • • • • • • • • • • • • • •

A rare night out with old chum David Niven in war-time London had its finale with a couple of Cockney prostitutes. They took the girls back, "for a few drinks and laughs and no hanky-panky, honestly". When they were recognized, the girls broke out the real – and rationed – whisky. Then one was called away, in black lace-underwear and very high heels, to attend to "The Major", a regular every Thursday. Douglas and David were invited to listen at the wall and heard the crack of a whip. "That's a fine pony, giddyap." The girl's heels clacked faster and faster and the whip snapped again and again, then they heard a high-pitched cry from the major, then a low, "Thank you m'dear, that was splendid, here's a fiver."

• • • • • • • • • • • • • • • •

Billie blows his mind

He made fifteen films between 1925 and 1928 although still in his teens. Mother was obliged by law to accompany him in the studios, and he had to grow a moustache to appear older. There were plenty of girlfriends, then he received a letter from a young starlet who had seen him in a play on the West Coast – Joan Crawford, not unused to making the first move, suggested they should meet. He called her Billie and discovered all the sexual education he would ever need was immediately available. He went a stage further, fell in love and married her. Douglas was still only 19, and Billie – or Joan – was 23.

The marriage lasted four years and he says, "I have no idea when those enormous hungry eyes of hers locked on to someone else." They were growing apart, but it was Joan who decided it was all over. She moved all his clothes out of the house into the Beverley Wiltshire Hotel, then sent a message to his agent. He discovered that for the past two years she had conducted a very passionate affair with Clark Gable, and one of their favourite love-nests was a portable dressing room Douglas had bought her as a wedding present and had only just finished paying for.

He crossed the Atlantic and fell for Gertrude Lawrence, the darling of London's theatre set. Her circle of friends and admirers included two Royal princes

> **ROYAL FRIENDS**
>
> Fairbanks received several American commendations for his bravery during the war, was decorated by the French and British forces, and was a staff officer on board the flagship USS Washington when King George VI paid a Royal visit. "What are you doing up here?" asked the king, then in an aside to the admiral, to the star's immense embarrassment, added, "We haven't met since we played golf together at Sunningdale."

who would both shortly become kings, Laurence Olivier, Ivor Novello, Noel Coward, John Gielgud, Beatrice Lillie, Cole Porter and Fred Astaire. All these soon became Douglas's friends as he wooed the older "Gee", though he was forced to compete with a British aristocrat, the Earl of Dudley. She romanced them both for over two years but then a new lover arrived on his doorstep, Marlene Dietrich. They were very secretive about their affair, but as he took his leave of her suite at Claridge's Hotel one dawn via the fire escape, he was watched with interest by a young policeman. "Morning Mr Fairbanks, trying out a scene for a new film are we?" he asked with a smile. Marlene then moved into the same block of flats where he was living.

MISTRESS SWAPPING

The Earl of Dudley had twin brothers who were so identical that they sometimes swapped girlfriends and took the unsuspecting ladies to bed, and were never found out. Both were in the RAF, and early one Sunday morning, with Douglas Fairbanks as an unofficial passenger, they repeatedly "buzzed" Noel Coward's weekend house guests in Kent. Coward had everyone line up on the lawn with their pillows to spell out "F**k off."

Their love affair continued back in Hollywood, but was going nowhere when he met Mary Lee, recently divorced from the fabulously wealthy Huntingdon Hartford, and three months later they married. When war began, Douglas Fairbanks went on to serve with great distinction in the US Navy on several warships. He helped found an elite beach attack group, commanded an amphibious landing unit, and joined a special intelligence group to plan major attacks on mainland Europe. After the war he continued to live happily with Mary Lee, who by now had presented him with two daughters.

Ava Gardner

She was gorgeous. Her dark eyes promising, the generous curves of her body so inviting, Ava Gardner treated life as a banquet, men were put there before her to be devoured. And the lady – dubbed the World's Most Beautiful Animal – was a glutton. There was never a more raunchy actress than Ava, she chalked up lovers on her sexual calender for forty years, the three she married were just as voracious. Actor Mickey Rooney, band-leader Artie Shaw and crooner Frank Sinatra who, together, amassed a total of twenty wives.

The story of Ava Gardner's break into the film business sounds like the corny screen-play of an old Hollywood '"B"'movie itself. Nevertheless, it's a true story and her potential shone from a picture in a photographer's shop window display. The photographer was 19-year-old Ava's brother-in-law who happily loaned the snapshot to a man who introduced himself as an MGM studio talent scout. He was a liar but often used the ruse to impress pretty girls but when Ava's picture eventually turned up in Los Angeles, the girl was summoned for a screen test.

Louis B. Mayer, the studio head, viewed the results and is reputed to have said, "She can't act, she can't talk but she's terrific. Put her on the payroll." From her home in Newport News, Virginia, the auburn-haired, almond-eyed woman with the perfect 36-20-36 figure, made the journey to the West Coast with her older sister Bappie as chaperone, a condition imposed by her ultra-strict mother. Within months she had

---

ALL MAN ...

Director John Ford hosted a dinner party for African politicians and diplomats in Uganda during the filming of *Mogambo* and cruelly tossed in the question, "Why don't you tell us what you see in that 120-pound little runt you're married to ?" Sinatra was not then the most popular man in Hollywood but Ava replied casually, "Well, there's ten pounds of Frank and a hundred and ten pounds of cock !"

---

met and married the cocky little star Mickey Rooney, and she was still only 19. Agent Milton Weiss witnessed their first meeting, "Mickey took one look at Ava and he was as horny as hell, he had to have her. And if that meant wedding bells, he just had to have her."

In the two years their marriage lasted Ava gained experience and poise, and acquired the serenity and sexual aura which provided magnificent fantasies for men from three different generations. Free again, she started to enjoy herself and among the stars queueing up to date her, Fernando Lamas, Peter Lawford and singer Billy Daniels were the most regular. But she had enjoyed a teenage crush on band leader Artie Shaw and when he wooed her she moved in to live with the four-times married, clarinet player. She soon became wife No 5 ... but only for nine months.

Then she met studio and airline owner Howard Hughes, eccentric and insanely jealous, he had her followed when he was away from home on business. They rowed when he accused her of staying out all night dancing at the Mocambo Club which she readily admitted, and he slapped her so hard her jaw was dislocated. She knocked him out with a brass ornament grabbed from above the fireplace. Their tempestuous on-off affair was widely publicized and years later, during the filming of *My Forbidden Past* with Robert Mitchum who was under contract to Howard Hughes, the actor phoned his boss and asked, "Would you mind if I went to bed with Ava ?" Hughes replied, "If you don't, everyone will think you're a pansy."

SHE WRUNG HIM DRY ...

In Italy for *The Naked Maja,* she had a wild affair with Tony Franciosa who was playing the eccentric painter Goya. He was then married to Shelley Winters who flew from California to confront the couple on the film set and the two women had a fight, swinging fists and pulling hair. Shelley accused, "She wrung him dry, she made love to him so often he lost weight. He needed two weeks recuperating in Capri to finish off the film."

Her career was progressing sedately but satisfactorily and Ava had discovered an insatiable appetite for sex, bedding more of her leading men like Clark Gable, Howard Duff and Robert Taylor who she used to meet secretly at his mother's house. She was seen out with David Niven and John Huston then along came crooner Frank Sinatra who ultimately became her third and final husband. Their life together, before, during and after marriage, was always stormy. He too was moody and jealous but that never stopped Ava doing exactly what she wanted to do, and with whom. Just prior to their wedding, in 1951, she went to Spain to film *Pandora and the Flying Dutchman* and briefly fell in love with bullfighter Mario Cabre but Sinatra forgave her.

The year after they wed she was off to Africa to film Mogambo, co-starring old flame Clark Gable and Ava was ready to rekindle the flames but Grace Kelly got to him first. The two women were natural rivals but became good friends and one day during *Mogambo*, as they walked past a group of Watusi warriors, Ava said to her, "I wonder if their cocks are as big as they say ?" and as Grace blushed she pulled up the loin cloth of the nearest African and commented, "Not as big as Frank's." In the middle of making that film she flew back to London for an abortion, she and Sinatra were having serious problems and there was no way she was going to have his baby, Ava confided to friends. Though he had been at the top of the music business for a couple of decades, it was Ava and his passion for the voluptuous actress that taught him how to sing a torch-song, said conductor Nelson Riddle.

The stunning actress always found difficulty sleeping at night so she gave up nights, going out clubbing, drinking and dancing and going to bed around dawn, she worked hard and played hard and there were few men on the Hollywood scene during her prime who could out-drink Ava Gardner. She bought a house in Spain and found another bullfighter to love, Luis Miguel Dominguin – "I speak no Spanish and he speaks little English but boy, can we communicate in bed," said Ava. By no means all her lovers were VIPs, Spaniards she met in bars and American officers stationed at local air bases frequently got lucky. A production assistant on one film told a biographer years later how he went to Ava's dressing room to deliver some dialogue changes. She said, "We'll discuss those later, let's go to bed first." And they did.

The Barefoot Contessa was filmed in Rome where co-star Humphrey Bogart gave her a wide berth so the come-hither look was turned on Italian comedian Walter Chiari. She went to India to film *Bhowani Junction* where, Ava admitted, she failed to seduce the male lead Stewart Granger, walking into his room wrapped only in a towel but he pleaded marriage vows – his wife was Jean Simmons.

She failed again in Mexico on Night of the Iguana but for different reasons. Ava

GOING DOWN ...

Ava had three days work – and blew the fifty thousand dollar fee on a water skiing trip to Acapulco – filming The Life and Times of Judge Roy Bean. Jokingly, she gave 70-something actor Billy Pearson the eye and the microphones picked up his response. "How would you like an old man to go down on you ?" Everyone on set froze, until Ava cracked up laughing and threw her arms round him.

wanted Richard Burton, confessing she was curious about his sexual prowess, but he was about to wed Elizabeth Taylor and she was right there, appearing in the same film. So Ava moved a 20-year-old local beach-boy into her apartment. In Rome again to make *The Bible,* she had a turbulent affair with

George C. Scott and during a row she punched him so hard, Ava fractured her collar bone and was forced to wear a neck brace. Omar Sharif, ten years younger, got the treatment as they filmed *Mayerling* but he was never one to kiss and tell.

In between films she was dating two more bullfighters Cumillano and Curro Giron and had a brief fling with a well-known playboy of those times, Porfirio Rubirosa. Then she went to Mexico, so much like her beloved Spain, to film *The Sun Also Rises* and by day dallied with screen-writer Peter Viertel, and by night partied with her co-stars Tyrone Power, Mel Ferrer and Errol Flynn. She was still in the final days of her marriage to Sinatra, then boy-friend Walter Chiari arrived. Ava was unfazed by all the potential complications, she had her choice of men.

Probably her happiest times were the years she spent living in Spain. She cared little for either the climate or the food but the wildness of the country, its culture and particularly, the practice of starting the day's revelries close to midnight and continuing until the dawn, suited Ava wonderfully. The constant party-ing gave her a taste for booze – anise, gin mixed with beer, cognac, all kinds of liquers and whisky. When finally she was forced to leave Spain and set up home in London and live life at a more sedate pace, she had first to dry-out at a health farm.

MOB HANDED

Ava Gardner spent money as fast as she earned it and only the continual generosity of Frank Sinatra allowed her to live her last years in some comfort. Sinatra was her protector, sometimes hiring bodyguards to keep her safe. When two more rows with George C. Scott left her black and blue, the actor returned to his hotel room and found all the sleeves of his coats, sweaters and shirts had been cut off – an anonymous warning that next time, it would be his arms.

Sedate meant fewer lovers, not celibacy, and London proved more accommodating for her discreet affairs with an actor, a comedian, a producer and then she almost made it to the altar again, with singer Freddie Davis, 22 years her junior and she is reported to have given serious consideration to his proposal. Ava was a long time coming to terms with television and turned down several opportunities, finally making seven episodes of *Knot's Landing*, at $50,000 dollars each. The fun and games were coming to an end, she was plagued by ill-health and having never been possessed by anyone, Ava now chose to live virtually as a recluse. She admitted, "Whatever wrinkles are there, I enjoyed getting them," and finally died in London early in 1990, aged 67, from pneumonia.

Audrey Hepburn

If anyone can claim to have "discovered" Audrey Hepburn, it would be the famous French novelist Colette. She was only 19 and had played bit-parts in four films, all made in 1951, when the ageing Colette went specifically to watch her filming another minor part in Monte Carlo. But the author of the book, now to became a smash-hit play, had to argue and pursuade the elphin-faced actress to accept the wonderful role on Broadway of Gigi — the young Parisian girl who is coached by two elderly courtesans in the ways-of-the-world. Though Miss Hepburn's sex life cannot begin to compare with many actresses of her day, it will surprise many of her fans to know there is even a hint of scandal in Audrey's closet.

> ## MONEY, MONEY, MONEY
> • • • • • • • • • • • • • • • • • •
> Director Billy Wilder was asked why Humphrey Bogart wound up with Audrey in the last scene in *Sabrina Fair*, instead of the handsome and younger William Holden. Cynically, he replied, "Because Bogey gets $300,000 a picture and the other guy gets $125,000".
> • • • • • • • • • • • • • • • • • •

A dozen years after *Gigi*, the role of cockney flower-seller Eliza Doolittle in *My Fair Lady*, made Audrey one of Hollywood's first million-dollar stars. The stingy producer Jack Warner fought tooth and nail against paying her such a fee for one picture but the star's agent won the battle and she received the money spread over ten years, for tax purposes, plus a per centage of the box office takings for one of the biggest money-earners of all time. But that image of Gigi never left her. She protested to Colette, "Madam, I am not ready to play such an important part, I haven't learned to act yet."

In Audrey Hepburn the writer recognized the very character she had invented — "a gazelle, a young colt, half-woman, half-boy, unformed, unself-conscious, surely a virgin, perfect !" said Colette. And on Broadway Miss Hepburn, the daughter of a Dutch baroness, was an overnight success. Yet the beautiful Paulette Goddard, who would become a firm friend out in California, first met Audrey in London and commented, "There has to be something wrong with that girl. Anyone who looks like that should have been discovered before she was 10-years-old." Her looks and the fame she soon achieved did not impress her, with New York applauding and Hollywood beckoning Audrey considered giving up her career to marry

James Hanson, later the industrial billionaire Lord Hanson, and settle down with him in Huddersfield where he then ran the family's haulage business.

It didn't happen. Acting fascinated her and as she finished in Gigi the opportunity to star opposite Gregory Peck in *Roman Holiday*, winning her an Oscar, was too much. He was the first of her many male leads to be romantically linked with Audrey but they were never involved. And in her next picture, *Sabrina Fair*, the irritable and hard-drinking Humphrey Bogart positively disliked this "young up-start."

Audrey didn't care for him either but the other male star, William Holden, now that was something else. The two instantly fell for each other, Audrey virtually engaged to Hanson was uncomfortable while Holden, very much married with three children, pursued her relentlessly. Their affair became public when both fluffed their lines in front of camera and the paranoid but word-perfect Bogart, exclaimed publicly, "They're conspiring against me because she's giving him a tumble. Look at those rings under her eyes, they're at it every night."

> ### THE HAND OF FATE
> • • • • • • • • • • • • • • • •
> Her second husband was a schoolboy of only 14 when they first met. Andrea Dotti shook the star's hand when she filmed an outside scene in *Roman Holiday*, near his home. He was twice that age, a psychiatrist specializing in female depression, when they met again on a Mediterranean cruise and soon married. Audrey was nearly ten years older.
> • • • • • • • • • • • • • • • •

The macho-Holden leaped to her defence and told Bogart to put his hands up. The screen tough guy was a moral coward and withdrew but that confrontation did William Holden's chances with the still impressionable young actress no harm at all. What ruined his chances, eventually, was the admission that if they were to continue the romance and ultimately marry, he could not give her children. The actor, a self-confessed hypochondriac who worried constantly about his sexual prowess and who played so many ultra-masculine roles, had had a vasectomy.

The man who would turn her into a mother, soon came along, husband No 1 Mel Ferrer, actor, writer and director who met Audrey the night *Roman Holiday* premiered in London. They fell in love, played Broadway together but her mother, the baroness, did not approve and issued several statements denying a romance. He had been married three times before, albeit twice to the same woman, and had four children. They wed in 1954 filmed *War and Peace* and *Green Mansions* together but during 13 years of marriage were frequently parted by their careers.

For the improbably named *Love in the Afternoon*, Audrey had two older suitors, on and off screen, Gary Cooper and Maurice Chevalier. If there was anything between her and the French actor, neither admitted it but he later confessed, "I did love her, I couldn't help myself." More rumours flew of another affair with Peter Finch but he was busy with an air hostess and reportedly with the other female lead Dame Peggy Ashcroft, quietly renowned as a man-eater. Marriage started heading downhill during *My Fair Lady* as she began to hear of Mel's affair with a young Spanish flamenco dancer.

Audrey was brilliant though out of character, playing the adulterous and promiscuous Holly Golightly in *Breakfast at Tiffany's* and later was tantalized by Peter O'Toole in *How to Steal a Million* — they had to film one scene trapped together in a closet, "very tempting" he said. Then came real romance with another British star, Albert Finney, and she abandoned her marriage vows to have a serious affair – "we met in a seductive ambience, in a very sensual time in the Mediterranean and there was an absolute attraction," he admitted.

Prince Alphonso of Spain was her next consort before her divorce and husband Number 2, Italian doctor Andrea Dotti, who provided brief happiness and she soon became pregnant with her second son. But the good doctor had too-good a bedside manner and he was frequently photographed night-clubbing with Italian models and starlets, but Audrey was able to treat him to similar medicine through a rumoured affair with Ben Gazzara, her co-star in two films. She finally found her ideal man, Dutch actor Robert Wolders. He was nearly ten years younger and whose first wife, glamorous actress Merle Oberon, had just died. They were together when Audrey Hepburn died in her early 60s in 1993, still trying to come to terms with the looks which dazzled so many men.

CHAPTER 2

THE GLITTERATI
ARTISTS, AUTHORS, COMPOSERS: THE VIRTUOSOS WHO WERE LESS THAN VIRTUOUS

☆ ☆

James Boswell

Two of England's great men of letters who lived a century apart, left ample records for researchers and biographers to piece together dramatic and shocking accounts of their sex lives. James Boswell had been dead more than a hundred years when his now-famous papers were discovered and in fine detail the parade of prostitutes, passionate mistresses and wealthy lovers are named and their escapades described in full.

He confessed, he enjoyed intercourse best when he was hurried, standing up and especially in public places – against a tree in the central parks of London and Paris or in a darkened side street off a main thoroughfare. When he felt the urge to copulate, which was frequent, he did not wait to reach his wife or the home of one of his latest lady-loves, he sought the company of the nearest available whore. These urges and the rapid coupling usually accompanied heavy drinking bouts with his literary friends when he might leave the party for half-an-hour, satisfy himself and return to the inn. When the evening finally ended, Boswell would often seek the lady's services again.

But the lecherous writer's treatment of these professional ladies was abominable. He names the whore who had him first; "Sally Forrester introduced me to the melting and transporting rites of love." She was the first but by no means the last and a succession of paid-for liaisons infected and re-infected him with venereal disease – his first dose came at the age of nineteen. He accosted one in a park and gave her sixpence, the woman was so offended to be offered so little money, she set about Boswell and her shouts drew a crowd around them. Her potential customer explained he was an officer on half-pay and could afford no more and with the crowd yelling encouragement, Boswell admits, "I forced myself upon the woman and abused her in black-guard style." That was his way of saying he raped her.

It seems he was always ready to take every opportunity to bed any woman who came his way. The pregnant wife of a soldier, selling chocolate to raise a little more money, called at his rented rooms in Berlin. She was soon on her way, "Our lust was satisfied in a minute," he recorded. His wife had a teenage, orphaned niece who came to stay with them for a while and with-out telling us whether his wife discovered the truth, Uncle James admits he "snatched a little romping pleasure with Anne". On the long journey from Italy, accompanying Jean Jacques Rousseau's mistress to England, he lost no time nor frequent opportunity to cuckold his old friend and bedded Therese le Vasseur. On their first night staying at an inn just outside Dover, he left her side to seduce a servant girl who had caught his eye downstairs.

BOSWELL'S CLAP

• • • • • • • • • • • • • • • •

Dr William Ober, chronicling Boswell's medical history, took a leaf from his subject's book when he entitled it *Boswell's Clap and Other Essays*, and tells us the man caught gonorrhoea nineteen times. Condoms in the late 1700s were made of dried animal's intestines so his partners risked conception and they both risked infection. The symptoms were, he wrote, "A little heat in the members of my body sacred to Cupid." The treatment caused almost as much suffering as the disease and he was only fifty-four when he died from complications arising from yet another bout of gonorrhoea.

• • • • • • • • • • • • • • • •

The cost of romping

He was still looking for a rich bride when he met Mrs Anne Lewis who was well connect-ed but unfortunately, still married. She had as healthy a regard for lusty intercourse as Boswell. His diary records they coupled successfully five times, staying the night at the Black Lion Inn. Food at the inn and the room for their fornication cost eighteen shillings, a sum he demanded the woman should repay when six days later he discov-ered she had given him gonorrhoea. His next mistress was also married, Mrs Amy Dodds who he describes as, "admirably formed for amorous dalliance, quite a rompish girl". We can safely assume she was well endowed, Boswell adored women with a big bosom. Two of these affairs produced offspring, a boy and a girl who both died in infancy.

Boswell's papers are written in eloquent though rather verbose style but he brought much original prose when dealing with his love life. He claims to have remained faithful to the buxom Margaret for the first three years of their marriage but when "she became averse to the hymeneal rites", he told his wife he must have a concubine. According to Boswell, she agreed at once, perhaps to ease the burden of his constant demands on her body. But they appear to have remained happy together for twenty years – and he was clearly grateful for her patience and support in helping him through a long period of impotence – until Margaret died of tuberculosis.

MARRYING MARGARET

James Boswell was short with heavy jowls but his dark hair and eyes, and a wicked grin, made him attractive to women. He tried hard to find a rich, well-dowried heiress, but at the age of twenty-nine he wed his penniless first cousin Margaret who bore him five children. Each act of love and the style adopted, with her and outside the marriage bed, was entered in his diary accompanied by a letter from the Greek alphabet. Margaret knew the code and had more than one reason to loathe his diaries.

The "multiplicity of women who fill my life" continued after her death but, though his fame as a writer was growing and his talent much admired, the dissolute, bawdy, licentious life James Boswell constantly pursued brought him public disgrace and in 1795, he at last succumbed to venereal disease. The public only knew the half of it, Boswell's papers were not discovered until the mid-1920s.

Lord Byron

Surely the greatest romantic poet the world has known and in his brief lifetime, Lord Byron assiduously practised what he preached, with a succession of wives, true loves, occasional mistresses and whores, even incest with a half-sister and, while a pupil at Harrow and a student at Cambridge, he dallied with homosexuality. Byron was a rogue, revelling privately in well-planned seductions and publicly in lewd and wild orgies. He went too far and London society, although growing more liberal at the beginning of the nineteenth century and by now well-used to scandal, hounded his lordship into exile, first in Venice then Greece where he died.

Byron was still at preparatory school when he acceded to the baronetcy and his first sexual experience came at the age of nine. The family nurse May used to fondle and arouse the young boy then allow him to watch as she made love with her more uninhibited partners, so he was more than ready when he became sexually active on his own behalf. His natural charm, the prose he constantly used in everyday language, the easy ability to awaken maternal instincts, particularly among his older partners, and undoubtedly, his wretched reputation, made him attractive to the opposite sex. Every woman who came into his company soon knew where his interests lay and many found him irresistible, despite his club-foot, his obesity and lack of stature. When the poetry and love-letters took over, the ladies in several corners of Europe could not get enough of Lord Byron. He was only 5ft 8ins yet he weighed 16 stones when he entered Cambridge, still in his teens. Later in life, though he always enjoyed eating and drinking among his wealthy companions, he often fasted to maintain something of a figure, living for weeks on hard biscuits and rice. Byron's satire and cynicism comes forth in two of his lines in a well-known poem:

> **BOYISH PRANK**
>
> To gain entry to an hotel in London's Mayfair where he was already well-known, he dressed one of his slender mistresses in boy's clothing and she was accepted as his younger cousin. But the cousin miscarried upstairs in a bedroom, causing absolute consternation among the staff, but Lord Byron survived and circulated the embarrassing story himself.

Let us have wine and women, mirth and laughter,
Sermons and soda-water the day after.

Seductive words and strange trophies

Though he enjoyed the conquests of younger and older boys at school and university, he was revolted by the prospect of having sex with men and satisfied his voracious appetite with a succession of mistresses and prostitutes in London. Perhaps his most famous, though easy, conquest was Lady Caroline Lamb, at twenty-seven the wife of a future Prime Minister of England. She was attracted by his reputation and verses of his recently published poetry:

> *Where the virgins are soft as the roses they twine,*
> *And all, save the spirit of man, is divine.*

Caroline was every bit as promiscuous as the poet and they exchanged unique gifts: locks of their pubic hairs. But when he tired of the affair he turned to her mother-in-law Lady Melbourne, to help him be rid of her. And the ageing Lady M was reputed to be yet another, grateful to share his bed.

Byron was not too proud to turn his attentions on to the "dead certs" of that era. He was twenty-four and happily accepted

HAVING A HALF SISTER

In 1813 Byron seduced Augusta Leigh. They shared the same father, Captain "Mad Jack" Byron, though they were brought up in separate homes. Years passed and when they met again, both in their twenties they rushed into bed and nine months later, Mrs Leigh bore the poet a daughter, Medora. That was the beginning of the end of his life in London, which turned its collective back on the licentious man of letters.

the invitation to move in for a while, from Jane Harley, forty-year-old wife of the Earl of Oxford. She had so many lovers and a succession of children who were known as the "Harleian Miscellany" as there could be no certainty about who had fathered each one. It was rumoured he attempted to rape Lady Oxford's thirteen-year-old daughter. To silence his many critics, Byron married Annabella who was convinced she could reform him. She gave up after one year and the birth of one daughter. He wrote in *Don Juan*:

> *Now hatred is by far the longest pleasure;*
> *Men love in haste, but they detest at leisure.*

For Byron, exile was a sensible answer but why should life change? In

Venice he bedded first his landlord's wife Marianna Segati, then the baker's wife Margarita Cogni. Renting the Palazzo Mocenigo he seduced a steady stream of married Venetians by day and hired local prostitutes at night. He wrote to friends in London, "Almost half my annual expenses are spent on women. This past year I have had 200 whores, perhaps more." The extra price he had to pay was the accompanying gonorrhoea which he poetically described as "The Curse of Venus".

Whether it was a shortage of money, the disease or a waning interest in sex, Lord Byron now entered a five year period of domesticity, though it must be said, with another man's wife. A marriage of convenience to Count Guiccoli did not suit nineteen-year-old Teresa. She fell for Byron and was delighted when the count invited him to move in, a ménage-à-trois which kept everyone happy. When they parted, the poet moved to Greece and lived for only nine more months. He was still only thirty-six when disease, mainly venereal, claimed him in 1824.

Guy de Maupassant

For a man on the threshold of a brilliant writing career, and who aroused not only passion but gratitude among his many loves, his death aged only forty-two, attributed to syphilis and in a lunatic asylum, was a tragedy. A greater tragedy lies in the probability that the killer venereal disease was inherited, though he still managed to be constantly sexually active for a quarter of a century. He was a talented author, quitting his law studies to become a government clerk in Paris and to give himself time to write. His short stories brought him fame and riches, plus four homes and enough periods of leisure to pursue lust with diligence.

Reputation can do wonderful things for a man or woman who enjoy their sexual exploits and willing partners are attracted to their sides, seemingly without effort. That was certainly the case for de Maupassant – women flocked to him in Paris in the latter half of the last century, prostitutes gave of their services free. For Guy, who remained a bachelor, was reported to possess tremendous stamina: he could go on and on without coming, rarely failed to bring a woman to climax and his short recovery period enabled him to have multiple orgasms himself. The bedrooms of France have rarely seen a more prodigious lover.

SIX TIMES A NIGHT

• • • • • • • • • • • • • • • •

A supremely extrovert and boastful young Russian writer came to visit him and de Maupassant, tiring of his bragging conversation, took him to the Folies Bergere. He picked up a dancer he already knew, took her to the nearest brothel for convenience and made love to her six times, before the Russian witness. The Frenchman later became boastful himself, claiming that afterwards he had gone across the hall and had sex with a young prostitute three more times.

• • • • • • • • • • • • • • • •

"All it needs is intelligence and some stamina to give a woman the greatest possible amount of pleasure," he said. Guy did not pursue his excesses beyond the bedroom to the bars and banqueting halls of the French capital, and achieved his fitness by rowing on the Seine, sometimes up to forty miles a day. Though proud of his endurance, he insisted it was really nothing extraordinary. "The fact that your stock of semen becomes exhausted, doesn't mean that your body is similarly exhausted. I am no more tired after making love three or four times as I am after twenty," he claimed. Clearly, he was able to sustain an erection long after most would collapse, and that was extraordinary and probably the greatest lure for the more demanding women.

Though father had left home, the family was not poor and at sixteen, still living in Normandy, he took rapid and successive lessons from prostitutes who operated around the port of Dieppe. He wanted to perfect his technique in readiness for the move to Paris, ostensibly to study law. There he moved on to wealthy society ladies, drawn to married women particularly if they were Jewish, "They were more passionate and more discreet" he said.

An amorous stamina

The established author Gustave Flaubert was a friend of his mother and became Guy's mentor in Paris. Even he doubted the stories of de Maupassant's marathon exploits in bed and with a group of writers, all at dinner together that day, struck a bet with the young man. The wager accepted and the meal over, Guy took the restaurant's book-keeper to a brothel as a witness, while the dining-group waited. They returned and the witness confirmed, "He had six girls in an hour." His friends paid up with a smile.

The great majority of the thousands of women he claimed to have had intercourse with during his life-time, were one-night stands. There were a few more long-lasting affairs, all with married women, though they were never the sole object of his carnal desires. Marie Kann lasted eight years, she was wealthy and "wonderfully impressed, then exhausted". Blanche Roosevelt Macchetta, a well-shaped, red-headed American, had a more than average appetite for sex and had heard all about Guy at home. Even before the opera singer turned novelist arrived in Europe to marry an Italian marquis, Blanche was determined to look him up. She persuaded her new husband to buy a Paris home and was soon able to copulate regularly with Guy at his country house in Etretat. "He provided the maximum sensual pleasure I ever found in bed," said Blanche.

> **EXTRAORDINARY MEMBER**
>
> Frank Harris, the Irish-American journalist whose frank autobiography *My Life and Loves* created an uproar with censors on both sides of the Atlantic, travelled to Paris to interview the man famed for his love life. Harris recalls walking with him when Guy said, "I suppose sexually, I am perhaps not quite ordinary. I can make my member stand at will." "Really?" queried the journalist. "Look at my trousers," said the Frenchman, laughing, and the journalist realized he was telling the truth.

Before he died Guy de Maupassant began to lean to the kinkier side of sex. A well-known Paris lesbian was Gisele d'Estoc who wore men's clothes and nearly went to gaol following a well-reported knife-fight in the street with a famous circus trapeze artist, Emma Bouer. Gisele represented a challenge but was sufficiently impressed after the first time, to introduce and sometimes share, a succession of her playmates to Guy's bed, including the trapeze lady. The last eighteen months of his eventful life were spent in an asylum after he hallucinated and tried to cut his throat. In 1893, Guy succumbed to the ravages of syphilis.

Alexandre Dumas Snr.

He owed much to the nobility of his parents and the family's connections. His father died when he was only three and he had a poor education, yet he still became a much-admired dramatist and historical novelist in the mid-1800s. He was given friendship and employment and introduced to Parisian society by Louis-Philippe, a future King of France and he never looked back.

DESCENDENTS

• • • • • • • • • • • • • • • • •

The author's grandmother was black, probably a descendant of the slave-trade, married a French nobleman serving with the Army in Santo Domingo. His father was a general in Napoleon's army at the time of the revolution. Dumas looked every-inch a Creole and once answered a cruel racist aside at a party, "Sir, my father was a Mulatto, my grandmother a negress, my great grandparents were monkeys. My pedigree begins where yours ends."

• • • • • • • • • • • • • • • • •

The predatory women who graced the French court found the dashing young man with striking looks and long, magnificently curly hair, a worthwhile pupil for the sexual instruction and exercise they were eager to bestow.

Not yet twenty, he realized a semi-permanent base was needed and though there was no intention of remaining faithful, he moved in with a dressmaker Catherine Labay, who was almost thirty. Two years later she bore him a son, similarly christened, and when he too became a writer they were known as Dumas père and Dumas fils. From the older man came such epics as *The Count of Monte Cristo* and *The Three Musketeers*, and he quickly became both a literary hero and a tireless womanizer. Many an actress accepted rooms on his estate which he called Monte Cristo, and was happy to pay her rent in time-honoured fashion. And there was never a doubt that Dumas père was happy to collect.

The man was generous to a fault, providing shelter on the estate to starving artists and penniless writers. When he caught his wife in bed with his friend Roger de Beauvoir, Dumas chided the man but said, "It's a cold night, move over and make room for me." In praise, de Beauvoir related the story to their mutual friends, adding, "Next morning he shook my hand and insisted two old friends should never quarrel about a woman, not even a lawful wife!"

Dumas once said, "I need several mistresses. If I had only one, she would be dead at the end of a week." Straightforward coupling soon lost its appeal. On one occasion he forgot a liaison he had arranged only two days earlier. When the woman arrived in his bedroom, she found there were already three others present – three naked young girls cavorting around the bed while the author whooped and hollered and revealed his readiness for action. She refused his invitation and fled. Word of this embarrassing scene soon reached his disapproving teenage son's ears. But Dumas fils would soon obey the rule – if you can't beat them, join them.

Theatre of lust

Dumas found most of his partners in the Paris theatre. He maintained few secrets and at one time, three of his current lovers found themselves cast in the same play. One, Fanny Cordoza, a dark-haired, voluptuous actress had a sexual appetite that was too much for her husband, an Italian count, so he wrapped wet towels around her in an effort to cool the woman down. Dumas knew a much better way to take care of her excess energy.

A longterm affair with Emilie Cordier produced a daughter. Then, before he could make a move in her direction, the latest sex symbol arrived in Paris, dancer Lola Montez considerably younger with plenty of experience under her belt, or beneath her petticoats. But like many before her, the lady was fascinated by the stories she had heard of his sexual stamina and keen to put this lascivious legend to the test. A couple of nights were enough. When they first embarked towards a convenient bed from the Paris salon where they had met "by accident", Lola made her intentions perfectly clear to the shocked, and probably envious, ladies and their partners sat round about.

The great writer was in his sixties and though still energetic, was only just hanging on to the last threads of his prestige. Then

LIKE FATHER ...

Alexandre Dumas not only gave his illegitimate son his name and his talent for writing, he passed on the same lust for women. An overheard conversation between them ran thus: "You know father, it's a great bore, you always give me your old mistresses to sleep with and your new boots to break in." Came the reply, "Why do you complain? It proves you have a thick prick and a narrow foot."

Alexandre Dumas fils never quite made his father's grade as a writer though Verdi based the grand opera *La Traviata* on his play *Camille*. But two later plays, *The Natural Son* and *The Prodigious Father*, were both interesting and amusing, clearly a personal interpretation of his father's character.

came Adah Isaacs Menken, a stage star whose fame and name, as the Naked Lady, had spread from America to Europe. She was an aspiring poetess and could give Dumas thirty three years, and made it quite clear she didn't want any English lessons from this prominent man of letters. Her act was a riot, her magnificent figure clad in an almost see-through leotard, strapped to the back of a cantering horse. And off-stage, she was reputed to be just as vigorous and athletic with two-legged companions. After so many years and thousands of weary but often appreciative partners, Dumas père had met his match. He was bent but not quite broken until finally at sixty eight, the risks he had so often taken caught up with him and syphilis led to his death.

Oscar Wilde

Ireland was just recovering from the long years of the great potato famine when Oscar Fingal O'Flahertie Wills Wilde was born, in Dublin in 1854. His slightly mad mother was convinced her second child would be a daughter and she dressed the new arrival as a girl, very nearly until he went to school. Hardly surprising then, these early days set him on the road to being the most famous homosexual of the last century. That earned Oscar Wilde two years hard labour in prison and inspired the lengthy poem *The Ballad of Reading Gaol.*

He might have been saved from arrest, trial and the infamy which his homosexual activities later earned, for the playwright was most certainly heterosexual in his twenties and ready to forget the string of affairs he had enjoyed with fellow undergraduates at both Trinity College, Dublin, and Magdalen College, Oxford. He competed with another writer for the hand of society beauty Florrie Balcombe and lost out to Bram Stoker, creator of Dracula. He threw himself at Lillie Langtry, the recent mistress of the Prince of Wales and now a famous London courtesan, but he had too little to offer, certainly in public life and maybe, in the privacy of her bedroom.

GIVING HIS ALL

He was a favourite among London's high-class whores who often entertained him all night. When he was asked about the risks of being robbed while in their rooms, Oscar replied, "One gives them all in one's pockets." This was a completely honest response – on occasions his payments amounted to a small fortune.

Three of Wilde's plays have remained classics, *The Importance of Being Earnest, An Ideal Husband* and *Lady Windermere's Fan,* and he developed a shrewd and perceptive eye as an observer of human behaviour. Tall and graceful, extremely humorous but probably over-dressed even in those Victorian, fashion-conscious days, he was the darling of London society. His remarkable ability with words kept him in great demand at dinner parties and at weekend, country house gatherings ... until scandal reached out to smother him.

But first came marriage, in 1884 to a very ordinary but sweet girl Constance Lloyd who soon presented him with two sons, Cyril and Vyvyan. His account of their honeymoon in Paris would have shocked even today's readers, had it not been couched is such beautiful language. But family life bored Oscar, coupled with a doctor's verdict that the venereal disease he contracted at Oxford, and thought he had conquered, was surfacing again. He treated himself with mercury, discolouring his teeth in the process, but managing to keep the syphilis at bay for more than ten years until finally it forced Wilde to give up sex with his wife.

Loving the Lord

He couldn't face going to bed with adult males and turned to teenage boys for his pleasures, and abroad some were even younger. The year was 1891 and Oscar Wilde was aged thirty-seven when he met the love-of-his-life, a handsome, young aristocrat almost half his age. Lord Alfred Douglas was known as "Bosie" to his friends, an aspiring poet who was equally attracted to the renowned playwright. Together they boldly flaunted their homosexual affair in the best restaurants and the finest hotels and when Wilde took him home to stay, even Constance admitted she found Bosie, "charming and excellent company".

Lord Alfred had enjoyed sex with women and even when Oscar came along, he still preferred small boys and neither man had any intention of remaining faithful to each other. They both wrote stories of their revelries in Algeria, a holiday undertaken specifically to romp with the inmates of the Arab bath-houses and male brothels. Bosie actually purchased a good-looking Arab teenager from his family, planning to return the lad to London, but he ran off before they departed. Back in London Bosie's father, the Eighth Marquis of Queensberry, was enraged and wrote brutal and insulting letters to both men. Ultimately, a card from the marquis bearing seven words and delivered to the Writer's Club in the centre of London, famously brought Wilde's world crashing around him. It read: "For Oscar Wilde, posing as a sodomite."

> **FIVE IN A BED**
>
> ● ● ● ● ● ● ● ● ● ● ● ● ● ● ● ● ●
>
> Wilde once boasted of having five messenger boys in his bed in one night. "I kissed each of them in every part of their bodies," he confessed, "they were all dirty and appealed to me for just that reason."
>
> ● ● ● ● ● ● ● ● ● ● ● ● ● ● ● ● ●

A self-inflicted demise

A furious Wilde pursued Queensberry for criminal libel, having assured his lawyers there was no basis for the accusing words. But private detectives had been following the two men, their private lives were about to be exposed at trial when the prosecution withdrew their case and the Marquis was freed. Now Wilde's friends and his wife urged him to flee the country but within a month, he was the man in the dock, charged with committing acts of gross indecency with various boys. His trial became one of the most sensational cases in British legal history.

In court several boys gave evidence and hotel chambermaids testified and it soon became clear that sodomy was rarely performed, but fellatio and mutual masturbation were the norm. At times Wilde brilliantly conducted his own defence; describing the homosexual nuances in his book *The Picture of Dorian Gray*, he uttered the celebrated phrase "love that dare not speak its name", and gained rounds of applause from the public gallery. The jury could not agree and another trial was called, culminating in a guilty verdict and the maximum sentence of two years imprisonment.

Bosie did not desert him and when Wilde was released, the two went to live in Italy and France where, shortly before he died at the age of forty-six, Oscar was persuaded to go to a well-known brothel. "The first these ten years, and the last," he asserted to his friend, poet Ernest Dowson. "It was like cold mutton but tell it in England, for it will entirely restore my character."

The Lecherous Men of Letters

Four men – all writers and contemporaries at the beginning of the twentieth century – were literary giants who laid claim to fame, and dwelled on sex in their private lives, the novels they wrote, or more usually both. Two were under-endowed and actually compared sizes in the search for reassurance, and two produced novels which became notorious, achieving far greater sales when they were banned in Britain and America, and more still when editions with the unexpurgated text were finally released.

DH Lawrence

The landmark court case in 1960 at the Old Bailey in London, which allowed full uncensored publication of *Lady Chatterley's Lover*, gave birth to the decade known as the swinging sixties. The gradual stripping of morals and the advance of a permissive society throughout the western world is often deemed to have started right then and there. D H Lawrence, the author of this startling novel, had been dead for thirty years and yet the influence he exerted on the literary world at that time was enormous. Here was a writer deeply affected by extreme motherly love – she doted on the boy and scorned her husband, a miner in the Nottingham coalfields.

His first sexual experience was not with one woman but a group; he described it as traumatic, being confronted by ribald, lewd factory girls who tried to pull off his trousers and expose his genitals. Lawrence avoided the ultimate embarrassment, but shorn of some of his clothing, he caught pneumonia. He was able to rid himself of the remains of his mother-fixation with his first successful novel *Sons and Lovers*, written as soon as he had finished mourning her and published when he was only twenty-eight. Naturally, when the book came out women were fascinated with the theme and anxious to meet him.

He had two girlfriends, Jessie Chambers and Louise Burrows, who like him were brought up in strict Victorian households, and they did little more than hold hands and kiss. Then a woman who worked in a local chemist's shop, the wife of the owner, recognized he was struggling for inspiration while writing a book of poetry. She seduced the twenty-three year old writer, which positively made his blood run faster, if not the ink in his pen. A number of rich ladies, some of them titled, learned he had other struggles trying to finance a second novel, and were eager to become his literary patrons.

> ### SEX ON THE BRAIN
> • • • • • • • • • • • • • • • • • •
> Curiously and capriciously, D H Lawrence accused his wife, and women in general, of having "sex on the brain". But when he wrote a letter in defence of the censored *Lady Chatterley's Lover*, he said, "I want men and women to be able to think sex, fully, completely, honestly and cleanly."
> • • • • • • • • • • • • • • • • • •

Income on two legs

They wanted little in return, just his time and attention and occasionally, to act out the passages he was writing. Lawrence called these ladies "Income on two legs". In disgust at his own behaviour in accepting the favours they willingly bestowed upon him, Lawrence lampooned these female patrons in his novels. He never quite identified anyone in particular, but it was an unkind way to repay their generosity.

Physically he did not cut much of a figure, painfully thin with straggly hair, but he had a vivid red beard and could exude a powerful personality. His friends and the literary world were amazed when he persuaded an aristocratic German woman to leave her husband and run away with him. They were well aware he treated married ladies as fair game, but this one had three children, and she left them behind as well. Frieda Weekley and Lawrence were an ill-matched pair. He was broke while she had a family income, he was frail while she was a blonde, Aryan amazon, and none of his lovers would describe him as virile but Frieda, six years older than he, thoroughly enjoyed a good hour's romp in the bedroom. Nonetheless they married, but the writer sadly confessed they were never able to reach a simultaneous orgasm.

Lawrence was a strange mixture, championing women's liberation through his writing while privately expressing his own chau-

> ### AMERICAN FRIEND
> • • • • • • • • • • • • • • • •
> Mabel Dodge Luhan, an American heiress and herself a writer, was infatuated with Lawrence, although never turned on by the man. She wanted to "Seduce his spirit" and wrote that "The surest way to the soul is through the flesh". Mabel gave him a 160-acre ranch in New Mexico, not big by American standards, but it surely impressed Lawrence's spirit and his flesh.
> • • • • • • • • • • • • • • • •

vinism. He even advocated beating a quarrelsome wife, though Frieda was more than his match in a fight as she proved many a time, smashing the odd dinner plate on his head. Writer Katherine Mansfield was shocked when Lawrence told her, "I do think a woman must yield some sort of precedence to a man. Where men go ahead, women must follow and be unquestioning." His heroes and heroines burned with passion, daring and baring all, consummating their illicit sex as they abandoned all the conventions while their creator would only make love in the dark.

He could never settle, living in Mediterranean countries and going to Australia and America. This involved long, arduous journeys by boat, but these provided material for a series of travel pieces. Nearing forty, the women he succumbed to were also a strange mix, including the eccentric Lady Ottoline Morrell, and Dorothy Brett, who was delighted to become his benefactor but dispirited when he entered her bed and proved impotent. Lawrence insisted that he could fulfil his sexual desires by "making love to a woman through my writing". Whether the target for these particular words could fulfil her desires in the reading is quite another matter.

Men considered Lawrence effeminate and he was jealous of a good physique which would have probably provided a better performance for him in bed. Instead, his well thought out scenes had to suffice. "Even if we can't act sexually to our complete satisfaction," he wrote, "let us at least think sexually, complete and clear."

F Scott Fitzgerald

When Francis Scott Fitzgerald wrote his first novel – *This Side of Paradise*, published when he was only twenty-three – it immediately shot him to stardom, and brought in a lot of money. It was considered scandalous at the time but very mild by today's standards, yet he was never able to repeat that success. His novels and most of his short stories appearing in New York's *Saturday Evening Post*, had a romantic basis and chronicled what he called The Jazz Age, almost autobiographical books of the life he was living himself. But his sex life was extremely complex. He was regarded by many contemporaries as a closet homosexual. He was a foot-fetishist, and obsessed with the dimensions of his penis. He asked prostitutes how it compared in size with other men and was never convinced by their universal answer, "It's technique not size that matters."

Fitzgerald's adult life lasted through only two decades, the 1920s and 1930s. The first, after marriage to Zelda Sayre, was savoured in extravagant style and at hectic pace, and the second was endured in debt and desperation. Though two more books, *The Great Gatsby* and *Tender Is The Night*, are considered classic pieces of literature now and were well received by critics at the time, they did not sell to the public. They failed to earn him a fraction of his first novel, and he suffered until he went to Hollywood under contract to MGM to write screenplays.

Scott met Zelda at a country club dance in Alabama. He had left Princeton without a degree to join the army. He was a lieutenant and she was just about to finish high school, a stunning blonde girl under siege from all the young men at the dance. But she fell for Scott, who was shy and reticent and as soon as he proposed, seduced him. "I was prepared, in fact I was on the point of insisting, we wait until our wedding night but with Zelda, refusal was impossible," he said.

Bearing in mind what she later said to her husband, it's surprising Zelda went through with the wedding, "Your problem is a matter of measurements. You could never satisfy me or any woman with that." Scott was well aware of his shortcomings in that department, though the other woman in his life, Sheilah Graham, the newspaper columnist he lived with after Zelda was committed to a mental institute, was more concerned about his shyness. "The penis thing never bothered me," she wrote, "but in all our time together I don't think I ever saw him naked."

LOTTIE'S SURPRISE

The prostitute Lottie surprised the racially bigoted Scott Fitzgerald. Learning his views one night she asked had he ever been to bed with a coloured woman. The man was shocked that she should raise such a question, and doubly shocked when she informed him, "Well you have honey, a dozen or more times. I may not look it, but that's what I am." He told Lottie to put on her clothes, and they didn't do it again.

Perhaps the reason he failed Zelda was the pace of his lovemaking. "He was always nervous as if he was afraid of losing his erection, and that made Scott very quick," said a prostitute he befriended. "I told him a thing or two and reassured him about size, he needed to know other aspects of lovemaking were far more important." He wrote the most romantic novels, but he was always personally uneasy about sex and his flirtation with booze didn't help – it eased the frustration and depression perhaps, but not the sex. He died in 1940, three months after his forty-fourth birthday, from a sudden heart attack.

Hemingway

Ernest Hemingway was very much a contemporary of Fitzgerald's. Only three years younger, a successful writer and later a Nobel prizewinner, he was another with a small penis. The two men discussed the subject on one occasion, and actually compared organs, Hemingway insisting they were both normal. But there the comparisons cease. "Papa" Hemingway was a big-game hunter and a deep-sea fishermen, he loved the bullfighting in Spain and Mexico and soldiering in Europe, though he was only a Red Cross ambulance driver in the First World War.

THE LIMIT

● ● ● ● ● ● ● ● ● ● ● ● ● ● ● ●

Hemingway had many strange theories about sex, which he discussed with his chums. He was convinced every man had an allotted number of orgasms in his life, which may have been a cover story, at least for himself, to explain his eventual impotence.

● ● ● ● ● ● ● ● ● ● ● ● ● ● ● ●

To maintain this macho image, he put himself about from his high-school days onwards as a great lover. He boasted of taking bromides to conquer his sexual urge, for otherwise he needed to make love to a woman – or different women – three times a day. Not true, said at least two who knew him well. Third wife and fellow journalist Martha Gelhorn said his singular talent was as a writer. Gertrude Stein, an American lesbian writer who was a close friend when he lived in Paris, commented, "He always made a big thing of trying to f**k me, but he could do that with safety, he knew my preferences."

When the author of such great novels as *For Whom the Bell Tolls* and *The Sun Also Rises* booked to go on safari in Africa, as he did many times, the agent in Nairobi was told to organise a harem of half-a-dozen girls so that Hemingway could take his pick each night, and whenever else he felt like it. But his male friends viewed this macho show with great suspicion, and by his own admission the man was a prude and disliked anything other than straightforward sex. He claimed to have bedded the German spy Mata Hari in Paris, a Greek princess in Athens, and an Italian countess in Florence, but more regularly he paid prostitutes at home in America, in Havana where he lived on a farm for a few years, and earlier in Paris. As a youngster he preferred older women, though once he reached fifty he went after much younger ladies. When he turned sixty he became anxious and depressed, and a few days before celebrating what would have been his sixty-second birthday, he ended his life with a shotgun.

James Joyce

Night Town, the red light area in the old city of Dublin, was no place for a fourteen-year-old boy, but it was there in 1896 that James Augustine Aloysius Joyce, the fresh-faced son of an alcoholic tax collector, first discovered the joys of fornication. That episode and several repeat performances eventually earned the lad a fortune as a writer as well as repeated bouts of syphilis. He was not much older when he considered becoming a priest and though he never swore in front of a woman, he felt no qualms about ladies reading his famous – or infamous – book *Ulysses*, which was considered so lewd and obscene that for nearly twenty years the full version was banned from publication in Britain and America.

Everything in that novel took place virtually within 24 hours on a very important day in the writer's personal life. June 16, 1904 was the day he "married" Nora Barnacle, a housemaid in a Dublin hotel. Having rejected the priesthood because it demanded a vow of celibacy – saving the Catholic church a good measure of embarrassment in later years – he also rejected any ceremony requiring a "Priest in a night-shirt" or a town hall clerk "With a pen behind his ear," so Nora became his common-law wife. June 16 was the day he told Nora he loved her, and twenty-seven years later they actually made it official.

They had little money during their first eight years together but living abroad, in Italy, Switzerland and France, allowed Joyce to scrape a living by giving private English lessons. This also allowed him to write and gradually, as he became better known, the royalty incomes began to flow. Nora ran his life and the man needed a woman's domination to survive. She was small-boned, trim with tiny breasts, but Joyce let his imagination run and wrote to her, "I wish you had a big, full, proud bosom and big,

KNICKERS, FINGERS *& SYPHILIS*

James Joyce had an underwear fetish, and for years kept a pair of doll's knickers in his pocket. In a bar or cafe he would sometimes slip them over his hand and ,using two fingers, walk the knickers across a table top, wave a "leg" provocatively, then walk them back again. The writer was probably still in his teens when he caught syphilis. Having studied medicine for a short time in Paris, in later life he treated the disease himself but he could never eliminate all the effects. which doctors told him contributed greatly to his chronic eye problems – at times he was nearly blind. Death however, at fifty-eight, came via the surgeon's table, following an operation for a duodenal ulcer.

fat thighs. I wish you would smack me, I would love to feel my flesh tingling under your hand."

Critics across the world admired *Ulysses* and the way the writer's words expressed his characters' inner thinking. But in real life where women were concerned, Nora maintained, "He's a simple weakling, he knows nothing at all about women." She stayed totally faithful despite his urgings that she should go to bed with one or other of his friends and allow him to watch, "So that I will have something to write about." In his letters to her, he had plenty to write about: "I long to feel your hot lecherous lips sucking away at me," and "I want to f**k between your two rosy-tipped bubbies". He often referred to various forms of corrective punishment, "I wish you would flog me" or "I would love to be whipped by you, Nora love".

Shortly before the storm over the publication of *Ulysses* broke, the author strayed from Nora's side and fell for one of his English students in Paris. Amalia Popper was the daughter of a wealthy Jewish merchant who warned the older man off, but the dark, hirsute nineteen-year-old aroused him and later that year, after moving to Zurich, he found her look-alike in Martha Fleischmann. He actually picked her up in a toilet. The central Europeans never worried too much about separating the sexes in their public facilities. James walked in on her, "At the very moment she was in the act of pulling the chain," he wrote to an Irish friend. They looked and they talked, and both obviously liked what they saw and heard. Later that night, "I was allowed to explore the hottest and coldest parts of a woman's body," he added in his letter.

Gabriele D'Annunzio

He was always very active, in and out of bed, and maintained so many facets to his life, merely reaching the age of seventy-five was probably the Italian writer's greatest achievement. Already a literary hero, he soared to prominence as a politician in the last years of his life, embracing the era and the ideals of Fascism and quickly becoming a supporter of Mussolini at home, and Hitler in Germany. He died shortly before the two dictators could combine forces and threaten Europe so forcefully, but in his early fifties and during the First World War, D'Annunzio was Italy's foremost flying ace. Sexually, he was on the warpath at a very early age, caned at school when he tried to guide the hands of a nun, who was fitting a new uniform, towards his penis. He was only twelve and barely four years later, pawned a watch recently given him as a birthday present, to pay for his first experience with a woman, a prostitute in Florence.

His father was the wealthy Mayor of Pescara who paid for his son's first publication, a volume of poetry, at the age of nineteen, to celebrate graduating from college where he had already started to gain a reputation as an ardent lover with a wide circle of admirers inside and outside the college walls at Prato in Tuscany. The poetry, the heroics and, of course, his growing prestige among Italian society women, gained him entry to many villas and boudoirs, often by secret notes from ladies he had seen and perhaps been introduced to at galas and celebrations, but with whom he had exchanged no conversation. The notes, delivered by loyal servants, were innocent enough but their invitations and their intentions were clearly stated.

There were added benefits. Quite apart from the variety of sexual preferences of these ladies at his disposal, D'Annunzio by now had extended his work into writing novels and dramas for the Italian stage. The

THE FLAME OF LIFE

D'Annunzio reached the peak of his prowess in a nine year affair with Eleanora Duse, an actress whose list of previous lovers was pretty well as long as the dramatist's with whom she set up home. He wrote plays for her to perform in, but secretly he was writing a novel containing the most intimate details of their time together. At the age of forty-two, "La Duse" realized the affair was over when she read the "The Flame of Life" and the passages revealing her ageing body and drooping breasts.

horizontal happenings provided plenty of material for the chapters and scenes he was currently writing. He was rarely so ungallant as to identify his co-performers, either by name or close description, but a few ladies were able to recognize themselves including the beautiful Barbara Leoni who told him "You have had a virgin in me", and promptly appeared in the pages of *The Innocent*.

PRINCE OF MONTE NEVOSE

• • • • • • • • • • • • • • • •

His wartime heroics cost him dearly and repaid him well. In the First World War, after flying several dangerous missions over battlefields, he commanded a squadron at Venice and on one sortie was hit by a bullet which blinded one eye. Then he turned soldier and capturing the town of Fiumi, he ruled the area, on the Yugoslav border, as the local dictator until Mussolini made him Prince of Monte Nevose, complete with local taxes and tithes, enough to afford 100 servants and a lavish lifestyle.

• • • • • • • • • • • • • • • • • •

Gabriele considered himself "the high priest of erotica", the passion and violence, superstition and immorality laced through his works upset many critics. He was labelled a vulgar dilettante, they objected to his arrogance and egomania and of course, to the erotica in his writing. Opposing critics saw another side, particularly in the poetry, and called him a genius. He made no self-judgement of his ability but did admit he was a sex maniac whose life and writings were guided by all this frenzied activity.

All this was carried out against a background of marriage, and apparently comfortable domesticity. He was only twenty when he married Maria, a year younger and already pregnant, the daughter of the Duke of Gallese who gave him three sons in the next four years by which time he had left her. She was tall, slender and blonde and not without a certain measure of dilettantism herself. Maria was given the title of Madone des Tantes – Madonna of the Fairies – for after Gabrielle, her preferences lay among the homosexuals in Rome.

Back at play with women, boys ... and lesbians

Now divorced and more free to pursue his libertine ways, he met his match in Naples when he bedded Countess Maria di Ramacca, by no means averse to a good helping of erotica and sexual mania herself. She was tall and strong, with a powerful but nonetheless attractive figure, and the stamina to go with it, and their frenzied affair led them into court, charged with adultery. The five months sentence on each was suspended and the couple had two children.

He tried homosexuality and admitted he became very excited by young boys. He set about "reforming" lesbians to show them the true way, and continued with his long series of semi-serious affairs. The religious and married Countess Mancini was consumed with guilt and went mad. Daughter of the prime minister, Marchesa Carlottie, confessed her adultery and "frenzied lovemaking" with D'Annunzio, abandoned her family, repented and entered a convent where she died as Mother Superior.

D'Annunzio spent more than he earned and he was forced into both bankruptcy and exile, moving to France. He was only 5ft 6ins tall but muscular and handsome until the age of twenty-three when he rapidly went bald, emphasizing his deep brown eyes which actress Sarah Bernhardt, though submitting more than once to his undoubted charm, described as "little blobs of shit". Charming yes, compassionate no, but that was the way of wealthy, society ladies around the turn of the century, young and anxious unmarrieds, dissatisfied wives and eager widows, to be drawn to the men who were attracting all the publicity for their sexual status. And Gabriele fell conveniently into that bracket.

He failed in his last ambition, "to ensure my actual death is as memorable as my life". He planned to have his ailing body fired from a canon and either disintegrate in mid-air or die from the shock of landing. The alternative, if an accomplice among the artillery troops could not be found, was to have himself immersed in a vat of acid. In fact, he died in 1938 from a more mundane cause, a cerebral haemorrhage while working at his desk, writing his memoirs, which are more accurately described as his confessions.

Kingsley Amis

The first of his twenty-odd novels was the hilarious *Lucky Jim* and this acerbic, complex and contradictory man went on to write poetry, radio plays, science fiction and detective thrillers, occasional political columns and restaurant reviews. In short, as his biographer Eric Jacobs tells us, the author Kingsley Amis was one of the grand old men of English letters. He was faithful to his talent, though rarely to the women in his life, and for more than forty years remained a conscientious hedonist while turning out thousands and thousands of brilliant words. His hands were equally at home at the keyboard of his battered typewriter or clutching a glass, more often the latter and usually filled with a large measure of malt whisky and a splash of water.

His favourite lubricant was the reason he avoided driving any form of motorised vehicle after leaving the Army at the end of the Second World War, those service years breaking up his time at Oxford University where soon after arrival, he flirted with communism. In later years friends claimed there were more selfish reasons for this political affiliation, "Kingsley was twenty and anxious to get laid and lose his virginity and the left-leaning ladies were easier with their virtue." Not for the first time, or the last, the writer used this experience to embellish a later novel. In real life the lass who agreed to introduce him to the pleasures of the flesh, wanted to be sure she had a good time herself and gave him a sex manual to read before they were due to meet and do the dirty deed. And in his book *You Can't Do Both*, the same thing happens to the leading characters. There are passages on foreplay and perversion and the need for men to understand women's different needs, learned from a sex guide, the lovers' encounter ends up in near-rape. What the writer failed to repeat was his trip to the chemist to buy contraceptives. He was so embarrassed, he asked friend and fellow-Oxford undergraduate George Blunden to accompany him. When the friend later

REVENGE IS SWEET

Discovering his latest infidelity, wife Hilly took her revenge when Kingsley fell asleep on a beach in Yugoslavia. She took a lipstick from her handbag and wrote on his bare back "One fat Englishmen" – the title of a book he was then writing – and "I fuck anything" then she photographed her handywork. Years later when his authorized biography was published, Amis gave permission for the photograph to be reproduced.

became Sir George and Deputy Governor of the Bank of England, he and Amis delighted in telling their respective versions of this tale.

Having made the plunge, Amis developed his sexual prowess and more escapades with the ladies, married and single, and some in khaki like himself, were served up in later novels, especially his memoirs. And many who knew him in those early student days, felt his first effort, *Lucky Jim*, was a parody on himself, enough there for even fringe associates to recognize and that book, later a very successful film, brought him lasting fame.

Kingsley gets lucky

There were very few university women in his day, the girls were mainly trainee nurses and secretaries or at the many minor schools of learning thriving around Oxford, and the 11,000 over-sexed but under-utilized young men seeking their degree as well as romance, followed a pattern which brought them together. They went to Elliston and Cavell's tearoom in the city. All very proper where it was acceptable to stop and chat to complete strangers or pass a message with a name and an address, there were very few phone numbers in those days. A pretty blonde student at art college, Hilary Bardwell, was the recipient of three messages one day. She chose Kingsley's to follow up and that changed her life.

It took him four months to seduce Hilly, and two years to marry her by which time she was pregnant. Before another year passed his promiscuity was running riot, as his young wife confirmed from the many notations in his diary. This casual security over his affairs as well as the constant infidelity, marked the fifteen years of their marriage. To accommodate his writing, Amis took posts as a lecturer at Swansea, Cambridge, Princeton and Nashville, and he took advantage of the many opportunities which came his way in the university social sway. At a weekend house party in America, Amis drunkenly escaped his wife and ended up in bed with another guest.

JOKER'S WILD

In the late 1950s the author used to borrow his friend Robert Conquest's flat in London for his sexual assignations. The friend, an American poet and ardent practical joker, would leave a note addressed to "Lucky Sod", a habit to which Amis referred in a poem called "Nothing to Fear". When Robert read the poem he decided to take matters a stage further, rigging up a tape recorder so that when Kingsley arrived and turned on the light, the words "Lucky Sod" loudly greeted him and his latest lady love.

Next morning at breakfast, he could not remember which of the few ladies present had satisfied him. In Swansea, at a small dinner party with his wife, and despite having recently bedded the hostess, he fixed a meeting with the third woman present only to discover she was a masochist. "One beating too many," he later confessed.

After divorcing he married another writer, Elizabeth Jane Howard and was no more faithful to her – any lady who took his fancy Kingsley considered fair game. This provided still more material for his books. At fifty-six Amis became impotent and followed his doctor's advice, but he did not submit to silencing embarrassment. In the book *Jake's Thing* he mixes real-life therapy with invented devices like the "nocturnal mensurator" supposedly to measure the night time rise and fall of Jake's erections.

The second marriage also lasted fifteen years, appropriately he met Elizabeth at the Cheltenham Festival where both had to speak at a seminar on sex in literature. When Elizabeth left him Hilly's affection, if not love, surfaced again and she moved him in, to live in the same house in London with her new husband Lord Kilmarnock. Kingsley Amis continued to write from there until the time of his death, aged seventy-four.

Natalie Barney

Of the many lesbian writers whose works flourished in the last two centuries, and who were drawn to make their homes in Paris, the woman known as "l'Amazone" was undoubtedly the most notorious. Natalie Barney was born into fabulous wealth in America and grew up in Cincinnati. Her grandfathers on either side had both been industrial magnates and when the two families merged through marriage, the famous Barney fortunes were the result. So Natalie was afforded an expensive schooling and at the age of twelve was boarded out in Paris where, even at such a tender age, she realized her predilections and later claimed, "My only books, were women's looks." Learning about herself was the most important lesson.

Back home in America after completing her education in various corners of Europe, Natalie did the social rounds in New York and Washington without ever submitting to any of many male suitors. But she was voracious, though secretive, in her pursuit of women until at the age of thirty, she decided to "come out" though neither the phrase nor the act was in vogue at the beginning of the twentieth century. To save the family embarrassment, she did this as she moved to Paris where she bought a large house on the Rue Jacob, almost next door to where Nino de Lenclos, one of the earliest and most famous French courtesans, had lived. Natalie knew what she was going to do with her life, realizing she could not rely on her earnings from publishing. In fact, her fame was never achieved by the pen – she wrote little witticisms, satirical poetry and later, her memoirs.

JAILBAIT

• • • • • • • • • • • • • • • • •

Natalie had as many as three dozen long-lasting affairs without ever promising to be faithful. When the latest lover, the passionate but jealous Renee Vivien whose poems revealed an obsession with death, refused to see her again, Natalie had herself delivered in a horse-drawn hearse to the woman, clothed in a white dress and lying in a white-satin coffin.

• • • • • • • • • • • • • • • • •

Prominence came to Natalie through her reputation and her activities in running the most celebrated salon in Paris, attracting every Friday afternoon – and running on well into the evening and next morning – artists, authors, poets, playwrights, actors and actresses, the French nobility, visiting Royalty, everyone who was anyone went to 20 Rue Jacob to be entertained by l'Amazone and her amazing friends. The title was bestowed not for her tall, strapping figure with its long, startling blonde hair, the lady achieved celebrity status when she was so readily identified in the novelist Remy de Gourmont's *Lettres a l'Amazone*; fictional love letters from Natalie to her fantasy partners.

Fellow American and poet Ezra Pound who was tried and convicted of treason in Washington for his activities in Europe between the two wars, became a close friend and advisor and he invited Mata Hari, the woman who would soon be executed as a German spy, to the famous house one Friday. She arrived completely naked on a white horse with the harness decked out in jewels. It seemed every newcomer to the salon's gatherings had to make an entrance.

Scandals avoided and outdoor sex

Dolly Wilde, the niece of Oscar, arrived and stayed but when she was eventually spurned by l'Amazone, took to drugs and then slashed her wrists. A maid averted this suicide attempt and the scandal, and Dolly accepted she would have to wait to re-enter her hostess's bed. Natalie would have sex in any place, at any time – in the open air, in public – the more avantgarde the better. A hunting party came upon her in the arms of a new conquest, both women were nude and entirely unaware of their audience at first. Her favourites, invited to accompany Natalie to the theatre or opera in Paris, were well aware they might end up on the floor of her favourite box, overlooking the stage and in the middle of a scene, doing what, to them, came naturally.

Three-in-a-bed to l'Amazone meant herself and two more women, a sex maniac of a different kind and when her lovers decided men were preferable as lovers, Natalie saw this as a natural challenge and occasionally brought them back into the fold. One woman who had gone off to get married, was delighted

FRIENDS AND LOVERS

The woman confessed she had an everlasting problem, keeping peace within the lesbian harem assembled at her house. Heterosexual men were always well received, though they were forever trying to entice Natalie and her friends to their beds, and were mostly unsuccessful. "I am a friend of men but a lover of women," she maintained. But the men who dressed as women were never welcome. "Put the hermaphrodites in the bushes," was Natalie's command.

to return and admitted, "I committed the delicious sin of submitting to her caresses, the woman is very good at what she does." She courted and, for a time, won the beautiful Liane de Pougy, very much an upper-class courtesan who described Miss Barney as "my greatest pleasure and my greatest sin." She came up with the perfect answer, for her, allowing Natalie to caress her, "only above the waist."

The celebrated author Colette became one of Natalie's lovers, then soon after the First World War ended American painter Romaine Brooks arrived and began to think of moving to Paris. Her mind was made up when she met l'Amazone and for the next fifty years they remained as companions, sometimes living together or in adjoining houses. Natalie continued to have other affairs and at the age of eighty-two, seduced the wife of a foreign ambassador in Paris, a woman who was twenty-four years younger and had never had a lesbian affair. That relationship lasted eleven years, embittering Romaine and finally breaking up their love nest. Both Romaine and Natalie were in their 1990s when they died, and one line in l'Amazone's will was obeyed to the letter. Like her regular salons, the funeral ceremony was on a Friday afternoon, in February 1972.

The Literary Lesbians

A passion for writing and other women, was shared by three notable writers who were all unashamedly lesbians at a time, through the turn of the century, when such love affairs were not easily tolerated. The first, Colette, was married three times and began her career writing near-pornography. The second, Gertrude Stein, went through a form of marriage with her life-long partner yet struggled mentally for most of her life to come to terms with her sexuality. And the last, Virginia Woolf, also married, had several loveless affairs with women, describing herself as a eunuch.

Colette

Sidonie Gabrielle Claudine Colette wrote a total of seventy-three books, regarded as one of the most revered of French authors whose much-acclaimed *Gigi* was published when she was aged seventy-two. This was the story of a young girl, a true French coquette, being trained for a life of love by two retired courtesans and was turned into a smash-hit musical on Broadway and by Hollywood. But her very first publications, the four *Claudine* novels, were erotic stories detailing the sexual adventures of an uninhibited, alluring and lusty young schoolgirl. The author was twenty just married to a man of thirty-five, Henry Gauthier-Villars, a rogue who called himself Willy and put that name on the *Claudine* books. Willy had a number of ghost-writers turning out lewd books under the same pen name. He sold pornographic postcards using his string of mistresses as his models, and was probably

A SECOND MARRIAGE

Colette was nearly forty when she became pregnant and married the father Henry de Jouvenel. This was her second husband and it was a mistake. He was as virile and as unfaithful as Colette, though he pursued only women, and they broke up when he accused her of "adultery and a half-incestuous relationship" – she quietly went off on holiday to Switzerland with her nineteen-year-old stepson Bertrand.

the first person in the world to see the opportunities of "branding". Willy made and sold a wide range of Claudine products in Paris and had his wife write two more books under his name to launch a line of sex-oriented gifts. Colette's early works undoubtedly spawned the cult in France of the sexually precocious, teenage girls who landed lots of older men into all sorts of trouble at the beginning of this century.

Erotic scenes on stage

She had thirteen years of marriage to Willy and following their divorce, she started writing under her own name, but first she became a music-hall performer. Instead of writing about love and romance and sex, she became a dancer and a sexual exhibitionist, miming erotic scenes on stage and often attracting audiences for all the wrong reasons. Colette admitted she felt the "thrill and luscious sensation" of baring her breasts on stage in an early play, written by herself, but went too far with a later seductive ballet scene. By now she was secretly embracing lesbianism, describing herself as "sexually impartial", and this called for an Egyptian-style mummy to arise from a tomb, unwind her bandages and, nearly nude, dance into the arms of her lover, ardently cuddling and kissing "him". When Paris discovered the lover was indeed her lesbian lover Missy, scandal erupted. The woman was a French aristocrat, the former Marquise de Belboeuf and a descendant of Napoleon who was also the choreographer of the ballet so she and Colette had both had a hand in producing this sensational scene.

MIX AND MATCH

Colette's first husband Willy encouraged her lesbian interests, especially after she found him in bed with Lotte Kinceler, a ribald, hunch-backed dwarf who was not averse to his sexual perversions. He was eager to remain free to pursue his conquests and introduced his young wife to one of his mistresses. She did not attract Colette but Willy's young, male homosexual secretary was most definitely interesting, and her sexual impartiality came to the fore again.

Colette returned to putting her sexual fantasies on to paper, though she could truly say not all the experiences of her heroines were entirely born of fantasy. Whether married or in between marriages, Colette enjoyed a succession of lovers, both men and women who frequently featured, under a pseudonym, in her novels. She was nearing fifty herself when another of her most famous books appeared, *Cheri*, the story of a tragic sexual liaison between a young gigolo and an ageing woman. *The Ripening Seed* was full of adolescent sexual initiation, there were more books, always a sexual theme to bind the stories together, with more details of the sensuous pleasures enjoyed by her well-drawn characters.

She moved in to live with Missy, there were two more marriages and a daughter, and several lesbian affairs. When she fell for another notable lesbian, Natalia Barney, she sent her a note saying, "My husband kisses your hands – and I, the rest." Colette continued writing well into her seventies and maintained, "The seduction emanating from a person of uncertain or dis-simulated sex is powerful." She always refused to distinguish between what was considered normal and abnormal sex. Colette was adored by five decades of readers, pouring out words from her apartment in Paris or her villa in St Tropez. She was made a member of the French Academie Goncourt and a Grand Officer of the Legion d'Honneur, honours women were very rarely graced with such honours, and died in 1954.

"THE LOST GENERATION"

The house in Paris was turned into a home-from-home for expatriate artists and writers, and Gertrude Stein coined the phrase "The Lost Generation" for the crop who surrounded her after surviving the war-torn years of 1914–18. She and art critic brother Leo befriended the new Cubist painters Picasso, Matisse and Braque, buying their works to help keep them going, from the Californian family fortunes. In 1969 the Stein art collection was bought for $6,000,000.

Gertrude Stein

Gertrude Stein also made her home and writing base in Paris, though she was born in Pennsylvania and brought up in Vienna. She dropped out of medical school in America, disturbed by her first lesbian liaison and dumped by her lover, another student, who was very passionate and readily accepted her own homosexuality. Her parents were wealthy and ready to grant her a comfortable, living allowance so Gertrude moved to Paris where she realised her sexual leanings would be more easily tolerated. Her first book *Q.E.D.* was completed in 1903, shortly before her thirtieth birthday, and chronicled the painful years of her late teens and twenties as she fought to come to terms with her lesbianism. But this book was not published until 1950, four years after her death.

A lover for life

She was working on her next book *Three Lives*, the story of three working women, when another American, artist Alice B. Toklas walked into the studio at the house to see the collection. For both women it was love at first sight and they remained together, in Paris, for thirty-eight years. While Stein provided for the home, through her writing and money she had now inherited, Toklas took care of the day-to-day running and worked virtually as a personal assistant. Alice was shy and slim, Gertrude a powerful personality, dark-featured and a robust fourteen stone. The two went through a form of marriage, shared the same bed and remained totally faithful.

They maintained the Paris salon for their gifted friends and visitors and Ernest Hemingway became a regular. "I always wanted to fuck Gertrude and she knew it, I tried often enough," said Hemingway. The two rowed regularly about lesbians. "The act male homosexuals commit is ugly and repugnant and afterwards they are disgusted with themselves," she admonished him. "With women, it is the opposite. They do nothing disgusting or repulsive and they lead happy lives together." That's exactly what these two lesbians did, surviving the German occupation of their beloved city through the second world War. Stein died in 1946, aged seventy two and Toklas in 1967, aged eighty nine lonely and still heartbroken insisting to her friends, "I still miss her very much."

Virginia Woolf

When Virginia Woolf committed suicide at the age of fifty-nine, the reasons had nothing to do with her sexual dilemma. She had already suffered four serious nervous breakdowns, each time hallucinating and hearing strange voices she could not identify, and each time – she had become a bestselling novelist – she was on the verge of finishing off another book. It was strange then that her demise came after completing her last book, but Virginia felt she was going mad once more and unable to withstand the experience again, she filled her pockets with stones and drowned in the River Ouse, near her house in Sussex.

She was educated at home by her father Sir Leslie Stephen, himself a writer and literary critic, but her childhood was marred by an initiation to sex from her two half-brothers George and Gerald Duckworth, fifteen or more years older than Virginia, and she quietly withstood their fondling, kisses and caresses from the age of six until she was twenty-two. By then she was already indulging in lesbian romance, beginning at sixteen with a local admirer Madge Vaughan then turning to a friend of the family Violet Dickinson.

Both women were considerably older and though they encouraged her to write passionate love letters, replying in similar vein, there was never any sexual contact.

The terror of a kiss

As she launched herself into a literary career, Virginia joined the Bloomsbury Set in London, a brilliant circle of writers, artists, critics, publishers and poets who had an enormous influence on British literature early in the twentieth century. They had considerable influence on Virginia too but when Lytton Strachey, famed for his astute biography of Queen Victoria, proposed to her, she was "in terror lest he would kiss me". Not for nothing was Strachey known as the Arch Bugger of Bloomsbury, he knew of Virginia's preferences and marriage would have provided excellent cover, perhaps for her but certainly for the promiscuous homosexual. She turned him down and he then introduced her to Leonard Woolf, the man she would marry and together they would set up Hogarth Press to publish all her books. Leonard was another of the Bloomsbury Set, surprised by her acceptance then staggered at her frigidity. "I find the climax is immensely exaggerated," she said and intercourse between them ended soon after their return from honeymoon.

VITA & VIRGINIA

As a lesbian, Virginia Woolf had one physical affair, lasting five years, with novelist and poetess Victoria Sackville-West, "Vita". She was a married woman of some standing but her husband allowed the affair to continue, "it is no threat to our marriage" he said. Victoria became the role model for Virginia's book *Orlando* and when the two women exchanged letters, Victoria wrote "I do not think of you as a sex object, that would be indecent." To which Virginia replied, "It's a great thing being a eunuch, as I am."

Virginia Woolf was a prolific writer with an extremely wide range. In *The Waves* she covered the progress through life of six different characters, from childhood to old age, while in *Between the Acts* and *The Years*, the action occurs in a single day. The view of herself and life was expressed simply in one of her letters. "I am not one thing or another, not a man or a woman. This vague and dream-like world in which I live, without love, or heart, or passion, or sex, is the world I really care about and find really interesting." Virginia and Leonard held on to their marriage for twenty-eight years and when she set out to kill herself, left him a note which said, "I don't think two people could have been happier than we have been."

Literary Lusties

Edna St Vincent Millay

Her first love was poetry, followed by men and then women. Edna St Vincent Millay was always a rebel, who broke every rule in the book when she was a student at Vassar. At the age of 20, her first poem "Renascence" was published and received rave reviews. After that the rules of life did not matter, and taking up residence in New York, she pushed the boundaries – even among the free spirits in Greenwich Village – to breaking point. She managed to keep her wild life mildly private, so that it did not prevent her becoming the first female Pulitzer Prize winner in 1923. But one of her bed-mates, author Edmund Wilson, did learn the identities of several of her other lovers, and called them the "alumni association". She suggested a unique three in a bed routine to the man, who would only be allowed to fondle the lower half of her body, while his friend John Bishop played with the upper half.

She was a petite, red–haired beauty courtesy of her Irish blood, and she captivated the men who came into her circle of friends, moving one to comment, "She is like a snow princess whose kisses leave splinters of ice in the hearts of the men who fall in love with her." Edna was one of three sisters born and brought up in Maine on America's east coast. After college she played bit parts as an actress on Broadway, and wrote magazine articles under various pseudonyms to pay the rent, for poetry, even prize-winning poetry, was never a big earner. This led her to pen the phrase adopted all over America and then the world … "My candle burns at both ends".

Edna was highly strung and lived, through her twenties and thirties, on the edge of a nervous breakdown. When she sought medical advice for recurring migraine attacks, her doctor suggested these might stem from the odd

LUST WEEKEND

Edna and another poet, Arthur Davison Ficke, fell hopelessly for each other, but he was married and trying to remain faithful. Practically, she suggested they go to bed for the entire weekend, consummate their passion for each other and never do it again. That is precisely what happened, and they remained close friends for several years without ever attempting to repeat this sexual therapy.

erotic impulse towards women. "If you mean I might be homosexual, I certainly am but I'm heterosexual too. What's that got to do with my headache?" By that time she had enjoyed more than a few affairs with older women, as a relief from sharing her bed with the many willing men pursuing her in Greenwich Village.

At the age of 31 Edna married Eugen Boissevain, a wealthy businessman who was totally devoted to her for the next 25 years, buying her a farm and an island off the Maine coast while insisting on an 'open marriage' to allow his younger wife to retain her freedom and the creativity which, he felt, clearly stemmed from that style of life. After that, Edna kept the identity of her lovers secret; they were anonymously re-created in her writing until she died aged 58. Eugen may have had a point.

George Sand

Armandine Aurore Lucie Dupin went to a convent school and wanted to train as a nun. But her wily grandmother had already recognized the signs within the passionate teenager, and took her out of school fast. Though that may have saved her from a life of abstinence, grandma can hardly have been prepared for what took its place – the girl had not reached her 17th birthday when she seduced a neighbour, who probably fathered her daughter, Solange, when she seduced him again eight years later.

The world knows this woman as the author George Sand; she took a man's name to pen her first novel *Indiana*, an overnight success in France in 1832. She was married at 18 to a man nine years older, but nearly all her later love affairs were marked by a difference in ages in the opposite direction – some were twenty or more years younger. These affairs, and her tremendous love and devotion for her son Maurice, gave her critics ground to accuse her of incest as well as being bisexual. The former claim was never proved.

Armandine, or George, had heavy, swarthy features. She was short with dark probing eyes. As early as the 1820s, she was championing the cause of women's liberation, calling herself the "Spartacus of

DEFENDING HER HONOUR

Gustave Planche, a literary critic, was another lover, and he fought a duel in defence of her literary honour. Another critic had savaged her latest novel *Lelia*, so the two men drew and fired pistols at dawn in Paris – and both missed. When news of the duel circulated in France, sales of the book shot up.

women's slavery". The heroines in her books were forever being corralled and controlled by their unhappy and unwanted marriages. Sand herself needed to be in love to enjoy sex; without love she was impassive to her partner and to the act itself. As love waned in each partnership, she became cold in bed. Jules Sandeau, her first Parisian lover, became bitter at the end and described her as a "graveyard". But the heroines in her books never had to suffer for long – their husbands and lovers suffered a convenient demise, dreadful accidents or suicides wrapping up their problems.

Her most famous lover was Chopin, who smoked opium, which did nothing for his sexual prowess, and when their affair ended after nine years, the egotistical composer told all their friends in Paris, "I am not sorry, the woman refused to go to bed with me, with me of all people." He was by no means the last man in her life – she remained active in bed until shortly before she died aged 71.

Robbie Burns

The poet – whose birth nearly 250 years ago is celebrated each year in every corner of the world where people with an ounce of Scottish blood in their veins can be found – achieved fame with the first book of his verses, called simply *Poems*, in 1786. His name found notoriety some two hundred years later with another set of verses. The lines from Robbie Burns' collection *The Merry Muses of Caledonia* were so raunchy, verging on the obscene, that they could not be published in uncensored form until the swinging sixties arrived. For a short time they occupied a place in the best-seller lists in 1965.

He managed to pack a lot of living and a lot of loving into his 37 years. His brilliant poetry rightly turned him into Scotland's national hero, and he left a lot of descendants around the highlands and lowlands, a string of children born both in and out of wedlock. He was raised on a farm in Ayrshire, the eldest of seven children, and made his living at farming until he became a tax inspector. He earned an income from his poetry but considered it his national duty, not a career, to write verses about his beloved Scotland as well as his other passion – fornication. His love letters as well as his poetry disclose the lusty exchanges this man enjoyed. Out in the villages and hamlets of Scotland in the latter half of the Eighteenth century, promiscuity was not unusual. Married women were expected to keep their infidelities reasonably quiet, but young maidens were not expected to deny themselves and remain virgins. It was almost the norm for marriage to follow pregnancy, but while Robbie had nothing against marriage, he did not see things entirely that way.

The women he loved inspired the rhymes he wrote from the very beginning. At 15 he fell in love for the first time, with Nelly Kirkpatrick, and though the girl remained chaste, the result was his very first poem. "Handsome Nell". Robbie had made his

A GUID WILLY

Another poem by Burns was called "Nine Inch Will Please a Lady," and the man felt he had proved the veracity of that maxim when he was reunited with a former mistress who he had left without saying good-bye. She was not pleased to see him again, he wrote to a friend, "till I cheered her up with vigorous lovemaking and she rejoiced with joy unspeakable and full of glory." He added, "What a peacemaker is a guid weel-willy pintle! 'Tis the sword of mercy, the horn of plenty and the tree of life between man and woman."

first approach and suffered his first rejection well before he seduced a servant girl in the family farmhouse and Elizabeth Paton became pregnant.

So did his next long-term lover Jean Armour, who prepared a document complete with a seal, signatures and witnesses to recognize each other as husband and wife. Her father had different ideas and destroyed the document. He knew her suitor's reputation, and sent his daughter to stay with relatives while he got rid of his potential son-in-aw. Mary Campbell was his next conquest, and she too became pregnant but died in childbirth. Following the publication of his poems, Burns was much in demand in the fine houses in Edinburgh and on the expansive Highlands estates to read his own works at festive balls and house parties. The invitation usually came from the lady of the house, who was not averse to a private reading, and delighted if she inspired new text for the man.

Burns proposed marriage to at least three women who were not expecting his babies before he turned his attentions to more experienced ladies. Frances Dunlop was a widow with 13 children, and Agnes Maclehose had a husband away in the West Indies, but Burns still had time for unattached working girls. May Cameron and Jenny Clow were both in service, and soon in labour as well.

THE FORNICATOR

Robbie Burns had three illegitimate daughters, all named Elizabeth. The mother of the first threatened him in the courts and was paid off, then disappeared leaving him with the little girl. Burns was publicly rebuked in his local church and he wrote one of his better-known verses to mark the occasion, called *The Fornicator*: "Before the Congregation wide/I passed the muster fairly/My handsome Betsy by my side/We gat our ditty rarely/By my downcast eye by chance did spy/What made my lips to water/Those limbs so clean where I, between/Commenc'd a Fornicator..."

When he returned to her side, Jean Armour forgave Burns and married him, and indeed they had four children, but her father's original instincts proved accurate. The poet continued to enjoy himself in various beds and managed to dirty his own doorstep in some style when he fathered yet another child by Anne Park, the barmaid at his local hostelry. His view of marriage was expressed in these immortal lines: "to have a woman to lye with when one pleases, without running any risk of the cursed expense of bastards." If only he had practised what he preached.

Honoré de Balzac

This prolific writer was very short and very fat, dressed scruffily, and had few social graces, yet he received 12,000 letters from female admirers. Many were proposals of marriage which he ignored; others included very explicit sexual propositions, and quite a few of those he readily accepted. A male admirer who later wrote Honoré de Balzac's biography said, "He slept with aristocrats, courtesans and trollops indiscriminately, displaying in his love life the same dazzling diversification that appeared in his writing. His yearning for romance was insatiable."

He put himself about among the ladies in some style and with considerable energy. At the height of his sexual activity, he was receiving as many as twenty letters a week from willing ladies in several of Europe's leading cities where his fame and his reputation had spread. They were eager to meet him and make love to him and they made it quite clear what they expected Honore to do to them. He kept these letters both to remind his mistresses of their requests, and to compare the theory with the practice when the fun and games were over. He kept them even longer than that, in fact – the best of the letters were made available to historians.

He was born just before the turn of the nineteenth century and studied law in Paris then, at 20, hell-bent on a career as an author, locked himself in an attic and poured out thousands of words, ghosting articles in magazines and re-writing other novelists work which he called "literary pig swill" until his own efforts were eventually published. But life was not all work. Even before his talent was recognized he set out on the seduction trail, though in truth seduction for this writer was rarely necessary. In between books he enjoyed two very different kinds of orgy – at the dining table and in the bedroom, or rather bedrooms.

In today's terms the man was a sexual athlete, taking his early instruction

---

A WOMAN SCORNED

"A woman is a well served table that one sees with different eyes before and after the meal," wrote Balzac. One lady he saw only with her clothes on. The elegant Marquise de Castries found the man revolting, and spurned him publicly. In return, de Balzac took his revenge, scornfully depicting a character in his novel *La Duchess de Langeais* who was easily identified as the beautiful marquise.

in the arms of a number of well-known Parisian courtesans. Of course, once his technique was perfected, this made him doubly attractive to potential partners, and the majority were ladies of more mature years and better social standing. He added to his formidable sexual armoury by personally circulating the opinion that de Balzac was a novelist who "understood" women. Once in their company, he would frequently draw on their maternal instincts saying, "I never had a mother, I never knew a mother's love."

In his early days soon after leaving law school, de Balzac made heavy play firstly on never having bedded a woman, and then on the chaste life he led, which to an extent, was quite true. Then at 23, he met Laure de Bernay, a young grandmother – she was almost exactly twice his age – and even a novelist with a fertile imagination had never guessed such passion and exhilaration existed. Chastity went straight out of the window. Though they enjoyed each other's company, particularly at night, for another 15 years, Laure encouraged him to have other mistresses. She advised him,

> ## COFFEE KILLER
>
> As he worked, Honoré was inspired by Napoleon. He kept a bust of the emperor on his desk, a portrait on his study wall and read constantly details of his life story. He died at the age of 51 from drink – coffee, no less – for as he wrote he drank endless cups of coffee, which doctors said hastened his death.

"Aim for the lonely, older women," and his next successful target was the alluring and tender Duchesse d'Abrantes. He was 25 and she was 40, a wealthy, blonde widow who paid off his creditors.

Now the man was in full stride. When Honoré wasn't writing he was ravaging, when he wasn't creating he was copulating. He did not consider his behaviour promiscuous; there were women to be pleased and he was only too happy to please them. The letters began to arrive from his unknown admirers and his goose-quill pens were put to tasks other than to fill the pages of his new novel – there were assignations to be made. One letter arrived from the Ukraine signed "The Stranger". This was in 1833, and the eastern European republics that would one day become Russia were even more of a puzzle then than they are today, and it says much for Honoré's diligence in research that he discovered the signatory was married to an elderly baron, the mysterious Evelina Hanska.

A year would pass before he was able to meet Evelina in secret in Lucerne, beside the breathtaking scenery of the Swiss lake. They would continue to meet in Europe's most romantic settings, with the baroness picking up the tab. Back home was Marie Louis de Fresnay, a much younger woman, who bore him a child, and whose unsuspecting husband was proud of their first-born. From Italy, the Countess Frances Guidoboni-Visconti surprised Honoré. Even to him she appeared over-sexed, but he managed to keep her happy for a period of five years. While these lengthy affairs lasted, there were still mini-affairs, one-night stands, casual partners, occasionally a pair of prostitutes to entertain together, and his correspondents to satisfy – and journeys in the early and mid-1800s were not easy; they were undertaken by horse and carriage or sailing ships.

In England, the amorous Lady Ellenborough had a reputation almost equal to de Balzac's. They wrote and agreed an encounter might be mutually enjoyable. The meeting, in Paris, lasted two months and there was only one subject on the hectic agenda. The noble lady liked to be mounted from the rear but then that was the preferred position for many ladies in that era, especially if neither the time nor a bed was available. They merely removed their under-things, hoisted their skirts and got on with the business. Both were devotees of sexual intercourse, but on the subject of exactly how it should be conducted, Lady Ellenborough and Honoré de Balzac could not see eye-to-eye, so to speak!

Creators of Fairy Tales

Literary historians and biographers have tried for the last sixty years to fathom the sexual proclivities of the creators of *Peter Pan* and *Alice in Wonderland*, two of the most wonderful fairy tales every written. J.M. Barrie, whose Pan was born of the bed-time stories he told to the children of his friends, liked little boys, while Lewis Carroll, as Alice's inventor was known, cherished little girls. There is not much evidence that either the boys or the girls suffered from the two men's strange adoration, but it could hardly be described as natural.

Forever young

Barrie was tiny, under five feet high, and went from news reporting on the *Nottingham Journal*, to freelancing in London, to writing novels and then plays in rapid succession. He worked furiously and was amply rewarded, already rich and famous still in his twenties. Those who knew him were aware of his tremendous mother–fixation, and at the age of 36 he wrote a book *Margaret Ogilvy*, the heroine based entirely on his mother, it was clearly an emotional tribute to her. One critic was savage in his condemnation of the book, calling it "Nothing less than a positive act of indecency." His next book was an autobiographical novel *Sentimental Tommy*, the story of a boy who surrounds himself with romantic dreams, and it had another little-mother heroine.

But this does not explain why the man's greatest pleasure lay in befriending numerous little children. Several were from fami-

FRUSTRATED AMBITION

The playwright Barrie hated being so small and he once wrote, "If I had really grown to six feet three inches, it would have made a great difference in my life. My one aim would have been to become a favourite of the ladies, which between you and me has always been my sorrowful ambition. The things I could have said to them if my legs had been longer, read that with a bitter cry."

lies he knew, but often, on walks through London's central parks, he would stop and talk to children out with their nannies or governesses, and his behaviour was that of a patronising uncle. Of course, the children inspired his greatest work, *Peter Pan*. From a successful play, it became a favourite Christmas pantomime. Here probably lies the truth behind Barrie, forever trying to recapture the very early, happy days of his boyhood at home in the village of Kirriemuir, in Scotland. *Peter Pan* is quite simply the story of a little boy who refused to grow up.

He loved actresses, and married the leading lady from one of his plays, Mary Ansell – but according to her the marriage was never consummated. Others had already compared notes and reached the opinion Barrie was completely impotent. In London's theatre world, he was given the title, "The boy who refused to go up!"

When he befriended the five sons of a London barrister – according to him, the role-models for *Peter Pan* – he fell in love with their mother, Sylvia Davies. He divorced his wife, but then Sylvia died in the following year. His life was constantly accompanied by tragedy, and he may never have made love to a women during his 77 years. But Nico Davies, the last survivor of the five boys he legally adopted, said, "He was the wittiest man I have ever known, and the least interested in sex."

HOW ALICE BEGAN

Alice Liddell was one of three children he took boating in Oxford. Returning to college, he wrote down the story he had told that afternoon and drew some accompanying pencil sketches. That was the start of *Alice* – and young Miss Liddell remained close to Lewis Carroll all through his life. He wrote to her often, but there was never any sexual connotation. There were rumours of an affair with a leading actress of the last century, Ellen Terry, but dismissively she said, "He was as fond of me as he could be of anyone over the age of ten."

Through the looking-glass

Lewis Carroll was a mathematician who also studied divinity. He was born at just about the time when the camera was making an appearance. He became a keen amateur behind the lens, and started to photograph the opposite sex, with his models gradually becoming younger and younger. Eventually, he discovered he adored girls between the ages of 6 and 10 – when puberty arrived, in his eyes the girls were ruined. Mothers trusted him implicitly, enough to allow their charges to go and stay with Carroll for a week or two at a time. Like Barrie, these little friends motivated his pen. At the age of 33, he had written *Alice's Adventures in Wonderland* and soon after, the sequel *Through the Looking Glass.* Designed as children's books, they were equally admired by adults.

He was very concerned and very proper about the right age at which a girl should be kissed, and he wrote to one mother, "Are your daughters kiss-able? With girls under 14, I don't think it necessary to ask the question, but I guess Margery to be over 14 and in such cases, with new friends, I usually ask the mother's leave." Again, like Barrie, the girls he took to early on were the children of his friends, but later he discovered new friends while out walking or on trains travelling to the seaside, or on the beaches. Undoubtedly, his approaches would not be tolerated today. What is just as certain is that Carroll died a virgin.

He entered Christ Church College at Oxford University at the age of 18, and stayed there for another 48 years, until the end of his life. He was ordained a deacon in the Church of England. but also worked steadfastly as a devoted mathematics don, writing fairy tales in his spare time.

H G Wells

It was the done thing in the last century for a young man to have his first sexual encounter in the arms of a prostitute. Indeed, fathers frequently sent their teenage sons to women they had known themselves, and paid well to have the youngsters expertly tutored. Novelist H.G. Wells had no such luck; he was all of 22 when he was initiated by an unimaginative and inattentive whore who left such a mark on the young man that he went three more years before setting eyes on another naked woman – and that was on his honeymoon night. His bride was cousin Isabel and he quickly set about making up for lost time, but she could not match his ardour and was thankful when he embarked on the first of a string of affairs.

Throughout his life Wells, the world's first science–fiction writer of note, was consumed with finding his ideal playmate, yet twice he married women who were sexually naive. His first marriage ended after four years. The second lasted 32 years, and again, his wife Amy – who he called Jane – was happy to allow him all the latitude he desired, as she could not endure the demands he made on her body. He was short, only 5ft 5ins, with a high–pitched voice, but a biographer who knew the man well summarized his personality. "No one could help loving Wells, with all his brains, bubbling with humour, full of charm, and there were many women who would have testified to this."

Herbert George Wells studied science and for a short time taught the subject, then

UNDERSTANDING WIFE

• • • • • • • • • • • • • • • •

At the age of 42, Wells became infatuated with Amber Reeves, a 22-year old London society beauty who quickly succumbed to the famous author's attentions. Within a month she was pregnant, and while friends on both sides stood back horrified, second wife Jane went out shopping for baby clothes for the new arrival.

• • • • • • • • • • • • • • • •

combined his learning with his talents as a writer, turning to journalism then to short stories. When his first novel *The Time Machine*, was published in 1895, he was only 29. The book immediately achieved enormous success. In the next six years *The Invisible Man*, *The War of the Worlds* and *Anticipations* were published, and for half a century were classics. Now he had the money, and he made sure he had the time, to go chasing women.

He was remarkably lucky in choosing Amy, or Jane, as his wife. She totally ignored his promiscuity – she even allowed him to keep framed photographs of some of his mistresses in his study – typing his manuscripts, sorting out tax affairs, arranging meetings and generally running his business life and the house. Friends ultimately persuaded Wells to be kinder to Jane, to be more discreet, and so he took a flat in London where he could stay overnight and entertain his ladies instead of taking them to restaurants and hotels.

Opinions are divided on whether this self-centred, powerful man had one true love of his life, but if he did, that woman was novelist Rebecca West. She was 20, a literary critic on the magazine *Clarion* who panned his latest book, *Marriage*. Wells, 46 – who always protested when bad reviews came his way – challenged the woman. But when they met, in 1912, he was smitten by her wit and intellect and by her sensuous looks. Over the next ten years they had a

> ## EGO AND CONQUEST
> • • • • • • • • • • • • • • • • •
> Author Somerset Maugham was a friend of Wells for years, and had very definite views about his lifelong sex hunt. "It was purely a physiological matter, it had nothing to do with love. He had a tremendous need to satisfy these strong sexual instincts. Ego and conquest did not come into it." These instincts were apparent from a very early age; in his teens, Wells was embarrassingly aroused by Greek statues.
> • • • • • • • • • • • • • • • • •

very passionate affair, and she bore him a son. This was one woman who could match his intensity in bed and his intelligence elsewhere; she certainly influenced his work. Amazingly, Jane accepted his first and now ailing wife Isabel into the family home, to nurse her and allow Wells to continue living comfortably with Rebecca.

But he could not remain faithful even to Rebecca, and their affair ended when another of his lovers tried to commit suicide. Varena Gatternigg was an Austrian journalist. At his London flat they made love, then had a tremendous argument and Wells walked out. She took an overdose but fortunately, Jane dropped by and found her unconscious but still alive. She managed to get the poor woman to hospital where she was saved. Wells had too many enemies in the literary and newspaper world to ensure a complete cover-up; Rebecca West's name was floated around this episode and she left him.

He had a brief fling with American Margaret Sanger, a career woman where sex was concerned. She led the birth control movement and despite being arrested in New York in 1916 for running a contraception clinic, toured the world and published several manuals advocating safe sex for women. Wells had an amazing introduction to Odette Keun, a former nun who turned to writing and sent him one of her books to review. They corresponded and arranged a rendezvous in Switzerland which took place in her hotel room. They barely had time to say "Hello", before he arrived at the door, she turned out the lights and then led him straight to her bed and they made love without setting eyes on each other. Later they built a love-nest on the Cote d'Azur and continued the affair for nine years.

Jane had died, and after Odette, there were other women in his life, casual affairs and longer-standing relationships. H.G. Wells remained sexually active almost until the time of his death, which came a month before his 80th birthday. A man with amazing drive.

Samuel Pepys

He lived to the age of 70, yet the diaries which brought him such fame were written over a period of only nine years in the mid–1600s. Pepys recorded great historical events, personal recollections and a vast amount of trivia to provide a brilliant picture of life either side of the Plague and the Great Fire in the City of London. But the diaries were so sexually explicit, detailing his love life with his wife and several mistresses, that they were not published for another 150 years, and certain narratives considered too bawdy and outrageous were censored out until 1970, when the full, unexpurgated version was finally released to the public.

Pepys was exceptionally mean and vain, with an enormous sex drive, and tried to keep his affairs a secret from his wife both by hiding his current diary and by using his own form of shorthand, also inserting words and phrases in French and Latin, Spanish and Italian. He carried on a "conversation" with himself in the quaint dialogue of that period, confessing all his flirtations, his intentions and dalliances with the many women who came into his life, his shame and promises to change his ways. Despite his behaviour, he remained the confidante of kings, a member of Parliament and held high government office in London. He was married young – at 22 – and that conveniently covered his extramarital activities, for Elizabeth did not discover her husband's true character until he was 35.

If Britannia ruled the waves, as she almost certainly did for some 250 years, the country owed much to Samuel Pepys. As Parliament's first secretary to the Admiralty, he had much to do with instilling discipline, setting the forms of court-martial, bringing about open recruitment rather than press-ganging unwilling sailors, and eventually doubling the size of the navy to control the

SEXY SISTERS

One woman made several appearances in his diaries, first as shop-girl Betty Lane then, after she was married, as Mrs Martin. When she was pregnant, Pepys moved his attentions to her sister Dolly Lane, and continued when Dolly became Mrs Powell. "Met Betty Lane and was exceeding free in dallying with her and she not unfree to take it" and later, "I had my full liberty of towzing her and doing what I would" and later still, "With Mrs Martin in idle and wanton humour, had two bouts within the hour." With Dolly, "Did what I would and might have done anything else."

increasing empire. Under Charles the Second and James the Second, he was one of the most powerful men in England. As he sought to rid the government of corruption, he was arrested and charged with treason then gaoled in the Tower of London. But his influence was too strong, and he survived even this episode. He still found time to keep his wife happy, find and seduce new women, and commit more than a million words to his diaries.

FAILED SEDUCTION

Ironically, Elizabeth Pepys discovered Samuel's indiscretions when she caught him embracing their servant-girl Deborah Willet, with his hand under her petticoats. Though he had kissed and fondled her, Samuel had so far failed to seduce the girl. According to his diary, "Elizabeth is angry – the truth is, I have a great mind to have the maidenhead of this girl which I should no doubt have, but she will be gone and I know not wither."

Pepys was a remarkable man, rising to a high position from a fairly ordinary start to life. His father was a tailor but he came from an old, well established family and after graduating from Cambridge, Samuel was sponsored by a cousin who later became the Earl of Sandwich. The diaries are one of the great legacies of English literature, an intimate and invaluable document, and his spicy revelations with their foreign phrases make amusing reading today:

> "And so to Mrs M and there did what *je voudrais avec* [I wanted with] her, both *devant* [in front] and backward, which is *muy bon plazer* [my great pleasure]."

So too Peg,

> "With me in my closet a good while, and did suffer me *a la besar mucho et tocar ses cosas* [to kiss her a lot and touch her things] wherein I had great pleasure."

These, of course, are not the expurgated passages which earlier publishers voluntarily restricted, first in 1825 then with a second version in 1893. With Mistress Ann,

> had a very high bout ... I rattled her up" [and then over a period of twelve months] "gently seduced Bagwell's wife, after many protestings I arrived at what I would, with great pleasure ...I tried to do what I would, and against her will I did enough for my contentment.

The diary entries were not confined to sexual conquests. He recorded several bouts of "Kissing and fondling breasts" in London's alehouses. A few fights occurred with Elizabeth, especially when he was confronted with evidence of his infidelity, but they made up their differences and he wrote, "A great sporting together in bed, we are a very happy couple again," and on another occasion, "I have made love to Elizabeth more times since this falling-out, and with more pleasure to her, than in all the time of our marriage before."

Failing eyesight forced Pepys to give up his diaries in 1669, very shortly before his wife died. He was aged only 36, but he didn't give up sex for a good many more years, though he grew more constant and faithful. He had an affair with unmarried Kitty Skinner that went on for twenty years before she finally moved in with him. Pepys had a second period in gaol, but was released without trial and died in 1703.

The Men
from Montmartre

At the highest point in Paris, to the north and on the right bank of the Seine, lies the district of Montmartre, dominated by the Basilica of Le Sacre Coeur, the Church of the Sacred Heart. In the alleyways and the small cobbled square behind the church are the tiny houses and tenement buildings where for two hundred years many of the world's most eminent artists lived and painted, men such as Pablo Picasso, Paul Gauguin, Toulouse-Lautrec and Vincent Van Gogh. Some of their graves lie in the huge cemetery on the hill here. The name itself is a corruption of mount and martyr, for a thousand years ago this is where Roman conquerors put to death their enemies. Montmartre, its fame spread through books, plays and films, is an essential stop on the tourist route, and what a story its walls could tell of its artists and their models, of the prostitutes who loved and fed young men who spent all their money on canvas and paint, and whose work now lines the walls of galleries and museums in scores of countries.

Pablo Picasso

There were very few women he took to bed who, before or after, failed to model for the Spaniard, surely the world's richest and probably the most influential artist in the twentieth century. Pablo Picasso made millions, in whatever currency his wealth is counted – pesetas, francs, dollars or pounds – and having started as an impecunious painter living in Paris, he spent millions. Sex dominated his life just as it dominated so many of his paintings. He expressed his rage at times, when he felt frustrated or growing tired of his current love, distorting the feminine figures on his canvasses, giving them gross, over-sized sexual organs and shrivelled breasts. This vengeance flowed into real life; a mistress, Alice Paalen, accused "One of his greatest joys is to make love to a woman then deliberately deny her the climax."

Fernande Olivier was one of his first loves, a partnership wrapped in a

Bohemian life-style and convenience. They were both 23, she was voluptuous and he was a randy artist. They lived in the same Montmartre tenement block and while he liked to paint, she preferred to pose, preferably reclining with a hint of her naked beauty. Without enough money to buy shoes, Fernande was forced to stay in her apartment for two months in the winter of 1905. Picasso had his own reasons for not paying for her footwear – "There was always love-making for entertainment," he said. "Pablo forced me to live like a recluse but I could not resist him," she confirmed.

ARTISTIC WORTH

He was born Pablo Blasco but following the Spanish tradition, he signed his paintings with his mother's maiden name and that is how he was always known. Picasso left an estate worth more than one billion dollars when he died. The vast amount of work he completed can only be estimated – some 14,000 canvases, 30,000 illustrations for books, and at least 100,000 prints and engravings.

When he changed women, he changed their form. Fernande had a full, rounded figure but she was followed by the petite "Eva" Humbert who he referred to as "Ma Jolie", an inscription he left on many paintings, though not of her. In Rome he met émigré Olga Koklova and they wed in a Russian Orthodox ceremony, but by the time their son Paulo was born, the marriage was falling apart. Olga, unwittingly, became the model for the first of his feminine ogres with the hideous bodies. Picasso admitted he saw women either as "Goddesses or doormats".

Then the blonde, vigorous Marie-Therese came on the scene. No longer deprived by his neurotic wife, his brushes created beautiful breasts again, and luscious, smiling mouths, and the figures, though not life-like, were strangely arousing. A daughter Maia was the result, and it was time to change models once more. Dora Maar was herself a painter, dark and intensive, intelligent and temperamental. Their impassioned arguments often left her in tears, and Picasso's many paintings of weeping women are usually of her. But like Marie-Therese, this model went into overdrive in bed and the man decided, on balance, she was worth a few more miles.

Picasso lived through two world wars

PEACE SYMBOL

Picasso spent most of his life in France, living in Paris or in the sunshine of the south, but made frequent visits to his native Spain until the outbreak of the Civil War in 1936. He was an ardent loyalist and a bitter opponent of Franco, especially when the general called on the friendly German air force to flatten a small town in the north west Basque country. This inspired Picasso's massive and harrowing painting *Guernica*, regarded by experts as his masterpiece. Later he joined the Communist Party and his Dove lithograph was adopted as the symbol of world peace.

and although sales of his paintings dried up for a while, he managed to keep his sex life intact. At the age of 60, another painter moved alongside, the nubile Francoise Gilot, nearly 40 years younger but with no reason to complain about her sexual exchanges. Picasso was delighted when she added to his brood; a son and daughter, Claude and Paloma. Francoise left after half-a-dozen enjoyable but stormy years, and another young woman, recently divorced Jacqueline Roque, moved into his bed and his homes. All this time, for nearly 40 years, he stayed married to Olga and frequently saw her, but when she died in 1955, he married Jacqueline who took over the running of his life.

> **FATHER AND SON**
>
> His father Jose was an art teacher in Malaga and Barcelona. Picasso's talents became evident when he was only nine, to such an extent that he was considered too bright to teach, so he had no formal training, only his father's influence. According to legend, when Jose recognized his son's brilliance, he gave up painting himself and just continued instructing his pupil.

Each of the women in his life had one thing in common – they were all beautiful. There are many judgements of Picasso, as an artist, as a businessman, as a husband and lover. Art expert Pierre Cabanne summarised, "Sex stimulation was his basic motive force. Desire, with him, was violence, dismemberment, tumult, indignation and excess." He died in 1973, at the grand old age of 91.

Paul Gauguin

Paul Gauguin was born in Paris, but was part Peruvian Creole. Soon after he learned to walk, mother took him to live in Lima in the mid-1800s. Even in the Peruvian capital, women went about the town in long, cloth skirts with bare breasts, and though he was 35 before deciding to concentrate on painting, the nudity surrounding Paul's childhood proved to have a dramatic effect on his art. He had toured the seven seas as a sailor and worked on the French Bourse as a stockbroker, but turning to painting cost him his ten-year marriage to willowy blonde Danish teacher Mette Gad, who went home with their five children. Never again would he have spare money in his pocket – just like the friends he soon found in Montmartre, like Cézanne, Toulouse-Lautrec and Pissaro. For a time, he moved in with Van Gogh.

He created most of his work in the post-impressionist period, exhibiting in Paris and able to sell many of his canvasses, never quite enough to live on but enough to pay for a visit to Martinique in the West Indies in 1887. Then in 1891 he sold two dozen paintings, enough to buy a passage to Tahiti where he set up home. Gauguin confessed to a powerful sex drive – he had hit some of the world's great flesh-pots as a sailor, but the days of free love only followed his marriage break-up. In this respect he obeyed the traditions of Montmartre without setting any records and for a time, moved in with a young seamstress, Juliette Huet. But when he moved across the world to the South Sea Islands, free love took on a new meaning. He rejoiced in the local custom of taking a different native woman to his bed each night.

At first this provided great inspiration, and the brilliant colours Gauguin deployed as he painted the native girls left their mark on the art world for the next hundred years. But this hectic promiscuity, night after night, soon took its toll. He put out the word: he was looking for a more permanent partner. Tehura was beautiful, in her early teens when she became his mistress, house-keeper and model. Little more than a year later he decided to return to France, leaving a pregnant Tehura behind. He moved to a fishing village in Brittany and made a dreadful choice with his new mistress, a quixotic 13-year-old Javanese girl named Anna, and after a short fling, it was his turn to be deserted. By the time he returned to Tahiti he had contracted syphilis. Still he found native women happy to enter his hut each night. "My bed has been invaded every night by young hussies running wild," said Gauguin, "yesterday I had three." He moved on to the Marquesas Islands and still the women flocked to his side. They came to be painted, to see the pornographic art and pictures decorating his walls, and to copulate with this strange man with a mighty reputation.

BELOW THE NAVEL

Gauguin's view on sex was expressed in the dissimilarities he found in two opposing cultures. "In Europe intercourse between men and women is a result of love. In Oceania love is a result of intercourse. Which is right? Women want to be free, that's their right, and it's not men who stand in their way. The day a woman's honour is no longer located below the navel, she will be free."

It is a tragedy that his work was of so little value when he lived, for today very few of the major art galleries of Europe and America are without a Gauguin in their collection. With his turbulent character, Paul Gauguin was used by author Somerset Maugham as the hero for his book *The Moon and Sixpence*, made into a film forty years after the artist's death from a heart attack in 1903, at the age of 54.

Henri de Toulouse-Lautrec

A vastly different life was laid out for Count Henri de Toulouse-Lautrec before he broke both thigh bones as an adolescent. He was crippled, his growth stunted at five feet and his features, distorted by the pain, never recovered. Father was an eccentric French nobleman who planned to take his teenage son out hunting – stag and deer by day, and loose women by night. By the time he was 20, Henri needed no one to guide him to the bars and the music halls of Montmartre. Bearded and bowler-hatted, in his baggy clothes and long overcoat trailing the ground, he soon became a well known figure in the artist's quarter where he felt most comfortable, spurning his high-born background to live among the down-and-outs. It was there he met Degas and discovered his true vocation, and his wealth allowed him to indulge his new passion, painting women and scenes drawn from the city's night life.

The Spanish have an old saying, "Big man, big prick, small man, all prick." That was certainly true of Toulouse-Lautrec. Underneath the voluminous garb, he possessed extremely well-developed sexual organs, entirely out of proportion to the rest of his body. He was described as a coffee pot "With a huge spout", and word soon got out when he bedded a young model, Marie Charlet, who boasted about the "Prowess and size" of her latest sponsor. Unperturbed by this grotesque near-dwarf with the strange appearance, models lined up to see if he was hung as well as he could draw.

He proved to be a brilliant artist and moved in with another painter, a woman

THE NOSE HAS IT

Lautrec reserved the same seat in a theatre for a month, so that each night he could watch Marcelle Lender dance the Bolero. His passion and his paintings concentrated on different parts of a woman's body but he always loved the fine lines of the female nose. According to a friend, "That was only natural, being so short when he looked up at a woman it was the first thing he saw."

more than twice his age – Suzanne Valadon, the mother of Maurice Utrillo. He still had his models, but discovered however good they were in bed, they were often like "Stuffed owls" in the studio. Brothels provided the perfect answer for both work and play, so he moved his rooms to live permanently among the prostitutes. They were surprised and impressed that he was so well endowed, for here was a man who could actually satisfy them. While paying for his pleasures, he could also sketch them nude and unposed as they sat and lay around the brothel waiting for their customers.

He also frequented the lesbian bars of Paris, and befriended their patrons, who constantly turned to him for advice – one of few men they were prepared to trust – and some trusted him enough to join him in bed. A full bosom was irresistible, and he was neither afraid nor embarrassed to plunge his face into a strange woman's breasts and purr like a cat. Win some, lose some; it occasionally earned him another conquest. He was wild about red hair and produced six paintings of a prostitute Rosa La Rouge, and he was pretty wild when she gave him syphilis, which eventually contributed to his death aged only 36.

Vincent Van Gogh

The last of this famous quartet was Vincent Van Gogh, the unorthodox Dutch painter who in his 37 years sold only one of his paintings, yet today the originals of his sunflowers, orchards and cornfield scenes are almost beyond price. He was a genius whose work could not be truly appreciated by his contemporaries, and he managed to live only by virtue of an allowance from his brother Theo. As a youngster he was kept on the straight and narrow by his father, a Calvinist pastor, and was himself a minor church minister for a time. He was never a successful womaniser, but when Van Gogh found one he loved, or thought he loved, he pursued her relentlessly.

His first rejection came in Amsterdam, from his landlady's daughter, Ursula Loyer. Then a widowed cousin Kee Stricker turned down his proposal of marriage and when her parents denied him access to the girl, he held one hand in the flame of an oil lamp, insisting, "I shall not remove it until I meet again with Kee." The poor man was sexually frustrated, and he was moody, and often depressed and poor company; "I must have a woman or I shall turn to stone," he plead-

POTENT ARTISTS

Van Gogh was fascinated by the behaviour of other artists and their claim that sex inspired their painting. An exception, he reported to a family friend, was Degas; "He does not like women, he knows if he loved them and f**ked them, he would become insipid as a painter." Rubens: "Ah that one, a handsome man and a good f**ker." Delacroix: "Does not f**k much, only has easy love affairs, devoting his time to painting." Balzac, Cézanne, Gauguin and several more were described along with their sexual peccadilloes, and he summarized, "Painting and f**king are not compatible, it weakens the brain. If we want to be really potent males in our work, we must sometimes resign ourselves not to f**k much."

SEVERED EAR

• • • • • • • • • • • • • • • • •

Contrary to the popular myth, when Van Gogh cut off a chunk of his left ear it followed an argument with Paul Gauguin, not with a woman. For ten weeks the two artists lived together in Arles in Provence, but Gauguin was more popular with the local prostitutes and Vincent was jealous. He sent the severed ear to a woman who actually preferred him, but she fainted and went right off the man after she had opened the envelope.

• • • • • • • • • • • • • • • • •

ed. Then, like many others of his calling, he found the prostitutes were kind and decent. In The Hague he moved in with Maria Hoornik, who was both pregnant and mother of a five-year-old girl. She posed for Vincent and also gave him gonorrhoea.

When he went to Montmartre, Vincent was taken under Toulouse-Lautrec's wing, had several affairs and bedded his share of prostitutes. He tried to get the ladies to pose for free but confessed, "Compared with Henri, I wasn't good enough meat to entice them." Increasing attacks of venereal disease made him periodically impotent and as his depression deepened, he became a voluntary patient in an asylum. He later escaped and shot himself in a farmyard, in 1890.

Victor Hugo

Adele Foucher had no idea what she had let herself in for when she said, "Yes" to Victor Hugo, a budding poet and author of 20 years, who explained he had saved himself for whoever became his bride. On the night of their wedding, the unfortunate lass had to say, "Oh Yes" nine more times, and after five difficult births in eight years, and constant daily bouts of sex with her ultra-virile husband whenever her pregnancies allowed, she abandoned sex with him forever. This was just the freedom he desired, and Victor set out to make love to as many women as possible for what remained of his life which, as it turned out, allowed him 55 years of licentious living. The man who wrote *The Hunchback of Notre Dame* and *Les Miserables* was moved to say, "Women find me irresistible" which was undoubtedly true, and he found the pursuit of women equally irresistible.

When Victor wasn't writing verse or thinking about the plots and sub-plots for his novels and plays, he was thinking about sex. Knowing he was a late starter, he set about learning what was needed to become a supreme lover. His choice of teacher was Juliette Drouet, a black-haired French

PEER'S PRIVILEGE

• • • • • • • • • • • • • • • • • •

In 1844 Victor was caught by police in the act of making love to Leonie d'Aunet, a married woman, and adultery was an offence, even in France. The woman's jealous husband had had the couple watched and followed. She was thrown into gaol, but Victor was the son of an honoured general in Napoleon's army, a former governor of Madrid, and he amazingly escaped, claiming "peer's privileges".

• • • • • • • • • • • • • • • • • •

actress with as many famous co-performers off as well as on-stage, and he chose well. She deserved her status, and taught him the varieties of sex which pleased her and were likely to satisfy any woman. With his prominence as a writer, his huge personality and a growing reputation as a lover, he had his pick of partners, but was really more interested in quantity rather than quality, and as long as they were young, he was willing.

Later in life he adopted certain principles. Married women were fair game, provided they weren't living at home with their husbands, an unusual stance for that era, and especially for men in his career. When Juliette came back into favour she knew, like wife Adele many years before, she would have to give Victor fairly free reign – she remained his mistress over a period of fifty years.

Juliette estimated he had sex with two hundred different women between 1848 and 1850, but she made sure she didn't go entirely hungry. With all his sexual activity they both felt more comfortable living separately but when in Paris, he visited her every day and she wrote him around 17,000 love letters, virtually one a day.

According to Victor himself, he savoured the days when he received a young prostitute soon after breakfast, bathed, and dressed in time to join an actress for lunch and make love to her either side of the meal. The afternoon was not wasted as he called on a courtesan he regularly courted, and back home in the evening he would still be ready for the mistress-of-the-moment.

His tremendous stamina helped him build up a personal fortune, yet he lived quite frugally, and did most of his writing while standing up. After writing the play *Ruy Blas*, he met the actress who was to take the female lead. Sarah Bernhardt had as much energy and desire for the business in the bedroom as Victor and the two roared into action. It was a fortunate coincidence that both needed only four or five hours sleep each night, though they spent much longer than that in bed together.

> **POET'S PENSION**
>
> ● ● ● ● ● ● ● ● ● ● ● ● ● ● ● ● ●
>
> Hugo could be a sycophant. During the reign of Louis XVIII, in the 1820s, he wrote poems and stories to please the French court. This won him the coveted honour of Chevalier of the Legion of Honour, and a pension of one thousand francs a year.
>
> ● ● ● ● ● ● ● ● ● ● ● ● ● ● ● ● ●

His writing had always reflected his political opinions, and after the 1848 uprising he became very wary of Luis Napoleon's rule and took himself off to exile, first in Jersey then Guernsey, in the Channel Islands, where he built a strange edifice full of hidden staircases and secret rooms. Mistresses were not so easy to acquire on the thinly populated islands, but he managed, and heightened his sexual pleasures by admitting his lady friends through these concealed doors. He also became a voyeur, and guests were viewed having sex through the secret peepholes he had installed.

Returning to Paris he managed, at the age of 70, to seduce a 22-year-old lass, the daughter of another writer Theo Gautier, and was delighted to find she was a willing recipient for the many tricks he could teach her. At the age of 80, his young grandson surprised Victor in the arms of a housemaid, and he quickly commented, "Look little Georges, that's what is called genius." Though he died three years later, in 1885, Victor's diary recorded four sessions of love-making in his final four months on earth. An outstanding author and athlete.

Stendhal

How often do we find among these talented heroes of the past two or three hundred years, a mother fixation, a first sexual encounter with a prostitute and a suffering through life from venereal disease? The writer born Henri Marie Beyle and known to the world as Stendhal had all three. Long after mother died when he was seven, he wrote, "I wanted to cover my mother with kisses, and that there not be any clothing. I always wanted to give them to her on the breast."

He was only 17, leaving home in Grenoble on a visit to Milan, when he paid a woman to provide his first sex lesson, and caught the syphilis which affected him on and off for the next forty years. But it did not cure his lust for women in between his prodigious output of words. Between 1921 and 1930 he published six books, including his masterpiece *The Red and The Black*, and the enchanting *Roman Journal*. He also wrote several short stories under a hundred and more pseudonyms.

He was not an attractive man, and was bald before he was 30. Paintings of nude women could always arouse him – no surprise there – but he was shocked and embarrassed when the sight of an aunt's thigh as she climbed down from a carriage produced a very noticeable reaction. This concerned him, for he was shy in his approach to girls and unable to begin any worthwhile relationships. So he joined the French army, served for a dozen years, and was lucky to survive the infamous retreat from Moscow with Napoleon in 1812. It was now he realized the pen really could be mightier than the sword, and he turned to writing. Unlike other novelists of his time, Stendhal did not immediately enjoy a gush of admiring women to his side. He had to work hard to find willing partners, and he was not always up to the job when he got them into bed.

Many an author has used personal experiences to fuel the themes of a novel, and this writer bravely recorded his lack of performance at a weekend orgy where he was a guest. Stendhal was completely impotent,

LIFE'S EQUATION

• • • • • • • • • • • • • • • • • •

He was born in France but adored his adopted Italy and when he died, had the tombstone inscribed, "Arrigo Beyle, Milanese, Visse, Scrisse, Amo" – He Lived, He Wrote, He Loved – which matched his equation for a full life, spelled out in some of his books: happiness = love + work.

• • • • • • • • • • • • • • • • • •

even in the hands of the female guests, all of whom were very accomplished prostitutes, but the orgy attended by noblemen and leading writers and artists in Paris in the year 1821 was the inspiration for his book *Armence*. It was very clear that the man knew what he was talking about. In other books he also faithfully recorded his rejections. He paid court almost exclusively to married women and was constantly spurned. They enjoyed his charm, his wit, and his embroidered manner of speech, but these attributes were not enough to get these ladies to copulate with him.

He overcame this problem, and wrote many times of making love to a woman several times in a night and on one occasion seven times, "Between dusk and the following dawn." In this respect he did resemble other writers, drawing much of his inspiration from the women who passed through his life, but he always suspected his work would be appreciated long after his death. He was right; nearly a century passed before his novels gained the recognition they deserved.

Stendhal never married, but he fell in love regularly. At the age of 52 he played a little game on the beach at Lake Albano, near Rome. He wrote in the sand the initials of all these women, and through his autobiographical work *The Life of Henri Brulard* and his private papers revealed their identities and exactly what they had meant to him.

Aa was Angelina Pietragrua, and when he first bedded her, he had his braces embroidered with her initials and the date. Ad was Adele Rebuffel. She was only 12 when Stendhal had an affair with her mother, but when the girl was 16, he managed to hold her breast for a second. Ai was Alexandrine Daru, his cousin's wife, who never gave in to him. Al was Angeline Bereyter, an opera singer and a tigress between the sheets. He once counted her nine orgasms before he was able to match her climax. Ar, Alberthe du Rubempre, was married, eccentric and a late love. After Stendhal died she tried to contact him during a seance – and failed.

C was Countess Clementine Curial, a very daring married lady in her mid-30s who had Stendhal hide in her cellar. Unknown to her husband, she fed him and bedded him down there for three days and three nights. G, Giulia Rinieri, was a 19-year-old virgin who tried to seduce Stendhal. When she was 20 Giulia succeeded, but turned down his proposal of marriage. M was Melanie Guilbert, an actress who granted his request on a picnic and bathed nude in a stream. It worked, but their subsequent coupling was a disappointment. Md, Mathilde Dembowski, was a revolutionary who inspired his novel *On Love*. The book and the woman were both failures. Mi was Minette von Griesheim, blonde daughter of a German general who spurned him. Finally, V was Virginie Kubly, a tall and lovely actress he worshipped as a teenager in his hometown – and never spoke to her.

With all these loves it is difficult to understand why Stendhal died a bachelor. A heart attack killed him at the age of 59.

The Music Masters

They came from France and Poland, Russia and Austria, Hungary, Germany and Italy, brilliant composers whose music will survive forever. During their lives they found time to make love to the hundreds of women who flocked to concerts, private lessons and recitals. These men were the original pop stars, and the admiring ladies their groupies, and there is not much today's sexy show biz stars could teach the swingers of the eighteenth and nineteenth centuries. The concertos, cantatas and requiems, the grand operas, sonatas and symphonies these men wrote were often commissioned for special one-off events, weddings or funerals, coronations or grand balls. Fortunately, these wonderful pieces have been recorded for the masses to appreciate. Of course, life in general, particularly sexual life, was a lot tougher to conduct then than it is now. When these pianists, violinists and conductors went on tour, a single journey might take a week or more, moving between Europe's capitals. They still found the time to indulge their passions.

Debussy

Claude-Achille Debussy was a child prodigy whose father owned a china shop in Paris, the profits of which allowed the boy to enter the famous Conservatoire of Music in the capital at the age of ten. Later, summer jobs introduced him to the joys of sex, teaching rich young heiresses to play the piano at first, and then he took a few lessons himself. Hired to accompany a married amateur singer, Alice Vasnier, they rehearsed more than music until her wealthy husband found out. Unlike many top composers in the late nine-teenth century, Debussy earned little money, yet among the fine pieces he gave us are the popular *Claire de Lune* and *La Mer*.

His brilliance attracted women, and he took his pick carefully. They succumbed to his dark, sombre nature and when he turned his romantic concentration in their direction, they were lost. Long-lasting mistress Gaby Dupont provided a home and meals for him for ten years, even while he was officially engaged to another singer, Therese Roger. She was less forgiving, and dumped Debussy when he had a one-night stand on tour in Brussels.

Gaby found he had enjoyed many brief duets closer to home and shot herself.

The lady recovered, at least from her bullet wounds, but Rosalie Texier came along and soon became Madame Debussy. They were so broke that the groom gave a piano lesson on the morning of their wedding to pay for the ceremony. Four years later her husband disappeared, and Rosalie too shot herself. Another singer Emma Bardac replaced her, first as mistress then as wife. She was neither young nor beautiful, but she was intelligent and rich and sustained him through ten years of marriage. He died aged 55, in the city where he was born, under German occupation in the last year of World War One.

Chopin

Frederic Chopin was another child prodigy, only eight years old when he gave his first concert in Warsaw, but he was in his 20s before he left Poland and launched himself at a wider audience. Paris drew him, and he drew the Parisian women, but his early experiences with a governess, coupled with the death of his mother, made the piano player ambivalent about sex – he was comfortable swinging either way. Countess Delfina Potocka had a great reputation, musically and sexually, seeing Chopin as a challenge and persuading him in the best way possible. He responded and wrote to her, "I would like again to plop something down your little hole in D flat major," and apparently he did.

Moving on, he asked Maria Wodzinska, the daughter of a Polish count, to marry

> **ABSTINENCE INSPIRES**
>
> ● ● ● ● ● ● ● ● ● ● ● ● ● ● ● ● ●
>
> Chopin's ego may have suffered when 'George' Sand kicked him out of bed, but he stayed on at her country house in Nohant for several years. Quite the opposite of most talented creators, the abstinence he suffered with neither women or men available must have inspired him for it was there in Nohant that Chopin produced the finest of all his piano solos.
>
> ● ● ● ● ● ● ● ● ● ● ● ● ● ● ● ● ●

him and she agreed. But the engagement fizzled out, and he met, then settled in with, French novelist 'George' Sand. It was said she too could swing either way, so perhaps the arrangement suited both partners, and he stayed for nine years. But their sex life was much shorter; she reported to friends, "He makes love like a corpse." The writer was 22 years older than Chopin and she hadn't got time to mess around. He never married and he never made much money from his beautiful music. Frustrated in both directions, he died from tuberculosis aged 39.

Tchaikovsky

Peter Ilyich Tchaikovsky was another bisexual. He went through an engagement and later still a marriage, but the Russian composer knew full well where his preferences lay. He was disturbed emotionally from early childhood, and suffered hallucinations and nervous breakdowns in his 20s, but his handsome looks and the musical imagination drew women like a magnet. When he discovered he was really a homosexual, he went to extraordinary lengths to keep it secret, referring to this side of his nature as "Z" in diaries and in letters to his brother.

He taught music at the Moscow Conservatory and fell for one of his male students, then for his nephew. He struggled with women until he met Desirée Artot, a French opera singer on tour in Russia. A month after they met he proposed and she accepted, but the lady stumbled on the truth and later on that tour, she married a Spanish baritone. Nearly ten years passed before Tchaikovsky became embroiled with another woman, one of his students Antonia Milyukova, and they were wed. Three months later he fled and, trying to obtain a divorce, admitted several untrue adulteries then attempted suicide, standing up to his armpits in the river waters of Moscow in late October. He spent the next 16 years trying to escape from that marriage, though he continued to support the woman until he died, aged 53.

MUSIC ADDICT

Under the patronage of wealthy widow Nadezhda von Meck, who paid him an annuity for fourteen years so that he could concentrate on composing, the Russian wrote his famous *Opus 45*, the *1812 Overture* and the classical ballet *Swan Lake*. She was addicted to music, and for a time Debussy was on her household staff, but although she and Tchaikovsky wrote several times, the two never met.

Mozart

Wolfgang Amadeus Mozart was born in 1756 and in the next 35 years he wrote chamber music, operas, orchestral symphonies and piano concertos. Proficient with both string and keyboard instruments, Mozart is considered one of the greatest musical geniuses of all time. Yet he died a debtor, killed by overwork and malnutrition, and he was buried in a pauper's grave. He was another child prodigy, giving concerts at home in Salzburg at the age of six with his sister. Women who came to know him as a child flirted with Mozart as a teenager, and propositioned him as soon as adolescence was passed. Reportedly the witty young man accepted many of these advances from wealthy Austrian admirers, but was too proud to accept any gifts of money.

Undoubtedly he liked to flirt, and wrote many love letters full of double meanings to these ladies, but when he came to write his long-admired opera *Don Juan*, he had to call in a true sexual virtuoso, Casanova no less, for authoritative advice.

Mozart fell in love with two of his cousins, Aloysia who also enjoyed flirting and said "No", then her younger sister, the faithful Constanze, who said "Yes", and they spent nine happy but impecunious years together before his death.

Liszt

At last we find a musical genius who became wealthy by virtue of his talents. Franz Liszt, was the son of a Hungarian man-servant who began his piano compositions at the age of eight; three years later, his concert debut in Paris was a sensation. As he grew up, playing privately for the crowned heads of Europe and publicly in the concert halls of Italy, France, Spain, Russia, Germany, Portugal, Turkey and Switzerland, the passionate young supremo had his choice among the aristocratic women who filled his audiences. They sent him notes, pieces of underclothing for him to caress and return, and locks of their hair to keep. After one concert, a woman was discovered carefully removing the cover of the piano stool on which he had just performed. Franz was under no illusions what these noble ladies really wanted, and he gave willingly.

A PIANIST'S TOUCH

The novelist George Sand obviously liked the touch of a keyboard artist's hands upon her body. Liszt took over playing where Chopin had left off. This strange, cigar-smoking lady liked to sit under the piano while he performed – musically, that is – and when challenged by his current long-term mistress to a duel, Sand's choice of weapons was fingernails – a fight that was never consummated.

Countess Adele de la Prunarede publicly acknowledged she was in love with him and not her husband, but when Liszt learned he was not alone among her extra-marital activities, he was off and into the arms of Countess

Marie d'Agoult. This lady left her husband and children to set up home with the now famous pianist in Switzerland, and together they had three children in four years before they separated. The writer "George" Sand was his mistress for a while, then the Spanish dancer Lola Montez. They were drawn together not only by mutual attraction but out of respect for the sexual reputations each had earned. Both admitted they were not disappointed, initially, but Lola had more capacity in her engine than Franz had in his tank, and they soon parted.

> **BRAHMS AND WHAT?**
>
> ● ● ● ● ● ● ● ● ● ● ● ● ● ● ● ●
>
> A pair of these composers, of course, make up the two halves of the famous Cockney rhyming slang adjective for drunk – Brahms and Liszt.
>
> ● ● ● ● ● ● ● ● ● ● ● ● ● ● ● ●

Some of his young pupils came on to Franz, but unless he was satisfied they had already lost their virginity, he would not take them to bed. Those who were experienced – and some were young enough to be his granddaughters – were allowed to stay behind for extra-curricular lessons. A princess from Italy, a baroness from Russia and a countess from Poland, high-born ladies with low-lying ideas, all came and went. A couple of well-known French courtesans, who got as good as they gave, kept the man's inspiration for his music intact. Then came the intellectual and ultra-sensual Princess Carolyne von Sayn-Wittgenstein, who arrived from Russia to live with Franz in Germany.

Her favourite habit was reclining on a bearskin rug wearing nothing more than a turban and smoking an Arab hookah pipe while Liszt played the piano. They were genuinely in love, at first. They wanted to marry, and by now Franz was rich enough to give up his earnings from his music to play entirely for charity. He was a Catholic, and journeyed to Rome where he thought he had sufficient influence to obtain her divorce. He failed, and then the attraction cooled and Liszt was free again to carry on his zealous pursuit – or receipt – of more mistresses. They continued to arrive at his door until shortly before his death at 75.

Brahms

The red-light district of Hamburg is where Johannes Brahms was brought up, and where he made his early living, playing pianos in seedy bars where the street prostitutes went to pick up their clients. This had a dramatic effect on his sex life. He fell in love often enough, though he never married, and he would only take prostitutes to bed. The love of his life was concert pianist Clara Schumann, wife of composer and friend Robert. Whether they went further than friendship, even after Robert was committed to a mental institution and died two years later, is open to doubt.

He wrote more than two hundred songs in the late-1800s, as well as his famous classical symphonies and requiems. Wherever he performed, Brahms found time to visit the bars, drinking copious amounts of beer and singing with the locals. But the girls from his early Hamburg haunts had left their mark. He explained to a friend, "To make the men wild, these half-clad girls used to take me on their laps between dances, kiss and caress and excite me. This was my first impression of the love of women. I cannot honour them as you do." Yet he was always courteous to these girls and he continued to fall in love, but if any woman endangered his bachelor state, Brahms was up and away.

Paganini

Niccolo Paganini spent every waking hour studying and practising the violin as a youth, and when he graduated to the concert stage, he vowed he would only rehearse or perform. He never practised, and that left him more time than most musicians to pursue the licentious life which brought him very nearly as much fame as his music. He was a gambler and womanizer. The Cote d'Azur, Vienna and Venice were his favourite flesh-pots, but Paganini suffered permanently from poor health, so he had to pace himself. When the wife of an Italian count captivated him and took the man off to her mountain villa, he found the perfect way to convalesce. The countess was proud of her contribution to harmonic splendour.

> **INSTRUMENTAL BACKING**
>
> ● ● ● ● ● ● ● ● ● ● ● ● ● ● ● ● ●
>
> Paganini was an excessive gambler, and serious debts forced him to pawn his violin during his early twenties. A French merchant was persuaded to lend him an expensive Guarneri violin to play at a concert, and after hearing him perform, gave the young man the instrument.
>
> ● ● ● ● ● ● ● ● ● ● ● ● ● ● ● ● ●

Princess Elisa Bonaparte Baciocchi was not a beauty, but she had a healthy appetite and decided if Paganini became director of music to the court at Piombino, she would not have to go hungry. Napoleon's sister was not to be denied on either account, and the violinist pleased her and himself, putting in a little overtime with a prettier lady-in-waiting as the princess took her daily siestas. All his women were well endowed in the bosom, and none more than Angelina Cavanna, a tailor's daughter from his home town of Genoa. He seduced the girl on a promise of marriage, then deserted her when she became pregnant, but her angry father had the violinist arrested and gaoled. Released again, he set up home with dancer Antonia Bianchi and this time thought so highly of their off-spring that he paid the woman to renounce all rights to their son Achille, and leave him to bring up the boy.

He was a brilliant composer, and gave the world scores of violin concertos and sonatas, and was virtually the originator of music set for string quartets. But his appearance, with a pale, waxen face beneath dark, curly hair, and forever wearing a long cloak to keep out the cold, helped the rumour that here was a man in league with the devil. His burial in consecrated land was delayed until 1845, fully five years after the man died.

Goya and Modigliani

As official painter to the Royal Court of Spain in the early 1800s, Francisco de Goya produced his celebrated and sensual Maja paintings. Although he survived the public displeasure of the infamous Inquisition, his work nevertheless attracted formal charges of obscenity. Later, when the Government in Madrid took firm action against the country's increasing progressive society, he fled to live in self-imposed exile across the border in France. In the previous century, before he was recognized, Goya had taken lovers wherever he went, in Spain, in Italy and France. He was studying in Rome when he fell for a beautiful teenage pupil at a boarding school which was actually part of a convent. One night he raided the convent and carried off the girl, and the pair had a long and satisfying affair.

Back in Madrid, the artist fell for the sister of a new-found friend, and rapidly seduced her. This was in 1773 and not surprisingly, the lovely blonde Josefa Bayeu became pregnant and was halfway to having her baby before Goya gave in to her family's pressure and married the girl. He painted a single portrait of his wife, who became pregnant five more times, but only one son, Xavier, survived childhood. The marriage was not a success, but his brother-in-law was well connected and Goya, for the first time in his life, had a steady occupation, producing designs for the Royal tapestry workforce in the Spanish capital. This position brought him to the notice of the married ladies surrounding the Spanish court.

A few found time to pose briefly for Goya, but their real interest inside his small studio was far from modelling. The Duchess of Alba was 20 and had already been married for seven years to the unpleasant and much older Marquis of Villefranca when she heard of Goya's studio attractions and called in one afternoon in 1795. The duchess wanted to pose and the artist wanted to paint, and from the very beginning, the

ADULTERY PROVED

• • • • • • • • • • • • • • •

In his late sixties, Goya was still having his way with various women and one was Leocadia de Weis, forty years younger and the lively and liberated wife of a local merchant. Her husband wanted a divorce, and he didn't have to wait long for proof of her adultery. Goya, at 68, was named as the father of little Rosarito, and the couple lived together for another 14 years, in Spain and in exile in Bordeaux.

• • • • • • • • • • • • • • •

magnificent duchess and the energetic artist both knew they would soon see more of each other, much more.

The marquis conveniently died the next year, and when the young widow retreated in official mourning to her estate in Andalusia, Goya went along to complete her portrait. The mourning lasted several months, and so did the painting. He sketched her and painted her hundreds of times in the next few years, clothed in her widow's black outfits, but more often unclothed. The duchess had the most beautiful buttocks and hips to which Goya was allowed to testify, in person and in paint. They split when she found another lover in Madrid, and the jealous artist then depicted her infidelity, giving one portrait two faces.

When they were reunited the duchess, still only 24, sat for him again and Goya completed the two portraits which gave him ever-lasting fame, *The Naked Maja* and *The Clothed Maja*. The nude was described by a notable critic as "Erotic without being voluptuous". Three years later, she died suddenly. Goya, remembered in her will, lived for another 25 years.

The birth of Amedeo Modigliani was nigh when his father, a Jewish merchant in Livorno, was declared bankrupt, but Italian law allowed a dispossessed family to keep the maternal bed "And all that lay upon it". The woman in labour, as was the local custom, was surrounded by all the goods and chattels and valuables from his storeroom that her husband could heap on either side, and Amedeo's arrival on July 12th 1884 saved what was left of his father's business. That business enabled him later, for six years in Venice, to attend art school, where he learned portrait painting and sculpture. He was a gambler, a boozer, a drug-user of some renown, and he made love to very nearly every model who sat for him nude. Modigliani turned out hundreds of paintings of naked ladies.

IN PARADISE

As Modigliani lay on his deathbed, aged 35 and suffering from tubercular meningitis, he suggested to his common-law wife Jeanne Hebuterne she join him soon, "So that I can have my favourite model in Paradise, and enjoy eternal happiness." She was pregnant and in despair, and following the painter's funeral she committed suicide, jumping from a fifth-floor window.

He moved into Montmartre, the artist's quarter in Paris, in 1906, and was both befriended and influenced by Paul Cezanne and Pablo Picasso. But he was wilder than either of them, and would occasionally be found asleep in the cobbled streets, drunk and sometimes naked. Hashish and cocaine replaced alcohol for a time and for fourteen years he kept up a life of debauchery which eventually killed him.

At 15 he surrendered his virginity to a maid in the family home, and while brothels attracted the man from time to time, he had a favourite line with the ladies which rarely failed. He genuinely preferred to paint peasant women, servants, barmaids, laundresses and seamstresses, who were flattered by his requests to pose and not at all alarmed when he asked them to strip off. Once undressed – and there were often many garments to remove – it seemed such a shame to waste all that effort.

He was 30 when he fell in love for the first time, with the wealthy English poetess Beatrice Hastings. They went to bed within hours of meeting. She was the original model for a series of nudes to form his first and only exhibition of paintings in 1917. Paris police considered the canvasses were so indecent that they closed the show. He often beat Beatrice, who fled after one drunken argument to be replaced by a tiny, slender art student of 19, Jeanne Hebuterne. She gave up her own career in return for a promise to marry and to become his model. They moved to the south of France, had a baby girl and little more than a year later, in 1920, he died.

CHAPTER 3

A FEW WHO
FOUND FAME
AND GAVE SEX
A BAD NAME

☆ ☆

Brigham Young

Two extreme and disparate views of the Mormon Church and its century-old doctrine of polygamy were held by its zealous president Brigham Young and one of his many daughters-in-law. "It is a divine sanction to enhance the population of the church and to eliminate spinsterhood, adultery and prostitution," said the man who was married at least 20 times and fathered 57 children. "If Salt Lake City were roofed over," the woman said of the Mormon headquarters in Utah, "it would be the biggest whorehouse in the world."

Young was a journeyman builder, a carpenter, and a sometime painter and glazier, when he read the recently published *Book of Mormon*. Two years later, he was baptized into the new Church of Jesus Christ of Latter-day Saints. What attracted him to its teachings is not entirely clear, nor is it known what success he had previously enjoyed with the opposite sex. But fifteen years later when he became its second president, he fervently preached and feverishly pursued the Mormon doctrine of polygamy. "Once the policy of plural marriages was revealed to me as necessary for survival, it was the first time in my life I had desired the grave. I knew the toil and labour my body would have to suffer," Brigham Young declared. His body had toiled and laboured plenty by the time he did reach the grave, for most of his wives were twenty, thirty or even forty years younger. Older women did not always become bed-mates, but he gave them his name and financial support.

As the Mormon movement spread out across America they were widely opposed, especially among the male population, and their first president was murdered in 1844 in an Illinois gaol. Brigham Young swiftly took over and led his flock to the Rocky Mountains, to settle in Salt Lake City and estab-lish the province of Deseret which became the territory and eventually the state of Utah. The man not only became the church president, he became governor of the territory too, but his performance in political office never matched that in the bedroom, and by order of the President he was deposed in 1857.

Young was a big, attractive man, deep chested with piercing blue eyes, a trimmed beard and a broken nose, and he was called "The Lion of the Lord". Many of his wives were dispersed around the city, but a num-ber were always kept together in the Lion House, with its first floor divided into a number of bedroom suites for wives with children and a central lounge for prayer meetings and relaxation. The floor above had smaller bedrooms for wives who were not yet mothers. During the day the leader would select his partner for the night and leave a mark on her door so that she would know what pleasures lay ahead, and he would not forget the for-tunate recipient.

He was naturally strong, and held a pri-vate belief that food from the cow intensi-fied virility, so he consumed vast quantities of cheese, milk and eggs. He fathered his first child at twenty-four and his last at sixty-nine. In 1862, three of his wives gave birth within a period of 25 days. Throughout his life he maintained a number of lengthy sex-ual relationships with some of his wives, and

> ## TEATIME
>
> Among his harem Brigham Young normally maintained one favourite. Emmeline Free was the first and bore him ten children, and she was replaced by Amelia Folsom, a headstrong young lady of twenty-three to Young's mature sixty. When her husband castigated Amelia on one occasion, she tipped an urn of tea into his lap – so the entire harem was neglected and went without for a few weeks.

> ## MATCH MADE IN HEAVEN
>
> There may have been others, but one woman was known positively and publicly to have spurned Brigham Young, a shapely and stunning actress named Julia Hayne. Unfortunately, she died young so the Mormon leader went through a proxy marriage with Julia – "So that we can be togeth-er eternally in Heaven," he said.

he tried to treat them all equally. "I have no desire to make a queen of one and simple courtiers of the rest," he said and it was only in his later years that younger wives complained about a lack of attention. Young insisted he was not promiscuous, as he would only sleep with one wife on any one night.

However, the best suite in Lion House, occupied by the current favourite, had a secret stairway and the restless, not-so-fortunate members of the harem were convinced he was making another call if the leader left their sides early.

In 1872 Young survived a federal investigation into his polygamous – or bigamous – marriages. The following year Ann Eliza, wife number 19, 27 or 56, according to which source one accepts, publicly sued for divorce. That could have been sorted out inside the Mormon movement, but now the

WIGWAM BAM

●●●●●●●●●●●●●●●●●●●●●●
He went through formal marriage ceremonies with many wives, while others were simply "sealed" to him, sometimes for the duration of a stay. He went among the Indian tribes hoping to convert many braves and their women, and visiting the Sioux on one occasion, he wedded not one but two pretty young squaws who stayed in his wigwam for a fortnight.
●●●●●●●●●●●●●●●●●●●

leader, forty years her senior, was in a cleft-stick. Young had to repudiate her right for divorce, pointing out his marriage to the senior concubine Mary Ann Angell was the one and only valid ceremony. To have done otherwise would have brought the feds back on the trail but his declaration virtually overturned the doctrine of polygamy he preached so fervently.

The man continued to live and love his wives until he died aged seventy-six. A dozen years later, the Mormon church officially renounced polygamy. However, in 1994 a new leader reintroduced plural living among the Mormons, and there are believed to be more than 400 families in and around Salt Lake City now practising what Brigham Young so eagerly preached a hundred and more years ago.

Sister Aimee Semple McPherson

America's major money-gathering evangelists of today have nothing on the faith-healer who founded the International Church of the Foursquare Gospel, an ardent holy roller who seduced her lovers in front of a candle-lit altar. She toured the country with her revival tent, but kept a "frat-flat" in Los Angeles. Fraternizing with the faithful was Sister Aimee Semple McPherson's neat way of describing her many affairs. Not surprisingly, the lady had an enthusiastic, devoted following, especially among the men, and not all of them came to hear her powerful sermons.

She was born in Ontario, Canada, and grew up in a farmhouse filled with religion seven days a week. Father was a Methodist bible-reader, mother a Salvation Army worker, and Aimee started to preach her own brand of gospel when she was only seventeen. She was rarely without an escort and the following year she married a Pentecostal preacher. They honeymooned in China working as missionaries, and there Robert died of typhoid. A widow at nineteen and already a mother, she returned to America and within months was married again, to shop cashier Harold McPherson. He became fascinated watching and listening to her at a faith-healing meeting, and a second child was the result. This young family of four, with two itinerant evangelists, travelled the length and breadth of America.

She was attractive, energetic and somewhat eccentric, and her prayer meetings had more to do with a Broadway production than a religious service, but her converts were numbered in tens of thousands. Harold soon tired of life on the road, though they lived in luxury. Aimee was soon attracting enough money to allow her to build their own church and settle down in one place. But he

SCANDAL SHEETS

The good sister was never far from scandal. At the age of forty-six she learned that nude photographs of herself, presumably shot by a former lover, were being touted round newspaper offices in California. *The Los Angeles Times* actually published the story but the pictures never appeared; the evangelizing Aimee was said to have made a better offer for the embarrassing negatives.

divorced her for desertion and before she reached twenty-one, Aimee had got through two husbands.

Finishing high school, Sister Aimee's early ambition was to go on stage, and she employed those talents first with her faith-healing clinics then in the pulpit, earning enormous adulation from her congregation. She dyed her hair blonde, and wore jewellery and couturier clothes, but there was still enough in the evangelical pot to pour $1,500,000 into the building of the Angelus Temple in Los Angeles, her headquarters for nearly twenty years and ultimately a tourist attraction. She also built a radio station, edited a magazine, wrote books and organized 200 missions world wide. Famously, the lady rode a motor cycle down the aisle of the packed temple, dressed in a policeman's uniform to emphasize her sermon on obeying God's Law.

She used various gimmicks and costumes to emphasize the themes of her sermons, but there was no television in those days to focus on Aimee and her bible meetings. Nevertheless, in 1926 radio stations and newspapers all over America reported she had drowned while swimming in the Pacific Ocean off a beach near Venice, California. For more than a week her followers set about organizing a dramatic memorial service and as they searched for the body, two were drowned themselves. A month later she turned up very much alive on the south Arizona border, with an amazing story of being kidnapped and held captive in Mexico. A grand jury investigated and learned that Sister Aimee had spent all that time enjoying sexual congress with one Ken Ormiston, a sound engineer from her own church radio station. They were shacked-up in a rented cottage in Carmel, close to the spot where she was supposed to have disappeared.

Within the Foursquare Gospel Church, remarriage was forbidden for a divorcee while the original spouse was still alive, unless you happened to be the church leader. Harold was alive, Sister Aimee was still using his name, yet she went through a wedding ceremony for a third time with David Hutton Junior – eleven years her junior to be exact. He was a spiritual-singing baritone, playing the part of Pharaoh in one of her more dramatic productions in the Angelus Temple, and they eloped. Two days later he turned high-falsetto, named in a $200,000 breach of promise suit by a former fiancee who worked in a massage parlour. Aimee went off key as well when she heard the news, fainted and fractured her skull.

The masseuse settled for five grand instead of two hundred, and Aimee kicked the man out. He went on the Californian night-club circuit, singing his own songs, billed as "Aimee's Man". Back at the frat-flat, Aimee continued to entertain. A ghost-writer turned real-life lover, and gave up the day-job preparing her autobiography in exchange for a far more interesting night-job. After him came a new comedian, the up-and-coming Milton Berle, who later described events at Aimee's love-nest. She was apparently "Passionate and very experienced", and they performed on the rug before her own can-dlelit altar, complete with a scene from Calvary and the Crucifixion.

The church had nearly 80,000 members. At fifty-four, she was still preach-ing but her days as a sex symbol were on the wane, and Aimee admitted she was lonely. Whether she ever found her perfect man, whom she described as "Six feet tall, with thick wavy hair, blue eyes, a big smile and plays the trom-bone" – why the trombone? – we will never know. She died from an over-dose of barbiturates, but the inquest verdict was "Accidental".

Sir Richard Burton

This explorer, adventurer, soldier, writer and some would say pornographer, reached for fame along many avenues, and his life was one long party. He studied sexual practices in Africa, India, America and the Middle East, and gained considerable first-hand experience among the native women and very likely with some of the men too. Sir Richard Burton's translation of *The Arabian Nights* included much of his own personal material, and covered subjects like castration, circumcision, various forms of birth control, harems, male brothels and aphrodisiacs in very fine detail. There were two schools of thought among the critics when they reviewed the 16 volumes – a brilliant psychological analysis said a few, while the majority thought it was the "Scrapings from the brothels".

He was an extraordinary linguist, able to speak fluently in ten languages, read in all of them, and even write moderately well in some. He started his travels early as his family moved around Europe, and grew up largely in France and Italy where he was taught the joys of copulation by many prostitutes in Naples. The year he reached twenty-one catapulted him into the nomadic life as he was expelled from Trinity College, Oxford, and immediately entered the Indian Army where he served for seven years. In Bombay he led raids with his brother officers on the Indian brothels, and they took no prisoners. On more private visits, he studied the sexual rites of the Mohammedans more closely then decided to switch religions and take a Hindu mistress. She was so skilled at prolonging love-making with Burton he actually complained, "It is impossible to satisfy her with less than twenty minutes," and he confessed, "Myself, I'm no hot amorist, more an interested researcher." This hardly explains his reasons for attempting to kidnap then seduce a Nun on one occasion.

The man raised an altogether different type of scandal when Sir Charles Napier, the senior British general in India, sent Burton

THE SULTAN'S WIFE

Burton loved to tell the story of a Sultan's wife whose robes slid up to her neck revealing her naked form underneath as she fell off her camel in front of a group of English visitors. But the Sultan was not the least bit embarrassed, "the visitors admired her body and the sultan was pleased, his wife had kept her face covered throughout the episode."

to investigate a homosexual brothel in Karachi. He wrote his report in such fine detail, accompanied by several drawings, there was little doubt he had acquired some first-hand experience. He might well have been saved as a het-erosexual by a beautiful Persian girl he met on the road back from Karachi. She was travelling with her family in a merchant car-avan and the affair lasted only a few days, but she so captivated the twenty-seven year-old Richard that he was still writing about her several years later. The man's literary output was phenomenal. He wrote 43 books covering his explorations, and 30 vol-umes of translations which can loosely be described as erotica around the world.

Leaving the army he moved to Arabia and in 1853, in the clothes of a Muslim pil-grim from Afghanistan, he entered the sacred cities of Mecca and Medina, where

THE PERFUMED GARDEN

● ● ● ● ● ● ● ● ● ● ● ● ● ● ● ● ●
The Scented Garden was also known as *The Perfumed Garden*, an Arabian sex manual written in the 1500s. When he had finished the translation, Burton told his publisher, "It is a marvellous story, full of Eastern wisdom, how the harem guards are turned into Eunuchs, what happens and what they do when they are married, female circumcision, the Fellahs [Arab peasants] copulating with crocodiles, yes crocodiles..."
● ● ● ● ● ● ● ● ● ● ● ● ● ● ● ● ●

he savoured the delights of the ladies behind their yashmaks. He moved con-tinents again to visit Africa, where he became the first European to enter the forbidden city of Harar, high on the plains of Ethiopia. One of his early books, *First Footsteps*, is based on his experiences here inside the ancient walled city, where he was enthralled with the savage custom of female cir-cumcision, making the 20-minute sessions with his Hindu mistress look like a swift sprint.

Then he went in search of the source of the White Nile, a fascination for several explorers of that period, and he was credited with the discovery of Lake Tanganyika, at 410 miles the longest freshwater lake in the world. This was where, 13 years later, the immortal words "Dr Livingstone, I presume?" would be spoken by Henry Stanley, the American journalist. On trips home to England he fell in love and wooed two cousins who both refused his pro-posals, but Richard Burton was rarely without a partner for his bed. He wrote of the Wagogo tribeswomen in East Africa, "They are well disposed towards strangers of fair complexion, and have no difficulty obtaining the consent of their husbands to be absent for the night."

At the age of forty he was finally married to Isabel Arundell, but there was to be no settling down and she promised to "keep up the romance of the honeymoon forever." Her husband immediately became a diplomat, holding consular posts in Fernando Po, Brazil, Syria and Italy, and continued his writing. Despite his marriage he also continued with his personal research, but Isabel insisted on accompanying him on a stage-coach journey across America to study the Mormons and their polygamous practices in Salt Lake City. Afterwards he declared, "Celibacy is an unmitigated evil, polygamy is the instinctive law of nature."

He crossed and re-crossed the Andes Mountains, canoed 1,500 miles down the rivers of Brazil, and voyaged up the River Amazon, forever restless and in search of adventure. Throughout his life, Burton could never come to terms with the strict conventions and morals of life in Queen Victoria's Britain or, at times, in the far flung corners of her Empire. He would point to his *Arabian Nights*, which was also known as *The Book of a Thousand Nights*, as an example of British bigotry and cynicism. Sales of the first expurgated edition flopped, but when the uncensored version appeared, it was an instant success. "Now that I know the tastes of England, we need never be without money," he told Isabel.

After such a wild and reckless career it was surprising that he was knighted, though that came late, at the age of sixty-four, just five years before he died. Lady Burton was left with an awkward decision. He had just finished translating the *Scented Garden* from the original Arabic and publishers offered her £6,500. But she felt his already-tainted reputation would suffer still further if she accepted, and she burned the steamy manuscript along with most of his diaries and journals.

CLOSE TO HOME

• • • • • • • • • • • • • • • • •

Not all of Burton's research was carried out abroad, nor all of his experiences gained at first-hand. One of his great friends at home was the eccentric Richard Monckton Milnes who, as Baron Houghton and a member of the Government, became a literary patron. He also had the biggest collection of pornography and erotica in the world, to which Burton contributed and extracted information from.

• • • • • • • • • • • • • • • • •

Simon Bolivar

As one of the world's first and most successful freedom fighters, the man was used to giving orders and seeing them quickly obeyed. When it came to the opposite sex, he was happy for them to assume command, and just as happy to comply with their wishes. Simon Bolivar was born into an aristocratic family in Venezuela, orphaned while very young, and went to live with an uncle in Caracas. He was surrounded by pretty young cousins who, when the boy was only twenty, decided to seduce him. As a teenager Simon travelled to Europe to complete his education. He did more than that – six years later, in a private audience, Maria Luisa, the fifty-year-old Queen of Spain famous for her sexual forays directed him to get his kit off. In the Palaces of Madrid, the monarch's word was law.

He repaid her favours most unkindly. During the early part of the nineteenth century, Bolivar managed to free six South American countries from Spanish rule – Venezuela, where he was born, Ecuador, Panama, and three more which made him their president, Colombia, Peru and Bolivia, a country which took his name. Along the way he was snared by senoritas and senoras alike, peasant girls and high-born ladies captivated by the slim handsome and all-conquering soldier politician another Maria in Madrid, a beautiful lady-in-waiting at the court, but Maria Teresa de Toro died of yellow fever within a few months, and her bereaved husband decided to dedicate his life to the freedom movement at home.

But he had a little more to learn, on both fronts. He was deeply influenced by Napoleon's activities in Spain and France, and in 1804, at the age of twenty-one, he went to Paris to learn more and where better than in the arms of Fanny du Villars. Funnily enough, Fanny was yet another cousin; in her forties, she was the wife of one of Napoleon's generals. He learned a considerable amount but had to leave when he was suspected of fathering Fanny's second child, something the general had failed to do. Back home he put all this learning to good effect, swiftly moving up in the ranks of the new Latin-American independence movement.

The man was a born opportunist who, after his marriage, rarely became emotionally attached to any of his lovers. They were there to be hunted, courted, pleasured and left. As most of them were themselves stalking Simon, the early phases of the romance were soon ended. Some took his eventual rejection very badly. In between battles he managed to make love to a young French girl living in Venezuela, and Anita Leniot claimed she waited 17 faithful years for him to return. He was reprimanded by General Francisco Miranda for risking capture by the Spanish armies when he had insisted on waiting for a current mistress to join the retreat.

That was the scene wherever Simon Bolivar fought, especially in Peru and Colombia. Never without a woman at his side or close by, he was known as "The Liberator", a title well earned. One woman managed to snare Simon, quite literally. Recently widowed Josefina Nunez was entertaining him in her villa one night when her home-town was suddenly taken over by the Royalist forces. As the freedom fighter had spent most of the day as well as the night inside those same four walls, he was not aware of their sudden arrival. Escape for the first few days was impossible, and Josefina was enjoying the unfortunate prisoner's attention so much that she neglected to tell him the army had moved on after she ventured into town for food. It was said Simon had good reason to forgive the lady.

In 1822, a lady appeared who would remain by his side until his death eight years later. In their own way Simon Bolivar and Manuela Saenz would save each other. He was thirty-nine and heading a victory parade in Quito, Ecuador, when the gorgeous, raven-haired senora from a balcony above, tossed a laurel wreath at Simon and hit him in the face. He was attracted first by the wreath and then by her looks and sent an invitation to the open-air celebration ball

WAR WIDOW

Isabel Soubletta was another widow who came to know Bolivar very well. She was widowed when her husband, a member of the Spanish Army, died in battle. The lady switched sides when the victorious rebels arrived and sent Simon two drawings, one of a battle scene, the other of her bedroom. Intrigued by this approach, he called on Isabel for supper, stayed for breakfast and dropped by for many a meal in the months which followed.

that evening. Manuela, 24, arrived accompanied by her husband but had eyes only for the fighter. They danced and disappeared and Simon learned she could not bear children.

He had always been careful not to leave too many traces or descendants of his love affairs, and now he found he could make love freely to Manuela, a great relief from his sufferings in the early stages of tuberculosis which caused acute irritation of his testicles. Well, in the words of a more recent courtesan, the young Mandy Rice-Davies of Profumo fame: "He would say that, wouldn't he?" Manuela, though sterile, was sexually extremely active and her much older, wealthy English husband could not satisfy her. She was apparently on the verge of a lesbian relationship with her maid Jonatas, who liked to dress up in a soldier's uniform. Simon's gain was the maid's loss and the husband's, for Manuela left him to follow her lover to Colombia.

There were other women to interest Simon on his travels around South America, but when the Spanish eventually gave up their Colonial rule, he moved in to live with Manuela. She learned of a plot by political opponents to assassinate him one night and, wearing a very low-cut gown, diverted their attention for long enough to allow Simon to escape. Though he was life-long president of three huge countries, he retired from political life and died in 1830.

Sigmund Freud

Growing up in a large Jewish family in Vienna towards the end of the last century limited the opportunities for a worthwhile career, so Sigmund Freud was more or less forced to choose medicine. The good doctor analysed his own dreams and probed the secrets of his friends, his students and scores of his patients, before determining the connection between our sexual origins and our later behaviour. Around the turn of the century Freud revolution-ized the world's attitude to diseases of the mind yet he managed to keep most of his own secrets to himself, including details of the relationship with his sister-in-law. He was probably summing-up his own life when this well-known statement was received by a startled medical world: "The sexual life of a civilized man is seriously disabled."

His days as a medical student were more or less uninterrupted by the opposite sex. At seventeen, he met Martha Bernays and they continued a four-year romance exchanging hundreds of letters, rarely meeting until they were finally married in 1886. In the next nine years she bore him six children and Freud later proclaimed, "Marriage ceases to furnish the sexual needs that it promised, since all the contraceptives available hitherto impair sexual enjoyment, hurt the fine sensibilities of both partners, and even actu-ally cause illness." Martha's sister Minna arrived to live with them in Vienna in the year her last child was born.

Though he desired sex almost as a daily diet, he appeared to be a strict moralist until his medical disciple Jung revealed the Freud family triangle. Carl Jung told an American psychiatric professor both women had admitted what was going on, and Minna confessed, "Sigmund is in love with me, at times we are very intimate." Jung confront-

ESCAPE FROM HITLER

When the Nazis annexed Austria, they labelled Freud's work as pornography and burned his books and papers. Princess Marie Bonaparte of Greece, a friend and former patient, negotiated his safe passage out of Vienna to London in 1938, paying a £20,000 ransom to the Nazi party.

FANCY A CIGARETTE?

Freud smoked twenty cigars a day and though he never analysed this personal addiction, he frequently stated, "Smoking, drugs and gam-bling are substitutes for the primal addiction of masturbation."

ed Freud and offered to analyse this triangle but Freud denied it existed, then conceded he was having continual dreams about American women, particularly prostitutes. "Why don't you do something practical about it?" queried the younger doctor and Sigmund, both shocked and embarrassed, exploded, "But I am a married man." Before he died in 1939 aged seventy-four, Freud burned hundreds of his letters but left a few to the Library of Congress in Washington, where they can be revealed to students and the world at large in the year 2,000.

Carl Jung

For seven years Carl Gustav Jung, the Swiss psychologist and psychiatrist, collaborated with Freud until they fell out forever after a bitter feud. Jung left his mark on the world with his original concept and development of the introvert and extrovert personalities. In his time he imitated both. As a young medical student in Basle he glimpsed a fifteen-year-old girl in pig-tails and was smitten. He asked her name and told a friend "One day I will marry that girl". He did, six years later, but he had his first sexual experience with the mother of a fellow student. Carl, a sturdy six-footer, was introduced to the woman at a university reception, and she arranged to meet him secretly at her home where he later made several afternoon visits.

He was faithful in the early years of marriage, and Emma presented him with four daughters and a son. "I have tried every conceivable trick to stem the tide of these little blessings," he wrote to Freud and asked him to interpret a recurring dream about two horses. Freud replied, "They reveal an illegitimate sexual wish that had better not see the light of day." With one patient he confessed their relationship had "Polygamous components", a rather unique description, and labelled another as his "Femme inspiratrice".

This was Toni Wolff, a young beauty with brains to match. The lady proved such an inspiration that Jung managed to persuade his wife to form a triangle, a sexual and intellectual triangle, with Emma as the "Simple cube" providing the everyday necessities, Toni the "Inspiring force" at the base, with Carl as "The many-faceted gem" on top, in more ways than one. Both women became practising analysts and the triangle lasted, in some form or another, for

HEIL HITLER

Jung is remembered for several famous sayings; "Show me a sane person and I'll cure him for you," he joked. But he was serious in his early admiration of Hitler, "A spiritual vessel", and the eruption of the Nazis, "The twilight of the Gods". By 1939 and the start of World War Two, Jung had changed his mind.

forty years. Retiring completely from medicine, Jung spent his final years alone in a retreat he built overlooking Lake Zurich, where he meditated and took to sculpture and wood carving. He carried on writing until he died aged eighty-five.

Friedrich Nietzsche

Friedrich Nietzsche is often associated with Freud and Jung, but their lives barely overlapped. He was a philosopher and a writer, and a study of his works was undoubtedly important to both doctors, but there the comparison ends. The German writer's most important book was *Thus Spake Zarathustra*, but his most interesting, *My Sister and I*, revealed the extent of his sexual repression, the rather mild activities and the wild exotic fantasies he endured throughout his life. The book was written in an asylum, and the red-hot manuscript was smuggled out by another patient but not published for another fifty years.

THE TRINITY

Nietzsche was introduced to a 20-year-old Russian girl Lou Andreas-Salome, who later became an associate of Freud's, and she moved in to live with him and Elizabeth. They called themselves "The Trinity", the core of an intellectual discussion group, but others in the assembly regarded them as a Menage-a-Trois. True or not, it infuriated the man who thought then his relationship with his sister was a secret.

"I did a great deal of maturing in Leipzig," he wrote, "a vast amount of masturbating and not nearly as much whoring as I should have. Elizabeth (his sister) crawling into my bed, made a habit of playing with my genitals as if they were special toys of hers, driving me to a premature and hopeless awakening." He had very few mistresses and was unfortunate in contracting syphilis from one of only two prostitutes he slept with. It may have been that his first experience traumatized him forever. At fifteen he was taken home by a thirty-year-old countess in Leipzig, a striking blonde woman who spoke to him outside a shop.

"I realized later the countess was a nymphomaniac, trying to quench the flame of her uterine passion. She was aroused by the taste of the whip and exhorted me to flog her, then rode me feverishly and beat my flanks in her frenzy. My conclusion is that cruelty intensifies the lust of a woman." Nietzsche died in an asylum aged fifty-five from a form of paralysis caused by syphilis.

Horatio Nelson and Emma Hamilton

With one eye, one arm, a skinny body and few teeth left after his constant sea-going diet, Admiral Lord Nelson was no catch for any woman, and had it not been for just one, Lady Emma Hamilton, his love life would have raised barely a ripple. However, if there is going to be just one woman in a man's life, what better than a classic beauty like Emma who modelled for three worthy portrait painters, posing as the Roman goddess Venus for Gainsborough, as the Greek enchantress Circe for Thomas Lawrence, and as the Biblical Mary Magdalene for Joshua Reynolds. Their affair shocked the nation. When they met in Italy in 1793 she was twenty-eight, married to the sixty-three year-old British ambassador to Naples, and Horatio Nelson, a mere captain, was thirty-five and wed to a faithful wife, Fanny, who stayed at home while he roamed the seas fighting famous battles.

What really shocked the British people was the indiscreet and scandalous behaviour of their national hero, the first man in all of Europe who stood up to and defeated the hated Napoleon. The man who allowed Britannia to rule the waves for the next one hundred years was reduced to a love-sick sailor on shore leave. Stories had circulated from abroad, and when they were first seen together in London, Emma was on Horatio Nelson's arm and very pregnant. To make sure no one got the wrong idea, the daughter she produced was named Horatia.

THE CELESTIAL BED

Emma's beauty was apparent in her mid-teens, and she was hired by a London quack-doctor to work at his Temple of Health. Dr James Graham was much in demand in the late 1700s, guaranteeing cures of impotency for his wealthy and aged clients. All they had to do was lie on the four-poster "Celestial Bed", which had amorous scenes embroidered on the canopy. Just in case the bed didn't do the trick, Emma performed erotic and naked dances around the room. There are no reports as to what exactly happened if the live back-up achieved success.

Nelson went to sea with the navy at the age of nine with his uncle, and at twenty was in command of his first vessel. Like many sailors, he soon had women in most ports. Then, out in the West Indies fighting the Spanish, he met Fanny Nisbet, an elegant and thoughtful widow who two years later agreed to marry him. They married in 1787 and set up home in England. Meanwhile, Emma was realizing the value of her looks, and at seventeen took her first sea captain to her bed. A young cousin had been trapped by the notorious press-gangs and forced to serve on a warship, so Emma went boldly to the commander and in return for the boy's release, promised him a night of love. Both were as good as their words.

There were many lovers until she became the official mistress of the Honourable Charles Greville, moving into a house in London's Mayfair. She was a "kept woman", and was sometimes offered to his friends. Sir William Hamilton was a rich uncle and Charles hoped to benefit from his will, and offered Emma to him as well. The young woman saw her chance and took revenge, marrying old Sir William and diverting the young man's inheritance to herself. She was delighted when they moved to Naples, and Italian society warmly accepted this vivacious English beauty. Then along came Nelson. He already had a mistress in Naples, Signora Adelaide Correglia, who saw the danger signals. Another five years and many sea-battles would pass before Emma could replace her.

> ### PUBLISH AND BE DAMNED
>
> ● ● ● ● ● ● ● ● ● ● ● ● ● ● ● ● ●
> Lord Nelson at Trafalgar and the Duke of Wellington at Waterloo were sailor and soldier, and together they were England's idols as they bloodied Napoleon Bonaparte's nose. Both had wives they did not love. The general was more discreet in his love affairs, but when a fashionable courtesan, Harriette Wilson, was writing her memoirs, she asked for £200 to exclude his name, and Wellington's celebrated epithet was "Publish and be damned".
> ● ● ● ● ● ● ● ● ● ● ● ● ● ● ● ● ●

Nelson's ship put into Naples, and he was badly wounded and ill. Emma fainted at the sight of her lover and nursed him at home, bathing the man in ass's milk and personally feeding him to build up his strength. We cannot be entirely sure of her motives. She stayed by his side for two months and for his fortieth birthday, organized a party at the embassy inviting two thousand guests. Sir William accepted the situation, telling the unfortunate and vengeful Charles Greville, "I shall not let my peace be disturbed." She left her husband in Italy, and Fanny had to learn the hard way that Horatio was not coming back to her.

The pregnant Emma and Nelson were not allowed much time together in London before he was despatched to fight another battle. He wrote her, "Prepare the dear thatched cottage in readiness for my return" – and the admiral was not referring to any place where they might live. Fanny continued to try and win him back, even entreating the king himself, George III, to intercede on her behalf. But Lord Nelson was smitten. Sir William forgave the couple, and they were both at his bedside when the elderly diplomat died. Before he took to sea for the last time, Nelson must have had a premonition of death for he rewrote his will, leaving everything to Emma and their daughter, and died aboard his flagship *Victory* as the French fleet retreated from the Battle of Trafalgar in 1805. Emma was distraught and used up all their money partying, spent nine months in a debtor's prison, and died penniless eight years later.

THE PATH OF LEAST RESISTANCE

In another famous remark, Lady Frances Shelley, a beautiful and popular society hostess at the time, was asked why she had spurned a wealthy Austrian baron and replied, "Know sir that I have resisted the Duke of Wellington." When this was repeated to him, the honest general responded, "I was never aware of such resistance!"

Marie Stopes

The idea that all women should be capable of enjoying sexual intercourse and allow themselves to become aroused and excited was taboo at the beginning of this century, until Marie Stopes elaborated her theories about birth control. Marie's books *Married Love* and *Wise Parenthood*, banned in America and panned in England, were nevertheless best sellers, the adverse publicity made sure of that. But when she took on the church after opening clinics and setting up the Society for Constructive Birth Control and Racial Progress, she lost her court appeal in the House of Lords. The challenge by a Catholic doctor, Halliday Sutherland, that she "Exposed poor people to experiment by offering them contraception", was upheld and she was ordered to pay the court's costs.

Marie Stopes was not a doctor. She was born in Edinburgh, studied botany at Munich University in Germany, then became an expert on coal mining. Her mother's ignorance of sex and her own failure in marriage prompted her, at the age of thirty-six, to study sex as an academic subject and constantly raise the question, "Why should only men – and rich ladies – be allowed to enjoy intercourse?" She knew what women had long suspected, that fornication could be fun, and from her contemporaries she learned of the female orgasm. The fear of pregnancy was overwhelming so the answer lay in birth control. She realized her own naivety – she had not been kissed until she was twenty-four, and only learned about masturbation at twenty-nine – and set about questioning hundreds of women and reading scores of books before writing her own manuals, an overnight sensation when they were published in 1918. In that same year Marie, now

LIKE A VIRGIN

A doctor giving evidence at her divorce in 1916 testified that Marie Stopes was still a virgin. She was thirty-six, but husband Dr Reginal Gates had failed to consummate their five-year marriage. This reported exchange in court with her lawyer astonished readers in London, not for the facts, but for the language used:

Q. "With regard to your husband's part, did it ever get rigid at all?"

A. "On hundreds of occasions when we had what I thought to be relations, I only remember three occasions when it was partially rigid, and then it was never effectively rigid."

Q. "And he never succeeded in penetrating into your private parts?"

A. "No, he did not."

thirty-eight, lost her virginity, as she was married for the second time to her partner in the birth-control campaign, Humphrey Roe.

They did not have women's emancipation entirely in mind, however. The purification of the British people in particular and the white race in general was probably more than a secondary target. At one time they proposed that the Government should pass a law "To ensure the sterility of the hopelessly rotten and racially diseased". Much later, when Marie's only son married a young woman who needed to wear thick-lensed glasses, she described the union as a "Eugenic disaster".

Twenty years after marrying Humphrey, she made him write a letter admitting his sexual inadequacy and granting her permission to carry on extra-marital affairs. The stable door was possibly already wide open, for Marie, who was then fifty-eight, had flirted with a number of younger men attracted by her fame and the prospect, they imagined, of being bedded by such an expert on sex. Her first two books were translated into more than thirty languages, and she lectured in various parts of the world until she died, aged almost seventy-eight.

Havelock Ellis

Between the years 1897 and 1928, *Studies in the Psychology of Sex* was issued in seven parts, a huge volume written by Dr Havelock Ellis. Dr Havelock Ellis ran his free sex clinics for forty years, for women and for men. He had obviously studied the subject very deeply, but he was certainly not writing from personal experience. By his own admission, Ellis achieved his initial erection and enjoyed sexual intercourse properly for the first time in 1919, when he was aged sixty. The life-story of this man who was widely acknowledged as an expert on sex is truly amazing. He never touched a woman until he was twenty-five, when he discovered his impotence. He married a lesbian, had a number of sexless affairs, kept a collection of photographs of nude women, and fell in love with at least three of his patients.

Ellis gave up medicine when he turned to writing, and his first book in this series, *Sexual Inversion*, dealing with homosexuality, was banned in Britain as "Obscene libel". He didn't have much luck with succeeding titles either; they earned him very little money, and he lived most of his life close to the breadline. Hundreds of women and rather fewer men flocked to his clinic where he gave free sex advice to anyone who sought it. The background to his own sex life was only revealed years later, and had a remarkable beginning. His first love was Olive Schreiner, a brilliant South African author using a male pseudonym. Ellis wrote praising his best-selling novel – and was delighted to receive her reply. They corresponded and finally met. When she was allowed to read through his diaries, Olive realized she could be his first-ever woman, so she planned a dirty weekend intent on seducing him.

Olive had lived a full life, with several affairs behind her, four years his senior, well travelled and a couple of books earning her good royalties, and Havelock was not at all unwilling. She stripped him in a country cottage she had rented in the dales of

THE FLAME OF LIFE

● ● ● ● ● ● ● ● ● ● ● ● ● ● ●

When the first volume of the *Psychology of Sex* series was published, the attorney general's ban for obscene libel was challenged in London's High Court, using the plea of "Scientific value". The judge ruled against, saying, "That is a pretence adopted for the purpose of selling a filthy publication." Other volumes were published in Britain and America, but until 1935 were only available to doctors.

● ● ● ● ● ● ● ● ● ● ● ● ● ● ●

Derbyshire and he kissed every part of her naked body. She became wild and passionate but he remained limp and flaccid, and finally came the ignominy of a premature ejaculation. This same scene was repeated time and again, and Olive was an experienced, sympathetic and determined tutor, willing to marry him at first, but the relationship gave way to a life-long friendship.

He was on the receiving end of author esteem when school governess Edith Lees, an admirer of his most recent sex manual, wrote a fan letter. She ended up proposing to him and did her best to arouse him, but three months after they wed, admitted her preference for women. Edith wanted Ellis to divert her from a life as a lesbian and give her a baby. No such luck. Their unconsummated marriage was marred by her frequent nervous breakdowns. The last in a long line of women who saw the learned physician and his sexless life as a personal challenge was a French enchantress Françoise Cyon. He was a widower of sixty and Françoise, half his age, succeeded where all others had failed, though it took her a year.

They spent hours and hours in bed, kissing and fondling, in mutual masturbation, wandering around the house naked, until at last he had his first full erection, and for the next 20 years Havelock Ellis was finally able to practice what he had for so long preached.

Howard Hughes

He was an oil-millionaire, owner of the TWA airline, war-time plane manufacturer, a director and producer of films, the owner of RKO studios, and according to some of the biggest male stars in Hollywood at that time, leading actors who worked for him or were contracted to him, Howard Hughes was "the greatest swordsman in town." Men like Gary Cooper, Errol Flynn and Clark Gable who were sound judges of the sex scene in Southern California, envied his success but accorded him their respect. Much later in his life few could ever explain why women found him so fascinating, though the money was the big attraction for many, he became an eccentric recluse so beset with avoiding disease and viruses, and all forms of publicity, he had an army of personal secretaries, assistants, nurses and bodyguards organizing his everyday living.

But in the 1930s and 40s his big black book had the numbers of actresses such as Carole Lombard, Constance Bennett, Katherine Hepburn, Joan Crawford, Olivia de Havilland, Lana Turner, Bette Davis, Ginger Rogers, Ava Gardner, Jane Greer, Ida Lupino, and more, and these are just a few we know about. He was rich – father had invented a drilling-bit for the oil industry which he leased out and brought in billions of dollars – he was handsome with a natural, boyish, Texan charm. In that advanced era of flying the man owned and piloted his own plane. And above all else, had a love-affair with the movie industry and was really very good at both producing and directing. But when he actually got all the lovely, leading ladies into his bed, apparently the performance started to go rapidly downhill. Too often he was indifferent to his partner's desires and his name was in the gossip columns so often, his playmates could easily compare notes.

He was frequently impotent with a new mistress, making the excuse of "first time nerves." But this would not do for Bette Davis who confessed "I

SEA AND SKY

• • • • • • • • • • • • • • • • •

Hotel bellboys and laundry maids regularly made extra bucks, tipping off newspaper reporters when Howard Hughes thought he was secretly slipping between the sheets with a new prize. So he bought a magnificent private yacht, 300 feet long, and turned the Southern Cross into a floating fornicatorium. With publishing heir William Randolph Hearst, he would board his seaplane in a foursome, alternating bewteen aviator and fornicator.

• • • • • • • • • • • • • • • • •

got to work on him, he wasn't going to fail me." And Howard Hughes showed his gratitude next day by sending her bouquets and bouquets of gardenias with the request, "Put them all in your bedroom." Not a few of these gorgeous ladies would later recall, "Howard was particularly adept at oral sex."

He was married at 20 to Houston heiress Ella Rice, soon unfaithful on a grand scale and divorced five years later. When friends noticed how many of his affairs were with recent-divorcees, he admitted a fascination for "wet decks" telling them, "I've noticed sex is so much hotter, much more intense with a new divorcée, particularly if the woman wasn't satisfied by the husband." Ava, Lana, Rita and Kate Hepburn fell into this category. Howard Hughes just had to get laid very regularly, and if the latest target was slow to give in, he proposed marriage. He didn't mean it but even if an expensive ring was part of the act, he got laid.

Flying was very much a novelty in the 1930s and Howard Hughes used another ruse, the cockpit-seduction, to great effect. He invariably introduced his plane and pilot's ability into the first or at least, an early date, then lavished gifts on his con-

TEENAGERS IN LOVE

• • • • • • • • • • • • • • • •

Faith Domergue was only 15 when Hughes, then 37 and only a year younger than her father, presented her with a huge diamond ring. They were engaged for the next five years and as she constantly discovered his infidelities, the teenage fiancée and her parents, were bought off by lavish gifts, new cars and splendid houses. Ten years later he installed another 15-year-old, schoolgirl beauty queen Yvonne Shubert at his home. "In between touring some of Hollywood's most famous bedrooms, it seemed Howard was trying to maintain his adolescence," said his p.a. after his death, "he was driven to possess entire groups of women."

• • • • • • • • • • • • • • • •

quests. Virginia Mayo was air-sick and too scared, and in any case, she rejected him. So did Ingrid Bergman who was very much married, though that didn't deter him, and when she refused the offer of a lift from California back to New York, he booked every last seat on flights from L.A. that day but the lady would only join him with Cary Grant alongside as chaperon.

The millionaire plagued with strange obsessions, was a devotee of romance and fascinated with big breasts, yet he never bedded the two women with the most-admired bosoms among his retinue of stars, Jean Harlow and Jane Russell. He sold Jean's contract to rival studio MGM for a mere $60,000 after making her into a star in *Hell's Angels* but when he spotted a snapshot of Jane, working as a chiropodist's receptionist, and her phenomenal 38-20-36 figure, the unknown was signed up immediately. All the pub-

ICE CREAM FOR AVA

• • • • • • • • • • • • • • • • • •

His pursuit of Ava Gardner was relentless. One evening he thrust a Cartier package at her, containing diamond bracelets, ruby earrings and an opal necklace. Another night she opened a battered shoe box revealing $250,000. On her 23rd birthday he asked, "What would you like, anything, just name it ?" Down-to-earth Ava whispered "Orange ice cream" then only available in New York's Little Italy, 3,000 miles away. It was flown across America and delivered in a solid silver bowl.

• • • • • • • • • • • • • • • • • •

licity surrounding her first big film *The Outlaw*, centred on the profile of her bosom, rising above a torn blouse. This became a landmark in the film industry and led to a series of rows with the censors. Hughes was so enamoured of the girl's chest, he gave her a 20-year contract worth $1,000 a week. And for those two decades she never made a film.

Jane Russell inspired his famous memo, "The fit of the dress around her breasts is not good and gives the impression, God forbid, that her breasts are padded or artifical. They just don't appear to be in natural contour. I am not recommending that she go without a brassiere, as I know this is a very necessary piece of equipment for Miss Russell, but I want the public to get a good look at the part of her they pay to see." So he designed a special half-bra for Jane – "he decided it was no more difficult than designing an airplane," said the well-endowed actress, "but I never wore it."

Rita Hayworth was ripe for his attentions and they would make love on the rug before a roaring, log-fire. This was a very secret affair, she was so recently separated from Orson Welles, and a surprise caller at his house, failing to achieve an answer to the bell they ignored, caught them in mid-act. He made Rita pregnant and persuaded her to have an abortion. He proposed to Gene Tierney and Linda Darnell on consecutive evenings. Gene was just about to wed fashion guru Oleg Cassini and said "No" then after her wedding, changed her mind. Cassini caught the couple returning from a weekend in Las Vegas and laid into Hughes with a baseball bat. Linda said "Yes please" promising to ask her cameraman husband for a divorce which scared off Hughes.

In his private cinema he repeatedly watched the sensuous new star Yvonne De Carlo do the dance of the seven veils in *Salome* then flew to Vancouver, gate-crashing a party to meet and woo her. Like several of his women, De Carlo had luscious thick lips. Unknown to either, the plane-maker was under surveillance by the FBI whose telephone wire-taps picked up an interesting conversation between the pair as Hughes tried to explain the difference between the male and the femal orgasm ... "yours is an implosion Yvonne, reacting to my explosion, and both are totally different in their physiological engineering." The lady did not sound interested, practice yes, theory no ! Describing their romance Yvonne said, "Howard would enter a girl's life, wine and dine and surround her with gifts, and suddenly, when he disappeared for a day or a week-end, you missed him terribly. It was quite deliberate, then would come the reunions."

He kept up the chase for screen-singer Kathryn Grayson for three years, and failed. He offered 19-year-old Liz Taylor's parents a million dollars for her hand in marriage, and failed. He succeeded with the beautiful, long-legged dancer Cyd Charisse and just managed to get starlet Terry Moore between the sheets, faking-up a wedding ceremony at sea on board a chartered yacht. Much later he and Marilyn Monroe enjoyed a few one-night stands.

On New Year's Eve in 1956 he planned an outrageous foursome, himself plus teenage sweetheart Yvonne Schubert and two actresses, the lovely, red-haired Susan Hayward and Jean Peters who would become his second wife. None of the females knew about the other two and dinner was set up at the Beverly Hills Hotel, for Yvonne in a bungalow in the hotel gardens, Jean in the dining room and Susan in the Polo Lounge. In a scene resembling a Marx movie or *Mrs Doubtfire*, Hughes dashed between tables – "important phone call darlings" – but despite an army of look-outs with walkie-talkies, suspicious Susan caught him at Jean's side. He married Jean but for four years they lived in different homes, her husband's eccentricities had begun.

In 1960 he tried to make a come-back, the 55-years-old ex-swordsman watched a Miss Universe contest on television, and took a fancy to ... Miss Belgium, Miss France, Miss USA, Miss Switzerland ... and his aides actually signed seven of these young beauties to contracts with a dummy film-production company, setting them up in their own apartments. They all vanished in a week except the hopeful Miss Belgium who remained for six months. Ironically, his final recruit Gail Ganley received the usual treatment, a home, a salary, drama training, and never came face to face with Hughes. Four years later, in 1962, she had the temer-

GIRL CRAZY

Hughes was such a fascinating character, not least to California's medical profession, and when he died Dr Raymond Fowler conducted a psychological autopsy, based on 300 depositions and official reports. The doctor decided he was a "maniacal collector" of women, trying to recapture the intense love he felt for his mother. *Confidential Magazine* had earlier published interviews enumerating 164 of his Hollywood play-mates.

ity to sue him for failing to put her to work and the court case exposed all, or nearly all, the secrets of his starlet factory.

In the last 25 years of his life, his well-paid staff had a torrid time but Hughes had a compassionate streak and was always incredibly kind to his former lovers, paying medical bills, settling damges in lost court cases, making planes available in emergencies. He was 70 and the second richest man in America, after J. Paul Getty, when he died intestate and 22 first cousins were eventually identified as his true heirs. Cause of death in March 1976, was due to kidney failure and tertiary syphilis but his dependence on pain-killing codeine plus injuries sustained in 14 plane and car crashes, may have had something to do with killing him.

CHAPTER 4

SEX MANIACS, NYMPHOMANIACS, COURTESANS AND GIGOLOS

☆ ☆

Giovanni Casanova

He died two hundred years ago, yet his name lives on to characterize any man who puts romance and the pursuit of women for sexual pleasure above all else. That is exactly what brought Casanova his fame, though he could just as easily claim the description soldier, spy, musician, diplomat, writer, traveller or gambler. We have to rely for the full chronicle of his sexual escapades on his own twelve-volume *Histoire de Ma Vie* ("Story of My Life"), written with a certain amount of embellishment, fantasy accompanying fact, dreams interwoven with dastardly deeds. On the other hand, more than enough corroboration exists among the confessions of many women who went eagerly to his bed during the eighteenth century.

Giovanni was born in 1725 in Venice. His mother was a local actress and father was a touring dancer who used the stage name Casanova. He lived with his grandmother and, according to his story, a maid named Bettina Gozzi aroused him at the age of eleven. He was perhaps too young for seduction, but she continued to play with the boy as she bathed him each night, setting him up for a *ménage-a-trois* with sisters Martha and Nanette

Savorgnan. He crept into their bed in his mid-teens. First time out for Giovanni, he delighted the older girls first by joining them in the bath, and then with his alternate lovemaking all night long. By his estimate he had each one three times. His early experience with Bettina probably did him a power of good, and he continued to wash and bathe many of his delighted paramours all through his life.

Amazingly, when he was at school at the St Cyprian Seminary, Giovanni was expelled for a homosexual escapade – by no means the last of his affairs with men – and then gained a law degree from Padua University. He joined the army, but soon left the ranks when he discovered his true vocation pleasing the ladies of Venice who plied him with money. For a short time he was a concert violinist, served a cardinal in Rome, then went on his first bout of travels to France, Germany, Czeckoslavakia, Austria and Switzerland.

In Geneva he called on an uncle and succeeded with two more sisters, Helena and Hedwig, who were his cousins, and while claiming to be virgins, they proved to be ardent athletes who enjoyed multi-orgasms. Then, he wrote, "... one of the girls, I forget which, brought me to the paroxysm of consummation as she kissed my pistol." He had long, dark hair with handsome, finely-chiselled features, a powerful figure, and the ability to speak many languages. For Casanova, romance was paramount. With most of his women, even his teenage victims, he liked to fall in love before he made love. His encounter with a fifteen-year-old he identified only as "C.C." brought him a barrel-full of exploits when she was incarcerated by her father in a convent at Murano as punishment for surrendering her virginity to Casanova.

LEMONS & OYSTERS

It is not surprising to discover Casanova suffered from venereal disease, though he tried to protect his partners with a crude form of covering. For their own sake, to avoid pregnancy, he advocated half a lemon be used as a diaphragm. The citric acid was supposed to act as a spermicide. One way or another, he was bound to make the ladies' eyes water. The oyster has long been regarded as a powerful aphrodisiac, and the oyster orgy was a game Casanova introduced to his wealthy partners. As the couple sat naked on the bed, he would suck the delicacy from the shell and pass it to the lips of his lady-love. If any oyster happened to slip and fall "between the alabaster spheres further, the delights of recovery were divine," he wrote.

He visited C.C. at the convent, and an attractive young nun he called M.M. took him to her apartments. They copulated but, unknown to Giovanni, this was primarily for the benefit of the woman's more permanent partner at the convent, Abbé François de Bernis, who was viewing their performance from a hidden chamber next door. He was also the French consul general in Venice, and when Casanova learned the man was an eager voyeur, suggested a variation. The nun agreed and brought C.C. to the room where "all three of us, intoxicated by desire and transported by continual furies, played havoc with everything visible and palpable," he wrote. Once more, the world had to wait the best part of two centuries, until 1960, to read the uncensored version of his memoirs which ran to 4,500 pages of tightly written manuscript. This was by no means his last encounter with a sexy nun, if we are to believe his account of events around the Venetian ecclesiastical establishments.

Casanova's story is a worthwhile read, if only to enjoy his descriptions of the social scenes in the grand old cities of Europe at that time. He was a clever raconteur, witty and charming, and took this ability to his writing, producing poems, books and even a translation of the *Iliad*. He also dabbled with the occult and when a jealous ex-mistress reported this to the police, he was denounced as a sorcerer and gaoled for five years in the Piombi prison cells under the roof of the Doge's palace in Venice.

A year later he made a spectacular escape, and turned up in Paris – where he is credited with introducing the national lottery in 1757 – then on to London, Berlin, and Warsaw, where he survived a duel with a Polish count, and afterwards to St Petersburg, where he says Empress Catherine the Great gave him an audience to discuss the calendar. Her reputation as a sexual hedonist was almost the equal of Casanova's, but he does not claim her as a lover. After nineteen years in exile he returned to Venice, where he acted as a spy for the Court of Inquisition, but he didn't give up the night job. He virtually advertised himself as an abortionist, telling his attractive and potential clients that repeated and lengthy bouts of fornication – with himself naturally – would end their pregnancies. They were not necessarily satisfied clients, not in every degree anyway.

The aged Marquise d'Urfe kept him in the manner he expected for near-

---

FAMILY VALUES

• • • • • • • • • • • • • • • • • •

Casanova was not at all embarrassed when he learned he had made love to his own daughter. Leonilda was the mistress of an Italian duke, a cover for the man's homosexual preferences, and after bedding the girl Giovanni discovered her mother was Lucrezia, a frequent lover around eighteen years earlier. A decade later he returned to her side when Leonilda was married to an aged and impotent marquis and desired a child. Casanova fathered his own grandson.

• • • • • • • • • • • • • • • • • •

ly three years. She was beyond child-bearing age but an enthusiastic trialist, and agreed Casanova should be allowed some stimulation as he attempted to satisfy her ambitions. It was back to the three-in-a-bed routine with Marcoline, who he describes as a "nymphomaniac lesbian", providing all kinds of vigorous variation. It was quality not quantity he desired; one or perhaps two women several times in one night was far more preferable than half a dozen different conquests between dusk and dawn. Casanova boasts that his longest bout of intercourse stretched through seven hours, and the shortest was all of fifteen minutes. He also claims one of his partners enjoyed fourteen orgasms before he eventually joined her. Five German sisters claimed his attention in London, though we cannot be sure each one joined him in bed for by then; as he approached fifty, Casanova was becoming exhausted and a little flacid. He lived to seventy-three, but his pen rather than his pistol was his chief occupation for the last twenty years.

Ninon de Lenclos

Among the many hundreds of lovers who flocked to her bedroom, we cannot estimate the number of father and son pairs Ninon de Lenclos enjoyed across the years. When she founded her Academy of Gallantry in Paris, the aristocratic adolescents who enrolled found that high on the curriculum came "the art of pleasing a woman." Many a male parent who remembered Ninon with gratitude as well as affection sent their teenage sons along in the mid-1600s, knowing they were going to be in good hands. Ninon, one of the very first and certainly among the most celebrated of courtesans, claimed 4,959 conquests altogether, not including repeat engagements, and living to the ripe old age of eighty-five, she must have been active for sixty of those years.

SPIRIT BEAUTY

Ninon was a striking strawberry blonde who gave currency to the legend that she was visited on her eighteenth birthday by a spirit who offered her eternal beauty, untold wealth or high rank. She chose the first and enjoyed the trappings of the other two. The jealous mother of King Louis XIV had her confined to a monastery, and though her influential friends had her released, the lady was in no hurry. Among her lovers she counted four-hundred-odd monks and abbots.

Her father was a musician who taught her to play various instruments and to appreciate art and literature. Women above the state of seamstress or maid were not expected to work, and he prepared her well for a life not of leisure but most positively of pleasure. Ninon established a salon, a regular meeting place, in Paris around 1645, financed by her admirers who gathered there almost daily to exchange views with artists, writers and political leaders, the people of influence. It was a practice followed by many courtesans who suceeded her during the next two hundred years. In other respects it was a high-class forerunner of the modern Singles' Bars, for the exchanges were often of the sexual kind. She loved gourmet food, adored fine wines, dressed elegantly and had a good, healthy appetite for fornication. She overcame the problem of admitting only the finest of gentlemen to her bed by granting her favours to those aged from seventeen to seventy, as long as they had the right pedigree. A natural extension to her salon, the Academy of Gallantry provided a steady stream of young lovers if ever the natural supply dried up.

Her father introduced her to a duke in Paris whose only interest in women was the seduction of young virgins. With that hurdle overcome, Ninon de Lenclos set about life in some style and at some speed. Her biography did not appear until a century and a half after her death, but it detailed many of the courtesan's affairs, starting with the Chevalier du Rare – a lavish lover but a mean partner – then Coulon, who proved a wealthy sponsor but was often too drunk to perform to her satisfaction. Before she reached twenty, Ninon fell in love with the very handsome Gaspard de Coligny, but he proved to be a poor performer and could not possibly keep up with her demands. In fact Gaspard was gay, so to make up for lost time, the lass took on two very active lovers, the Abbé Dessiat and Marechal d'Estres, and when she became pregnant had no idea which one was the father.

SONS & LOVERS

• • • • • • • • • • • • • • • • •

Among the young men allowed to call on her, when she was past sixty but still giving a few "lessons", was her own son. She realized his identity as he spoke of his father, but before Ninon could stop him, the youth professed his love for the elderly but still beautiful courtesan. When she revealed the truth, young Guillaume de Gersay went into the garden, plunged his sword into his breast and died instantly.

• • • • • • • • • • • • • • • • •

Blood tests had not been invented, so paternity was decided by the roll of the dice and Marechal won – or lost; at any rate he was named as the father. These were all men who lasted the distance, for most who were lacking in the virility expected of her suitors were dismissed after one or two sessions with Ninon. There were no orgies but more than a few erotic renderings, and Ninon was able to maintain her appeal for decades. The Marquis d'Andelot almost persuaded her to marry, then Louis de Bourbon took over as her sole financier for a time. She moved out of Paris to live with the Marquis de Villaceaux for two years at his country house and when he fell ill with fever, stayed in bed with him for an entire week. The marquis recovered from the fever, but was relieved when Ninon returned to the capital.

Friends of both sexes had good reason to be grateful to the lady, as she passed on some of her spent lovers to less-demanding women friends. Villaceaux stood in for the king when his mistress, Madame de Maintenon and a confidante of Ninon, was forced to go without for a time. A letter from Madam de la Suze revealed that Madame de Lenclos had not only advised her on which of her ex-lovers were now available, but also what each man had to offer beneath the blankets. She was not slow to put down the average or inadequate.

Two counts and a duke rated very poorly. De Sevigne was so incompetent and pompous, with such skimpy equipment, that "I could not commend him to a teenage virgin," she wrote. The Comte de Navailles fell asleep as she prepared for bed on their first assignment. He was a soldier who woke up to find he was under attack and totally unable to defend what the lady was holding. The affair was never consummated. The duke was bedded merely in revenge, his mistress was an actress, "and more than welcome to this inadequate man."

Though she retired as a courtesan at fifty-one, Ninon continued with her salon and bestowed her favours with great deliberation, eager to educate young men more on a part-time basis, and happy to put back some of the pleasure she had taken out of her sex life. The father of Voltaire, the brilliant writer, had long been a friend though never a lover, and when Ninon died in 1705, she left funds in her will to buy books for the rising young man.

204 ☆ SEX MANIACS, NYMPHOMANIACS ...

Aly Khan and Aristotle Onassis

Their vast wealth was acquired by very different means, inherited fortunes and property versus shrewd gambles and investment. Yet both these men, born within five years of each other in the early 1900s, used their riches to attract some of the world's most striking and well-known women. Aly Khan became an international playboy, costing him the spiritual leadership of twenty million Ismaili Muslims. Aristotle Onassis was a lusty young schoolboy whose hot-blooded passion gained him suspension and expulsion. It is probably true that neither man would have changed anything in their lifestyles – particularly the sexual conquests which attracted reputations and headlines in equal and well deserved portions.

> ### "ISMAK"
>
> ● ● ● ● ● ● ● ● ● ● ● ● ● ● ● ● ●
>
> "I think only of a woman's pleasure when I am making love," said Aly Khan. As a teenager, father had sent him to a clinic in Cairo to learn the Arab sexual technique called "Ismak" , which he seemed to have perfected. One of his mistresses explained, "He seldom reached a climax himself. He could make love by the hour, while the woman lost control and had her orgasms he stayed in command. Aly could climax himself but only when he wanted to."
>
> ● ● ● ● ● ● ● ● ● ● ● ● ● ● ● ● ●

Prince Aly Suleiman Khan, son of the Aga Khan of India, saw very little of his homeland. He was born in Italy, schooled in Switzerland, bred racehorses in Ireland and France and polo ponies in Venezuela, raced cars all over Europe, hunted big game in Africa and lived much of his adult life between London, New York and California. Ostensibly to study law, he arrived in England at eighteen, the precise age when the daughters of dukes and earls and innumerable lords "came out" at their debutante balls. The year was 1929, and Aly Khan was on every deb's mother's invitation list. Fat chance of catching this young man – hell-bent on scratching every corner of London's playground, he pierced a few maidenheads and broke a few hearts and went happily on his way.

Aly soon moved on to bedding married women, which he did successfully and secretly, and when brewing heir and British M.P. Loel Guinness went through a very public divorce in London, he confessed he had no idea wife

Joan had enjoyed a two year affair with the prince. Joan became Aly Khan's first wife and gave him two sons – Amyn and Karim, who leap-frogged his father to became the Aga Khan on the death of his grandfather in 1957. That was no surprise, for by then Aly had moved on to more fertile playing fields in Hollywood and crowned many sexual triumphs by conducting a wild and outrageous affair with the beautiful film star Rita Hayworth.

Hayworth was then married to the equally prominent and furious Orson Wells. Before her, Aly had delighted Juliette Greco, Grace Kelly and Kim Novak to name but a few, and Hollywood's rising stars agreed, "At that time, you didn't exist if you hadn't been to bed with Aly Khan." When Gene Tierney met him and instantly picked up his vibes, her reported reaction was, "That's all I need, some Oriental super-stud chasing me." The lady had more than enough experience, but was soon smitten and hoped to marry the man before Rita Hayworth carried off the prize, soon to her own disappointment. They wed and rapidly divorced. For Aly Khan, marriage did not dictate a change in lifestyle. He lived and he died in the fast lane, at the age of forty-eight, behind the wheel of a car in a road accident.

> **DOOMED LOVERS**
>
> • • • • • • • • • • • • • • • • • •
>
> When Onassis met Maria Callas, she had been happily wed for ten years to Italian opera patron Giovanni Meneghini. Within a month the marriage was over. The lady clearly preferred older men – her husband was thirty years senior and her lover eighteen years, but after joining the shipowner Maria conceded, "We were very rich and very happy but we were doomed. We had only one thing in common, but he didn't like opera and I didn't like travel."
>
> • • • • • • • • • • • • • • • • • •

Expelled

Being thrown out of school was a fairly regular event when Aristotle Onassis, the Greek shipping tycoon, was a boy. Nothing wrong with his brains – he was a self-made millionaire by the time he reached twenty-five, he was ready for the opposite sex before he reached his teens, and he was just as bad at home. At the age of eleven Onassis tried to seduce the family's laundry girl. At twelve, a teacher complained he had pinched her bottom, and twice at thirteen a school matron and a teacher's wife reported he had fondled them through their clothes. Then at fourteen a French mistress wearing a light, summer dress was more receptive, and he explained, "I cannot help myself, you are arousing me and nothing can stop me violating you." He was right, nothing and no one, certainly not the mistress, did stop him.

His family were tobacco merchants, but were forced to leave most of their possessions behind when the Turks and Greeks clashed in 1922. Aristotle was sixteen when he left Athens and arrived in Buenos Airies with $1,000, and quickly turned from tobacco to shipping. He was soon chartering oil tankers to supply Europe, then buying and building his own ships, but always dividing his time between making his fortune and making love to a succession of South American beauties. He moved north and savoured what New York had to offer, in business and pleasure, and met a wealthy, classic Scandinavian blonde, Ingeborg Dedichen, who disclosed, "He was huge yet he was gentle. He would stroke and kiss every part of my body then take me so swiftly and urgently, the room would shake."

For Ingeborg, the shipping magnate was not her only port of call, and she suffered a few beatings from the enraged and jealous Greek until she attempted suicide. Onassis recognized it was time to move to Hollywood, and had his share of starlets before deciding it was time for marriage at the age of forty. His choice was a great surprise – seventeen-year-old Tina Livanos, daughter of a shipping competitor, to whom he stayed married, though not faithful, for thirteen years. She ignored his affairs as he travelled America and Europe, but was present on a Mediterranean cruise aboard their own yacht *Christina* with Sir Winston and Lady Churchill, when Aristotle met his great love, world famous opera star Maria Callas. Either side of his eventual divorce, their love affair was featured and photographed in newspapers around the world. The former sixteen-stone singer was just as wild and just as passionate, and just as surprised as the rest of the world when he re-married.

His bride was Jackie Kennedy, the black-haired, beautiful widow of the murdered American president who had borrowed his privately-owned Greek island to overcome her grief five years earlier. But America's former first lady did not share his passionate nature. She was twenty-three years younger, and their marriage contract stipulated separate bedrooms while allowing certain visiting rights. She enjoyed his wealth, he enjoyed her fame, but they were rarely happy. He turned to the opera star again, for comfort and advice, and Onassis was considering divorcing Jackie when he died in 1975.

La Belle Otero

The lady was described as the last of the great courtesans. While others of her persuasion organized their regular salons, the places where people of note met and where sexual intrigues began, La Belle Otero became a dancer and music hall star, privately entertaining wherever she happened to be at the time. At the turn of this century, in Paris, London, Brussels, Madrid, Moscow or New York, she moved easily among the ranks of high society, receiving her lovers with her own pleasure and satisfaction very much in mind! She was also described as a nymphomaniac – if she was, then Otero put her desires to very good use, and her passion and lifestyle certainly agreed with her. Carolina Augustina Otero Iglesias, the illegitimate daughter of a Spanish prostitute, lived to the ripe old age of ninety-six.

The names of men who could testify to her passionate qualities read like a chapter from an International Register of Royalty ... King Leopold of the Belgians, Czar Nicolas of Russia, Prince Albert of Monaco, Prince Alfonso of Spain, the Prince of Wales and future King Edward the Seventh of England, the Khedive of Cairo, Prince Nicholas of Montenegro, and the Shah of Persia are only some of those we know about for certain. There were others, millionaires and industrialists without the Royal connection, and all these men loved her, gave her expensive gifts, set her up in houses or apartments, and seemed to have no regrets when she moved on. "I was a slave to my passions but never to any one man," she told an interviewer many years after she retired.

She started dancing as a child. At eleven she so excited the shoemaker in the village where she grew up that the man raped her. Through her teens she was a part-time prostitute, but danced and sang whenever an opportunity came along. At twenty she moved to the Cote d'Azur, where she developed another passion, gambling in the French casinos. Otero went into the music

UP, UP & AWAY

A French nobleman promised her an undisclosed sum to accompany him in a hot-air balloon, and he made love to Otero on and off for an hour one summer afternoon in 1902 flying above Montpellier. In between his exertions, Baron Lepic also had to pilot the balloon, and in her autobiography she recalled, "It was an experience every woman should enjoy." The baron was more than satisfied, for the lady gave him back the money.

hall full-time, going abroad as the lead dancer with a touring company two years later, but there was always time to indulge the afternoon-job. At the height of her fame and in the sexual prime of her life, she demanded 10,000 dollars in cash or kind for a one-night stand.

With her long-term lovers it was different of course, though she never entertained any man who could not afford to keep her in luxury. The extensive roll of her Royal playmates was quite extraordinary. These were proud men with their own reputations to uphold, men who undoubtedly knew where the woman had been and, presumably, where she was likely to go later. They must also have known they would be compared, their technique, performance and stamina would be noted, and when Otero published her autobiography some years later, while the majority were still alive, the lady spared no blushes. She revealed that several of her ex-lovers conspired together to give her a very private thirtieth birthday party hosted by Prince Albert of Monaco, and among those who attended were the Prince of Wales, King Leopold and Grand Duke Nikolai of Russia.

BELLE'S BUST

● ● ● ● ● ● ● ● ● ● ● ● ● ● ● ● ●

La Belle Otero's bust was famous, accentuated by her very slim waist, and drew men's eyes wherever she went. She was radiant and startlingly beautiful, nearly six feet tall, with rich, black hair, and her dark Spanish eyes sent men weak at the knees. Colette, the writer and lifelong friend, said Otero's breasts reminded her of elongated lemons, "very firm, and upturned at the nipples." An admirer said they preceded her into a room, "by a good quarter of an hour."

● ● ● ● ● ● ● ● ● ● ● ● ● ● ● ● ●

Formidable

Albert had good reason to be grateful to Otero. The head of the tiny state on the Mediterranean where in later years actress Grace Kelly would become First Lady had great difficulty getting an erection. But the practised courtesan helped him succeed, and then told his highness that the performance was "formidable", and the prince moved her into a Royal apartment, gave her nearly half a million dollars worth of jewellery, and was happy to be seen in public as her constant escort. "He was not virile enough to get his money's worth, but that wasn't my fault," she wrote. When she visited Prince Nicholas of Montenegro, part of the old Yugoslavia, Otero spent three weeks cooped up in his palace, "He was fifty and very strong, and all he wanted to do was make love. I saw nothing of the countryside." He gave her silver bracelets and gold watches.

The Shah of Persia liked to visit for three hours most afternoons. "He was a dirty, smelly old man, but very generous." Soon after leaving Otero's apartment, a servant would arrive each time with a single jewel, a diamond or emerald or perhaps a pearl. King Leopold was mean, "but he learned fast, and he did provide some splendid homes." In America, William K. Vanderbilt came up with the goods – $250,000 worth of jewels – but she declined his offer of a yacht. In London, Bertie, the Prince of Wales, "was surprisingly virile and generous," but gave her up in favour of actress Lillie Langtry.

Surrounded by bodyguards, the Czar of Russia would receive her in his Moscow apartments, as would-be assassins made it too dangerous for him to visit Otero. "It was like undressing in a Spanish bullring or an army barracks," she said. Her reward for three days and nights of non-stop lovemaking in Cairo was a ten-carat diamong ring encrusted with pearls, worth 500,000 French francs, from the Khedive. Otero's added attraction to these noble lovers was the fact she could not bear children, a hangover from the childhood rape.

SPEND, SPEND, SPEND

The hundreds of gifts of jewellery were constantly sold to pay her gambling debts. By her own estimate she went through $20 million at the casinos, and one night on the Riveira, convinced she was on the verge of a winning streak, she took men to her nearby hotel to earn more money to replenish her stake. When dawn arrived, a croupier told Otero she had left and returned to the tables eleven times.

Otero was nineteen-year-old King Alfonso's first woman, exactly twice his age, and he showed his gratitude then, and again eight years later when he laid on an apartment in the centre of Madrid where he continued to visit her. She moved back to France and, still attractive, maintained a regular sex life well into her sixties, but she was alone, living in Nice, when she died from a heart attack in 1965.

Marquis de Sade

Whips, rope, canes, belts and even chains were wielded by this French noble-man on his naked victims to such an extent that he gave his name to the sexual perversion of causing pain. Sadism sounds too mild a word to describe his activities, and when five prostitutes conspired to stop him, accusing the Marquis de Sade of using drugs before trying to sodomize them, his mother-in-law was so appalled that her additional evidence persuaded a judge to gaol him for twelve years. That was not his first time in prison – "outrageous debauchery" had earned him various terms inside, from magistrates in Paris – considered a hot-bed for licentious behaviour 250 years ago – and in Marseilles, Vincennes and Milan, when he fled France in favour of Italy. The extent of de Sade's well-orchestrated orgies is beyond imagination.

He enjoyed both receiving and inflicting pain, and while he loathed homosexuals, he preferred sodomy to straightforward sex, probably not for any physical reasons but because it was unlawful. The majority of the victims of his perversions were prostitutes, and the owners of brothels in Paris received official warnings from police they too would be arrested if they sent any more girls to de Sade. He lived at Charenton, close to Paris, but kept a house in the city exclusively for his orgies, and when the supply of professionals dried up, he resorted to amateurs. Among the ranks of the ruling classes he found more than a few ladies eager to volunteer who reasoned, "What's a little pain when so much enjoyment is available?" The advantage, which de Sade later recognized, was that although they might be one-off orgiasts, they were far less likely to make official complaints than his paid-for partners, for fear of the ensuing publicity. According to the marquis, he had no trouble indulging his evil passions with a different woman every day.

REIGN OF TERROR

The marquis passed up a unique opportunity to revenge his lengthy gaol sentence. During the first French uprising he was made a Revolutionary Judge during the infamous Reign of Terror, but could not bring himself to order his mother-in-law's execution when she appeared before him as a member of the aristocracy. Subsequently he escaped the guillotine himself, when he lampooned Napoleon and his mistress Josephine in a booklet, but was brought to court by the Government censors for his erotic book *Justine*.

Donatien Alphonse Francois, Comte de Sade, was born in 1740, and born to the saddle, a young cavalry officer who rode women just as easily as his horses. A riding crop was one of his first weapons of flagellation, but from where his perversions derived has never become clear. He was ably assisted by several young men, sexually depraved members of the French aristocracy, but none had his organizational ability, his enthusiasm or devotion, or the permanent setting for these orgies. The special house had rooms draped in black, with effigies and crucifixes, restraining straps, low couches, pornographic drawings, erotic passages from books in frames, and all manner of flagellation kit hanging from the walls.

With a prostitute Jeanne Testard and an unwilling amateur Rose Keller, he had already been before the courts when he met and married Renée-Pelagie de Montreuil in 1765. He was virtually wed to two women, for her blonde sister Anne-Prospere was part of the bride's dowry, and very fortunate that turned out to be, for the younger woman was an eager recruit to her brother-in-law's erotic menagerie. She saw more of the marquis, in every sense of the word, than her sister, and especially when Renée became pregnant. Anne was frequently chief whipper-in at his orgies, but was absent one afternoon when he brought home a thirty-year-old widow. This latter was thrashed so frenetically that she ended up in hospital and de Sade in prison. His release was ordered after his wife made an official visit to his cell... and became pregnant again.

School for Sadism

A condition of his parole was that he leave Paris and live in the countryside in Provence, so he took the two sisters, and his valet, Latour, to set up home at the family chateau La Coste, outside Marseilles. He engaged a professional procuress to round up prostitutes for his more outrageous escapades, and a wicked old monk from a nearby monastery to recruit young girls "in need" of sex education. The monk told the parents of teenage girls they would be well taught and very well disciplined, and by now Renée-Pelagie was a fanatic flagellist as well. Of course the girls were given a choice – cane or whip – and uniquely in the education profession, the pretty young students were given the chance to hand out corporal punishment to their superiors.

Two of the girls complained and were able to produce some pretty good physical evidence, and the marquis was under investigation again when the incident with the five prostitutes, a highlight of his sordid career, was brought to the attention of local police. They were aged between eighteen and twenty-six, and were taken to the chateau by Latour who throughout the evening handed out liquorice-flavoured sweets. These were laced with the aphrodisiac Spanish Fly, which at first had the required effect on the girls, as they were offered the choice of anal or vaginal intercourse. They were whipped and did some whipping, had a few more sweeties, and remained naked and more or less horizontal all night. But the valet had overdone the Spanish Fly, and when the prostitutes started vomiting violently, the men attending the orgy were afraid some of the girls were going to die.

The nobleman fled to Italy, and when he dared to return he was immediately arrested and eventually confronted in court by his mother-in-law. No parole this time, and when he was finally released, he was a divorced and nearly penniless frail old man. The revolution brought him to prominence again, and his time inside assorted prison cells had been put to good use. The Marquis de Sade turned to writing, and the successful novel *The Adversities of Virtue* was followed by a noticeable book of short stories, *The Crimes of Love*, and it was through his literature de Sade was able to find more sexual satisfaction and indulge in far more sinister and diabolical orgies within the walls of his evil imagination. Not surprisingly, he spent the best part of his last twenty-five years in an asylum, where he died in 1814, at the age of seventy-four.

Countess di Castiglioni

On February 1, 1856, this young woman was visited in her grandfather's palace in Florence by two Italian noblemen. They had a task for Virginia Oldoini, who was known as Nicchia and had recently become the wife of Conte Francesco Verasis di Castiglioni. The countess was stunningly attractive and not yet twenty-one. Her fidelity to the count was of no importance, she was to go immediately to Paris and seduce Napoleon III, the new Emperor of France. One of the men was her cousin, the Island of Sardinia's prime minister, Camillo di Cavour. He knew her beauty bowled men over and that she was highly-sexed – she had lost her virginity at sixteen by going to bed with three brothers. The other man was her husband's boss, Victor Emmanuel, the ruler of Piedmont and Sardinia.

Their aim was to elicit the help of Napoleon to boot the Austrians out of the north and unite the various states in the south under one flag. They reckoned Napoleon would be unable to resist the looks and the charms of the magnificent countess, and Nicchia would be unable to resist the importance of the mission they outlined for her. They were absolutely right. The countess ended up in bed with the emperor, and Victor Emmanuel ended up as King of Italy. Thus were the affairs of state handled in Europe a hundred and fifty years ago.

Nicchia's family were so worried about her behaviour after the episode with the three brothers became public knowledge that they decided to marry her off as soon as possible. She was gorgeous, few men would reject her and, not unnaturally, they chose an impressive noblemen with very highly-placed connections. The nineteen-year old bride's impression of Francesco was some-

FOREIGN CORRESPONDENCE

● ● ● ● ● ● ● ● ● ● ● ● ● ● ● ●
The countess undoubtedly had political influence, in Turin, Paris and London, wielded in time-honoured fashion. But a bashful Italian government in the early part of this century decided that should remain a secret forever. Her "diplomatic correspondence", or rather the letters she wrote home detailing her major conquests, were all officially burned.
● ● ● ● ● ● ● ● ● ● ● ● ● ● ● ●

what different – she thought him a weak imbecile, especially when he later sanctioned her first diplomatic mission – and after producing a son, Nicchia refused to sleep with him again. Although the seduction of Napoleon was her cousin's idea, the future king decided he should personally check out her credentials, but after bedding the countess himself, he sent her off to Paris with excellent references.

The lady stayed on in Paris after Napoleon succumbed, and managed to put her husband two million francs in debt. The emperor remained her lover for three years, and gave her emeralds, rubies, pearls and a house in the rue de da Pompe, which he visited regularly. The empress was well aware of the affair, and Nicchia made sure she stayed in imperial favour, confining her outings to the days so that she was always available at night. However, Napoleon was not the sexual adventurer she craved, and the lady had a voracious appetite. Her daylight outings took her to several different beds in Paris, and she removed the monogrammed underwear the emperor had given her a few times too often. The most powerful man in Europe heard about this but unable to resist her passion, he carried on calling. Then one night a would-be assassin caught the couple "in flagrante dilectii" in the rue de la Pompe, and though he survived the attempt, Napoleon decided "enough", and sent the young woman into exile.

QUEEN OF HEARTS

Nicchia was a daring and dazzling young woman. Attending an official ball for the emperor in Paris, she appeared almost naked. The ladies were in fancy dress, and the countess chose to appear as the Queen of Hearts, with two small hearts stitched into a gauze strip across her breasts to hide her nipples. A third heart set in a transparent skirt was supposed to hide her vagina, but her pubic hair could be clearly seen. Napoleon was clearly amused but his wife, Empress Eugenie, sent her a caustic note saying, "We think your heart seems a little low."

He kept his word to the Italians though, and Nicchia was rapturously received back home. In fact the recently crowned king decided on a dual reward – a life pension equivalent to 1,000 French francs a month and the honour of becoming his official mistress, setting up the countess in the Pitti Palace in Florence.

The king used his influence and had her re-admitted to France, for he had another diplomatic task for the countess to fulfil and she promptly bedded the foreign minister in Paris, reporting back directly to Victor Emmanuel in Italy. Her affairs were not at all confined to official business. Nicchia needed to boost her dwindling fortunes, and seduced the elderly Baron James de Rothschild, considered at that time to be the richest man in the world. He overcame her financial needs and she overcame her sexual needs by promptly bedding, in turn, each of his three sons, who presumably decided the lady was worth sharing.

Her fame had spread far and wide across Europe, and the countess was in her thirties when she was summoned to London. The Marquis of Hertford was also fabulously wealthy, and he wrote, "Give me one night of love, include all your erotic refinements, and I will give you one million francs." It was an offer she could not refuse, but she was totally unaware the marquis was much younger than the baron and much stronger than the three sons put together. The one night of love lasted from dusk to dawn and when he left, Nicchia remained in bed, very sore and completely exhausted, for three days.

Soon after turning forty, in fear of her fading looks and charms, Nicchia became a recluse in a Paris apartment in the Place Vendôme. She kept the windows shuttered, and the few friends allowed to call reported she had put sheets over all the mirrors. She remained there, living on her well-earned savings and the King of Italy's pension, until she died aged sixty-four.

Rudolph Valentino

He arrived in New York in 1913 unable to speak the language, an eighteen-year-old Italian farmer's son sent abroad by a family embarrassed by his behaviour. When he died in 1926, the queue of women waiting to see his body was eleven blocks long, and a dozen or more suicide victims in America and Europe were reported to have left notes citing Rudolph Valentino's death as their reason. In the space of thirteen years, he had gone from a lonely and involuntary immigrant youth, to gardener, dishwasher, dance-hall partner, model, potential blackmailer, gigolo and finally, Hollywood's greatest screen lover, whose studios protected their asset with bodyguards and private detectives to vet the unknown women determined to meet and seduce him.

He was handsome, suave, sleek and available. At first he was too proud to ask his conquests for money, but elegant and extremely rich Joan Sawyer recognized the young man's dilemma and, for a few weeks during 1915 after picking him up in a dance-hall, she kept Rudy as her exclusive lover. But she revealed too much in her pillow talk and Valentino took her money, and more still from another woman. He gave evidence against Joan, who was named as correspondent in a well-publicized divorce trial. Rudolfo Alfonzo Raffaelo Pierre Filibert Guglielmi di Valentina D'Antonguolla had come a long way. Waltzes and tangoes would keep that hungry wolf from his door, but Rudy was seeking his fortune. His dancing ability took him into cabaret and then vaudeville and he joined a touring act with jazz singer Al Jolson. Trouble with the police in New York drove him to Hollywood where, after playing bit parts and more dance routines, his potential as a screen romeo was finally recognized in 1921.

Tinseltown's publicity machine went to

JUST A GIGOLO

Vice squad detectives in New York learned a number of clients at a high class bordello run by socialite Mrs Georgia Thym had later been modestly blackmailed. They knew the lady sometimes brought in gigolos to service her friends and other wealthy women in the afternoons, at the same establishment. They suspected twenty-one year old Rudy was one of them. The madam was arested and so was he, but he was released after spending a few days in police cells. His involvement was never explained – police said he was detained as a "material witness", but never gave evidence. He left town and surfaced in California a few months later.

work and hysterical, swooning women flocked to the cinema to see the silent Rudy playing in *The Four Horsemen of the Apocalypse*, *Blood and Sand*, *The Eagle* and his most famous roles in *The Sheikh* and *Son of The Sheikh*. Strangely, the woman who captured his heart was thought to be a lesbian. Natacha Rambova posed as a Russian ballet dancer and choreographer, but was really the daughter of an Irish emigrant.

Under her thumb

The lady dropped her Russian image, left the ballet business and virtually took over Rudy's life and married him. Though he was already an acknowledged screen star and would eventually play named parts in fourteen full-length features, she wanted bigger and better parts and fought his battles with the studios, so that for the best part of two years he made no films at all. What really infuriated Paramount and United Artists was the publicity she attracted as his wife and agent. They wanted America's women to see Valentino as still available – to them! Worse still, she took to directing some of his parts, hoping to emulate the image and idolatry Douglas Fairbanks had built up, and managed to portray Valentino as effeminate.

MARRY IN HASTE ...

Valentino's encounter with the marriage ceremony was unsuccessful, to say the least. In 1919 he wed Jean Acker. Both were seeking their big opportunity in Hollywood, but the actress had barely said, "I do" when she realized her mistake. Back at their apartment she quickly said, "I don't", and dashed inside, bolting the door. That marriage was never consummated. Valentino failed to wait the stipulated time for the annulment, and when he went to the altar with Natacha Rambova – whose real name was Winnie Shaughnessy – he was arrested for bigamy and spent his honeymoon night in another police cell. Another court heard his story of the unconsummated original marriage and charges were dropped.

In *Monsieur Beaucaire* his performance was acclaimed but the critics were shocked to see him wearing wigs and a beauty spot, in silk outfits and lace cravats and they savaged the man all the ladies adored. He was never popular with the male critics nor the male population and with Natacha, he became an easy target. But the movie-moguls won and the couple were divorced after a five-year partnership. Her real interest in Rudy lay outside the bedroom door.

The studios moved in the bodyguards to maintain their idol's image as he returned to single status and they put considerable pressure on Californian newspapers to keep any unwelcome items out of their gossip columns. One affair they most certainly did not want to report was his brief but passionate romance with Marion Davis, for the lady was publicly known as the mistress of William Randolph Hearst, owner and publisher of the huge chain of newspapers right across America. She decided to give the man up and introduced him to her close friend, one of Hollywood's hottest female properties, the star Pola Negri. The actress resisted him but Valentino, who could have had any one of thousands of attractive women in his bed at this time, was still a devoted romance seeker. He knew how to win a woman's heart and secretly entered Pola's apartment to sprinkle hundreds of rose-petals on her bed. She invited him back to clear them up and when she wrote her autobiography, years after his death, Pola conceded, "He took me that night in a perfect act of love. The way he used his body, the concentration in his eyes, his true sexuality just captured me."

How much more impact Rudolph Valentino might have had the world will never know. He died suddenly in New York at the age of thirty-one, his "lying-in-state" and eventual funeral accompanied by unbelievable scenes of hysteria. For many years after a strange, anonymous woman in black laid flowers on his grave and sat there silently for hours on end.

Mata Hari

If only the stories were true about the woman executed by the French towards the end of the First World War for acting as a double agent and spying on behalf of their German foes. If they were true, her persecutors would have raised a statue to her memory in the centre of Paris, rather than send Mata Hari before a firing squad. When police arrived to arrest her at a Paris hotel in February 1917, it was said she greeted them in a first floor suite, draped across a settee without a stitch of clothing. Inside St Lazare Prison, she performed nude dances for the pleasure of the guards, claimed another report. A lover is supposed to have tried to bribe the firing squad to use blanks and before the order to "fire" was given, she is alleged to have wriggled and shaken off her coat to reveal her naked body.

What proved to be true was that the phial of "invisible ink" found in her possessions turned out to be a solution of cyanide of mercury used, as she explained, for a self-injection after intercourse to avoid pregnancy. She also faced her executors without a blindfold, "so that I can look these men in the eye and they will know I have done nothing wrong," she said. It is also true that she slept with senior officers on both sides, but she confessed to "a love of the uniform," and even when she was operating as a prostitute in peace time, she would frequently go to bed with a soldier for nothing. No one claimed her body for burial after the execution so it was given to a Paris medical school for dissection where it was found there were fewer bullet wounds than there were rifles in the firing squad.

The evidence of espionage against her was thin. The French Government have kept the file and transcript from her court martial at Vincennes a secret for eighty years, and she always maintained her inno-

SCARRED FOR LIFE

Though she was supposed to be the first completely nude dancer to appear in public in Paris, others in the cabaret and stage line-ups claimed she wore a thin, gauze body-stocking to cover marks on her breasts. These were supposed to have been caused by her husband, who bit her so deeply that he left permanent scars.

cence. She was brought up in Holland, agreed that she promised to spy for French intelligence in Nazi-occupied Belgium, but denied accepting money from the German high command. "I gave them old scraps of information to make them believe I was on their side," the woman claimed. Officially, she expected to collect a million francs from the French who trained her as a seductive spy to obtain information from German officers.

She was born Margaretha Geertruida Zelle, and set out to become a teacher after leaving school, but found a husband by answering an advertisement in an Amsterdam lonely-hearts newspaper column. He was more than twice her age, a balding captain in the Dutch Colonial Army, but life with Rudolph MacLeod promised adventure. He was due to return to the old Dutch East Indies, to Java and Sumatra. The magic of marriage did not last long out there – he was unfaithful with the native girls and she flirted with his younger fellow officers. This is where the fascination for the uniform was born. MacLeod began to drink and beat her, and as a diversion, the young wife who was now a young mother of a son and daughter began her self-taught dancing lessons.

EASTERN PROMISE

She had very full, luscious lips with dark eyes and raven hair, a sultry and sexy look she perfected in the Far East. There she learned to dance by watching the native oriental girls perform religious ceremonies in their Hindu and Bhuddist temples. Mata Hari took big money for her favours from wealthy businessmen in Paris, and at the height of her fame, shortly before the war began, claimed she could earn 25,000 francs "for one night's performance."

From the temple dancing girls she took the name she would later use on stage, Mata Hari. In Malay language that means "Eye of the Day" – quite literally, the sun. She perfected the oriental dances, copying their rich costumes and dazzling jewellery so that when the couple returned to Europe she could leave her army husband and turn to show business in Paris. It was 1904 and the lady would soon be thirty. Her debut performance against a background of palm trees and mystic statues on stage turned into a reckless, unplanned striptease which sent her audience wild. Even the women stood and cheered and critics applauded her act. "Mata Hari ripped off the jewels covering her breasts, her naked body entwined with the flames and with the shadows, a shattering performance," one of them enthused.

A young German officer Lt. Alfred Kiepert recognized the pull of the uniform when he met the dancer in Berlin. "Don't take it off," she commanded back in her hotel room. He was rich, owned family estates, had a handsome face marked with a duelling scar, and was married. Mata Hari had to be content with moving into an arranged apartment. Back in Paris, there were other soldiers of varying rank and in Holland, a colonel in the Hussars

Wilhelm van der Capellen, held her attention for a while. When the war began in 1914 she was back in Berlin. Movement around Europe was much eaier than in the war which followed twenty-five years later, and it was at this time that her spying activities are believed to have begun.

Double agent

Undoubtedly she used her sex appeal to lure officers from armies on both sides into bed. She didn't need much training or too much luring. The fornication was very much two-way traffic but the important information went only one-way, she claimed, from the Germans to the French. But her masters in Paris didn't trust the woman. She was secretly followed to Madrid and witnessed in several meetings with Germans who were known intelligence agents. She met a Russian captain, Vladime de Massloff, who fought with the French, and fell in love with him as he recovered from battle wounds. It was too late – a few months later she was arrested.

At her trial she was defended by a former lover, elderly lawyer and magistrate Maitre Clunet. Her chief witness was another ex-bed mate Jules Cambon, a civil servant in the Foreign Ministry, but a third man failed to turn up. Recently retired General Messimy dictated a letter to the court through his wife, "I never knew this lady," it said and the defendant refused to expose him or their affair a decade earlier. Arrested in February, she was found guilty in July but did not face the firing squad until October. An unknown high-ranking officer volunteered that he was the father of her unborn child and, according to French law, such a woman cannot be executed. She denied pregnancy but the authorities waited, to be sure.

The Duke of Queensberry

Known as "Old Q", this leading member of the infamous Hellfire Club remained a bachelor and paid his doctor a daily retainer to keep him alive. The doctor was delighted to see William Douglas, the fourth Duke of Queensberry, continue his life-long vices of gambling and pursuing amorous women right up to the age of eighty-five. But the randy aristocrat helped his own cause by maintaining fanatical fitness, going to bed early with or without company, and ensuring his long line of partners were clean, which sometimes provided a secondary task for his physician. In the early days that meant he bedded as many teenaged virgins as possible and never took a prostitute, and by the end of his long, sexually active life, he had managed to escape venereal disease. For such a man, that was a rarity in the eighteenth century.

The Douglas family hailed from huge estates in the border country in Scotland and he had another title, Third Earl of March. Before his reputation as a rake and seducer became public knowledge around 1750, the mothers of several becoming young ladies sought him out. He accepted their invitations to dinner and week-end house-parties, but marriage was the last thing he had in mind, and when the Duke's true mission in life was discovered, the order to lock up your daughters went out. Later in life, the widows and divorcees went in pursuit, deciding they could look after themselves or better still, abandon themselves, but right through his life the Duke of Queensberry was never attracted to older women. It was the poet William Wordsworth who was so appalled at the man's complete disregard for public opinion that he gave him the title of "Degenerate Douglas".

Soon after a group was formed calling themselves the Friars of St Francis,

PLAYING BALL

Old Q was an inveterate gambler and instituted many renowned and unique bets in the mid-1700s, most of which he managed to win, but often at tremendous personal cost. He bet a group in his club a message could be delivered fifty miles in one hour, then set about hiring hundreds of farm workers. The message was secreted inside a ball which was then thrown, one to another, right across country.

he was a natural to be invited as a member. They became known as the Medmenham Monks and later as the Hellfire Club, a collection of profligate, middle-aged men who were members of Parliament, wealthy dukes, earls and baronets – the brainchild of Sir Francis Dashwood. The club had as its motto, "Do what you please. Dare to despise convention," and members obeyed that very edict. Meetings of this highly clandestine club were held in a secret chamber at the old Cistercian Abbey beside the River Thames at Medmenham. The Dashwood estates are at High Wycombe in Buckinghamshire, and the well known caverns in the chalk hills of the Chilterns where more meetings were held, are close by. They were nothing more nor less than very well planned orgies for the exclusive pleasure of the noble members gathered there. Masked women – some of them paid prostitutes and others titled ladies known by one or two members for their licentiousness – would appear dressed in nun's habits. The masks stayed in place but the habits were soon cast off as the night's amusement began and the random coupling got under way.

A BALCONY SCENE

In his eighties, the duke used to sit on the balcony of his flat immediately overlooking Piccadilly. He would ogle passing young ladies and drop notes down to them. The older prostitutes would wave up to him, and it was said that if a man could sit for a day with him on the balcony, the result would be a night to remember.

No one knows when the club held its first meeting but it was dissolved in 1763 when stories of the final orgy became public, the year after its founder, Dashwood, was made Chancellor of the Exchequer. The club was supposed to worship the devil, holding the occasional Black Mass, and a newly elected M.P. John Wilkes dressed up a monkey as Satan and released the animal into the meeting. It frightened the life out of everyone present but the jape was the last straw for the old Earl of Orford, and it sent him insane. As a reprisal, the Earls of Queensberry and Sandwich identified Wilkes as the author of an "obscene libel" – he had written the pornographic "Essay on Woman" – and he was forced to flee abroad to avoid prosecution.

Degenerate Douglas was not sorry to see the Hellfire club disbanded, as it had always appeared to be an elaborate and unnecessary way to gain a woman's favours. With his wealth he could afford to be a patron of the opera and Italian singers visiting London held a definite attraction for him. He was also a patron of half a dozen theatres and from the ranks of their actresses, he would hold beauty parades in his bedroom. Those he selected over the years were often thankful for his company and accommodation, and dutifuly showed their gratitude.

From Rome came the Countess Rena, who stayed on in London for two years and introduced him to a beautiful friend, Marquesa Fagniani who had been a famous opera star in Milan. The lady's husband had huge gambling debts when they met – the marquis got paid and the marquesa got laid, an arrangment which suited Queensberry perfectly. When the woman unexpectedly decided their affair should end, Old Q took the marquis back to the tables to run up a few more debts. He lived according to the aged Italian proverb, "A man with an erection is in no need of advice." Throughout his life many women had loved the old duke and wrote passionate messages of thanks for their times together, and his last act was to read through nearly a hundred of these letters found strewn across his death-bed.

The Lascivious Ladies of London

The oldest profession in the world could be classified as almost a noble calling two or three hundred years ago. Certainly the noblemen called more often than most on these ladies in the upper echelons of their career, and they were frequently publicly adored and regarded as minor heroines. Abroad they were given the grander title of courtesan, and were revered and admired. In London they became escorts of Royalty, even wives of the nobility, their company was sought at parties and their advice heeded in the fashion houses. None was so famous as Nell Gwynn, the orange seller who became an actress and the acknowledged mistress of the King. Kitty Fisher started life as a lowly milliner, and was soon able to charge a hundred guineas (£105) for a night in her bed – an absolute fortune as long ago as 1760. Fifty years later Harriette Wilson, who turned professional at the age of fifteen, settled a £1,000 debt with half an hour of her services.

Nell Gwynn

Nell was brought up in a bawdy house run by her mother in Covent Garden, close to where London's famous opera house stands today. Her father died in a debtor's prison in Oxford and she never learned to read or write. But Nell had an amazing personality and she was reckless, entertaining and witty, with a constant infectious laugh. Her dresses, cut low, exposed a magnificent cleavage, her fine features topped off with an amazing head of chestnut-coloured hair. She was a barmaid before she reached her teens and joined her sister selling oranges outside the Theatre Royal in Drury Lane, where the leading actor Charles Hart soon took her to bed. In return, he allowed her to play small parts and her natural talent allowed Nell to become the first actress with a talking part on the London stage – until then, in 1667, fresh-faced, adolescent boys had always played female roles.

She was a brilliant comedienne, a fine singer and dancer and "pretty, witty

ITCHING AND SCRATCHING

A sheet of printed poetry, unsigned, circulated in London capturing the scene. It might easily have been delivered by the lady herself before an appreciative audience:

Hard by Pall Mall lives a wench called Nell

King Charles the Second he kept her.

She hath got a trick to handle his prick

But never lays hands on his sceptre.

All matters of State, from her soul she does hate

And leaves them to the politic bitches.

The whore's in the right, for 'tis her delight

To be scratching just where it itches.

Nell" rapidly became the darling of London and mistress of Lord Buckhurst, the 6th Earl of Dorset, who introduced her into Royal circles. This was London two years after the Great Plague had taken thousands of lives, a year after the Great Fire had decimated the City's grand churches and buildings, and Charles the Second had been on the throne six years after a long period abroad in exile.

The queen was unable to bear children, and the king needed cheering up. Enter Nell, who was now making a name for herself delivering cheeky and sometimes vulgar monologues. After a few visits to the Royal bedchamber, His Majesty set her up in a house close to the palace, and she was happy to be but one of his many mistresses and mother to two of his several illegitimate children. Nell spent the best part of twenty years entertaining the king and his friends, and the common people of London loved her.

She was never granted a title herself but persuaded the king to make the elder of their two sons the Duke of St Albans. The king's deathbed request in 1685 was "Let not poor Nelly starve." She had always remained faithful to her Royal lover and now, at the age of thirty-five, was deeply in debt. The new monarch, James II, paid these off and settled her with a pension of £1,500 a year, but in 1687 she suffered a bout of apoplexy, was partially paralysed and died. Her funeral sermon at the imposing church of St Martin's in the Fields in Trafalgar Square was delivered by a future Archbishop of Canterbury. Its theme: "Joy

THE PROTESTANT WHORE

A celebrated story depicts Nell Gwynn's popularity among the masses. She had a serious rival in another of the king's mistresses, the haughty and high-born but nonetheless beautiful, Louise de Keroualle, the Duchess of Portsmouth, who was both French and Catholic, not a popular mixture at that time. Nell's carriage was mistaken for her rival's one day and was being stoned and jeered by passers-by when she poked her head out of the window and declared, "Pray good people, I am the Protestant whore," and departed to their cheers.

shall be in Heaven over one sinner that repenteth, more than over ninety and nine just persons who need no repentance."

Kitty Fisher

A hundred years later, another young lass became the darling of London's society. She was never a Royal mistress or anyone else's mistress, accepting all-comers and levying fees according to the services they required until she married a former client. Kitty Fisher was born in central London. Her parents were poor German emigrants, but made sure she had an education before sending her out to work as a dressmaker. She was petite, pretty and provocative, drawing the attention of husbands accompanying their wives to the shop where she worked.

Kitty was not slow to appreciate opportunity and after a brief affair with a handsome cavalry officer, set herself up in a flat in fashionable Mayfair. A hundred guineas to stay the night was paid by leading politicians and titled gentlemen, including the Nation's favourite soldier, General Sir John Ligonier, and leading sailor First Lord of the Admiralty George Anson, who in turn introduced her to the Duke of York, younger brother of the reigning king. This was how fresh clients arrived at her door – personally introduced by their friends – and Kitty decided to charge no more and no less than her usual fee for her new Royal patron. In the morning, before Miss Fisher had time to announce the price, the duke handed her £50, which she took between finger and thumb and, accompanied by his blushes, placed it on a muffin and ate the note for breakfast. Hearing this story, another client and former Royal aide, the Earl of Pembroke, was so ashamed he settled a pension of £1,000 a year on Kitty, which also allowed him certain visiting rights.

The lady was not aware she was so well-known in public eyes until an accident occurred in St James Park, outside Buckingham Palace. Kitty was

HIDE & SEEK

● ● ● ● ● ● ● ● ● ● ● ● ● ● ● ● ●

Kitty regularly entertained Lord Montfort, a dwarf whose head did not quite reach the level of her navel. He was just about to leave her home when a messenger preceeding another of her clients, the Earl of Sandwich, arrived to say his lordship was on the way. Hurriedly, she hid her dwarf lover under her hooped skirts, walked him to the corner of the street and let him go. The story was related to Parliament, in the House of Lords, by an angry peer taunting the earl – probably yet another client.

● ● ● ● ● ● ● ● ● ● ● ● ● ● ● ● ●

thrown from her horse, and the incident was reported in verse in the *Universal Magazine*:

> *Dear Kitty, had thy only fall*
> *Be that thou met with in The Mall*
> *Thou had deserved our pity;*
> *But long before that luckless day,*
> *With equal justice might we say,*
> *Alas, poor fallen Kitty!*

A client paid the eminent Joshua Reynolds to paint her portrait, then another, a wealthy former member of Parliament named John Norris – himself one of the leading rakes of his day – fell in love with Kitty and, much to his family's fury, they were married in 1766. Sadly, his bride succumbed to tuberculosis and died five months later.

Harriette Wilson

Harriette Wilson could not be more different to her illustrious predecessors, though she shared their manner of living. She was born into reasonable wealth in London's Mayfair in 1786 and to the day he died, Swiss scientist John Dubochet was totally unaware that four of his seven daughters earned their living on their backs. The Dubochet sisters were famous for their parties. They were talented musicians and fluent in both German and French, attracting a host of London's leading young men to their beds. Harriette, who adopted the name Wilson from one of her first clients in her mid-teens, was tutored by her sisters and soon outstripped all of them. The Dubochet sisters did not come cheap, but Harriette's fees were easily the highest and so was her lifestyle.

Her wardrobe was reputedly the most expensive in London, and forced to pay a gown-maker's bill in a hurry, she claimed the £1,000 was settled by half an hour in bed. Apparently she was not one to lie back and let her partner enjoy himself – she entered the fray with abandon, determined to achieve her own pleasure, and while her sisters took comfortable and accommodating husbands, Harriette relished her role as a well-paid, well-admired prostitute. She sometimes tested her lovers with a brisk, two hour long walk in the park, on the grounds that if the man could not keep pace with her in the park, he had no chance between the sheets. She lived briefly with the Marquis of Lorne, "an excellent walker," she reported, maintained a long affair with Lord Ponsonby and then the youthful Marquis of Worcester, an infantry lieutenant, asked her to marry, which set off a peculiar merry-go-round in her life.

The young man's parents, the Duke and Duchess of Beaufort, were infuriated. They refused their permission and, learning of his intention to move in with Harriette until he reached twenty-one and didn't need their consent, father had him posted to the Duke of Wellington's staff in Spain. Old Beaufort met his potential daughter-in-law and proposed she should forget the young man in return for an annuity of £500. She agreed, then the duke knocked it down to £200, so she took him to court and won a settlement of £1,500. In Spain, Wellington learned of this arrangment and paid Harriette a call on his next trip home, making a few more forays before he returned to battle. The Duchess of Beaufort recounted the story to her then secret lover Richard Meyler, a farmer and landowner who decided to see what all the fuss was about. The duchess was furious again when Harriette moved in with him.

At the age of thirty, she started to believe her best performances were in the past and left for Paris to find a fresh, if somewhat older, string of suitors. From there, now married and recognizing the inevitable as she approached fifty, Harriette Wilson

A WOMAN OF MANY WORDS

• • • • • • • • • • • • • • • •

It was Harriette who drew the renowned retort from the Duke of Wellington – "publish and be damned" – when she demanded £200 for his name to be left out of her autobiography. He was not alone in this view but the book, entitled *Harriette Wilson's Memoirs of Herself and Others*, was a sell-out, and she made a £10,000 profit from its sales, and more still from those who paid up for anonymity. At the age of eighteen, the bold and lusty Harriette had become a kept-woman in a country house. She dared to write to the Prince of Wales, who replied in three lines, proposing nothing more than a simple meeting. She dashed off another letter, "to travel fifty miles in this weather, merely to see a man with only the given number of legs, arms, fingers and so forth, would be madness. If you can do anything better, in the way of pleasing a lady, than ordinary men, write directly. If not, then adieu, Monsieur le Prince."

• • • • • • • • • • • • • • • •

decided to write her memoirs which began, "I shall not say why and how I became, aged fifteen, the mistress of the Earl of Craven." The book went to thirty reprints and continued to sell well in spite of a rival publication, written soon after, by a long-time adversary and high-class whore who titled her own memoirs *Confessions of Julia Johnstone, written by Herself in*

Contradiction to the Fables of Harriette Wilson. According to Julia, the portraits in the other woman's book were true and lifelike, "as to the rest, so much of the truth has been distorted so as to conceal her shameful and scandalous behaviour." She failed to mention that much of the scandalous behaviour complained of was probably omitted because those present at the time had paid good money for the details to be left out.

Rasputin

A group of Russian patricians took no chances when they decided this Siberian peasant should die. He was a seducer, a flagellant, a healer and holy man, with undue influence on their ruler's wife, the Empress Alexandra. Among the assassins as the great Russian Revolution dawned were Prince Feliks Yusupov, related by marriage to the Czar, Grand Duke Dmitry Pavlovich, the Czar's nephew, Vladimir Purishkevic, member of the Duma parliament, and Dr Lazovert, their adviser. Their intended victim was a man of forty-five, Grigori Yefimovich, who grew up in Pokrovskoye where as a youth, the villagers had given him the name Rasputin meaning "debaucher".

Yusupov invited the holy man to his home where they plied him with food and wine, poisoned with cyanide by the doctor. He failed to die and was shot twice, by his host and by Purishkevic. The doctor pronounced Rasputin still alive so they tied him up and cut a hole in the ice covering the Neva River in St Petersburg. They threw him in and were finally satisfied he would drown. The date was December 30, 1916. His crime was not truly the power he wielded inside the Royal palace. In male-dominated Russia, the religious Rasputin had phenomenal success with the ladies who admired his sexual accoutrement, a massive penis measuring thirteen inches long at its proudest moments. He had the sex drive to go with the equipment.

ALEXANDRA'S ADVISOR

By the year 1911, Rasputin's behaviour was virtually a national scandal. Church and government leaders tried to intervene but if they put pen to paper, these men might find themselves transferred to remote spots in Russia, such was his influence at the palace in St Petersburg. When the Empress Alexandra acquired more powers in 1915, she adopted Rasputin as her chief adviser and some of his detractors disappeared forever. The servants at the palace merely added to his conquests, and there was room to wonder whether the first Lady had joined them.

As a youth, he liked to swim at a lake near home and in hiding, the beautiful wife of an army general, Irina Danilova Kubasova, watched him strip and swooned in delight at the sight of his body. The woman decided she must have him and quickly planned the mass seduction of sixteen-year-old Grigori with the help of six of her maids. One girl lured him to the house and up to the bedroom where the others and their mistress waited. He was hooded, doused in cold water and dragged to the bed, where he was soon a willing participant in his own initiation rites. In the months and years that followed, there were few maids in the village left in need of initiation, and a good number of the married ladies had also discovered what this young man had to offer.

At twenty he married Praskovia Dubrovina and at twenty-six he had fathered four sons, but by then he had joined a religious sect, the Khlysty. A visit to the same lake where he sported with three local peasant girls is said to have sent him on the religious trail when he noticed a reflection of himself on the surface of the water. The sect were flagellants who indulged themselves in all manner of sexual practices, and from them Rasputin acquired a novel approach to women which secured an amazing response rate. This was along the lines that in order to be redeemed, one must first be a sinner. Infidelity for a married woman and the forbidden pleasures of the flesh for a virgin were as good a sin as many, and more enjoyable than most. Through fornication lies the route to redemption became the regular theme of his sermons. There was plenty of redeeming going on around Rasputin and all the while Praskovia maintained home, brought up the children and stayed faithful.

HOLY RELIC

• • • • • • • • • • • • • • • • •

At the time of his death, one of the assassins is supposed to have castrated Rasputin and a servant girl at Yusupov's home recovered the severed phallus and kept it. Fleeing Russia at the time of the revolution, she went to Paris where the organ was kept, presumably preseerved and mummified by an expert, in a polished oak box and appeared, said an alleged observer in 1968, "like a blackened, overipe banana, about a foot long."

• • • • • • • • • • • • • • • • •

Randy redemption

This strange man with deep staring eyes who claimed he could see into the future cultivated a very real skill administering homeopathic medicines. As he crossed Russia, the sect acquired many converts, mainly female, and he cured many ailments as well as their biblical psychological problems. He developed and extended the Khlysty's traditional sex practices, encouraging wife-swapping and congregational orgies, but life was not always selfish indulgence for Rasputin. The redemption he offered allowed scores of women ridden with guilt to enjoy their sexual release for the very first time. If that happened to be with the preacher, then both sides were happy and relieved. An apartment for more private prayer in St Petersburg was made up of a waiting room downstairs with the "holy of holies", as he called his bedroom, upstairs.

His faith healing brought Rasputin to the notice of Nicholas and Alexandra, the Royal couple whose son Alexis Nikolayevich was heir to the Imperial Throne of Russia and a chronic haemophiliac. He sincerely eased the boy's suffering and impressed the Czarina so much, it was said she too fell under the holy man's spell. Her letters to him bore sexual overtones, but it was more than any Russian leader's life was worth to publicly add that to the long list of his misdeeds.

To an outsider it seemed all his women, aristocratic consorts, military wives, prostitutes or maidservants, were all the same provided they could cope with his equipment and satisfy his huge lust. But with a head of state at the Royal palace, it was a different matter. Whether it was his mysticism, his religion, his homeopathy or his thirteen-inch member, the political conspirators decided enough was enough and Rasputin must be despatched. It was an ignominious – if astonishingly well-resisted – death for a man whose exploits have inspired a film, songs and several books in the last seventy five years.

Adah Isaacs Menken

She was tall and slender, with magnificent legs and high breasts, an intellectual actress who could write praise-worthy poetry. Yet her fame spread across the Atlantic to Europe because at outdoor shows she liked to perform near-naked, strapped to the back of a running horse. Adah Isaacs Menken achieved stardom as she repeated the scene indoors, as a stage-exit, playing a dramatization of Lord Byron's poem *Mazeppa* all over America and in London and Paris. What was a nice Jewish girl from New Orleans doing on stage without any clothes on? Acquiring a legion of fans, that's what, and allowing a few of those fans to keep her in the luxury she cherished. She loved champagne and fed her dogs sugar cubes soaked in brandy. Adah was some lady and in the mid-1800s could have commanded much more than the $200 she asked her over-nighters.

A few years earlier, stranded in Cuba, she could be had for the price of a meal. Austria's baron Friedrich von Eberstadt picked her up when she was eighteen and her name was Dolores Adios Fuertes. He offered her family financial support and Dolores a wonderful free holiday in the Caribbean, and perhaps a little spending money. Impressed with his title and wealth, both mother and father urged her to go to Cuba with the baron. Deflowered and then dumped on the beach, she was desperate for the price of a return ticket to New Orleans and made the money in time-honoured way in Havana, competing with the local girls. Fortuitously, the sweetest revenge would come her way though she had to wait ten years and travel six thousand miles to achieve it.

> ## DUELLING LADIES
>
> Adah had travelled with circus shows in her early days in show business, and learned to become an excellent pistol shot. Unaware of this expertise, a woman in Paris accused Mrs Menken of making eyes and then an assignation with her man. Adah challenged her to a duel and, just to let the Frenchwoman know what she was in for, pulled a pistol and plugged a shot through her hat. "Je m'excuse, je m'excuse," cried the would-be duellist.

That became her way of life, a paid prostitute in between the highly-acclaimed but not so well rewarded time on stage, but her exotic show-business career attracted the nocturnal patronage. The mining boom of '49 was still going strong when she took her mildly erotic *Mezappa* on tour, first in California then in Nevada. Silver miners in Virginia City threw nuggets up on stage, the mayor announced a new find would be named Adah's Lode, and a reporter on the local Territorial Enterprise came to call. He was better known in later years as Mark Twain. He showed her his and she showed him hers – poetry that is – and the two became lovers.

The change of title came when Dolores was twenty-one and she married a Cincinatti merchant, Alexander Isaac Menken. She added an "s" to the middle name and retained that for the rest of her life, even though she went through two more marriages. In New York she married Tom Heenan, the bare-knuckle boxer, and she was at the ringside when he fought a forty-two-round draw for the world heavy-weight championship in London. It was a luckless marriage – Adah didn't realize she was still officially wed to Menken who reported her to the police. But the scandal only served to make her more popular with an adoring public. Avoiding arrest, they had a wild honeymoon and a wild two years together before they divorced and she met a riverboat gambler Jim Barkley. He agreed to marry Adah when she was six months pregnant by him, but seventy-two hours into that honeymoon, the hot-blooded actress realized her mistake and left for Europe, never to set eyes on him again. Young Louis was born then Adah, realizing her opportunity for vengeance, decided to see if she could find that wretched baron in Vienna.

MAGAZINE MACHO

The woman known as the Naked Lady met the senior Alexandre Dumas in Paris, where she had read of his waning prestige as a ladies' man. He was, after all, well into his sixties, but Adah persuaded the writer to have a photograph taken for a magazine, with her in a tight-fitting and revealing dress draped all over him. The result was a return to his macho glories, and a more than satisfied bed-mate.

Having become a famous actress and accepted in the highest social circles, Adah was able to trap the man and arranged an innocent-looking meeting. He again tried to seduce her. She put him off but promised a night to remember if he would take her to a palace ball later that week and introduce her to Emperor Franz Joseph. Friedrich still held memories of Cuba and agreed. Unsuspecting, he waited beside her in the glittering line-up at the reception and as soon as her introduction was completed, Adah curtsied then dropped her cloak to the ground and stood before the emperor in a flesh-coloured body-stocking. To all intents and purposes she was naked, doing an Imperial Streak for the emperor who strode from the room in a fury. The baron was ruined. ·

However, Adah had a serious side to her nature and her poetry was good enough to be praised by Charles Dickens and Algernon Swinburne who offered a little criticism and some useful advice. In return, she sorted out a problem for Swinburne, who suffered periods of impotence unless he was spanked with the bare hands of the woman who happened to be lying beside him. Her syntax improved and so did his circulation but he realized he had not enough to offer a woman like Adah and introduced her to another writer, the wily and randy old novelist Alexandre Dumas senior. He was more than twice her age and had probably had twice as many women as she had men, but the two found they were sexually and intellectually suited, and Adah was with him when she died from an internal abcess tragically young at only thirty-three.

Cora Pearl

Gin, the drink which makes some women happy and some women cry, is widely known as Lady's Ruin and was certainly the downfall of this young lady. Enticed into a pub near her home in Devon, the teenage girl had her first taste of gin and unknowingly, her first taste of fornication. She woke up in bed next morning beside the merchant who had plied her with drinks and accepted the £5 note he offered. There were fifteen brothers and sisters at home, as well as an angry father, and she left that same day to start what amounted to an apprenticeship in a London brothel. Emma Eliza Crouch who was born in 1835, the same year as Adah Menken, learned well and learned quickly. Moving to Paris, she changed her name to Cora Pearl and was soon charging ten thousand francs for a night in her bed. On those occasions she was expected to remain conscious.

There were prostitutes a plenty and enough elegant courtesans to keep the men in Paris in raptures, yet Cora rose to the top of her profession with a string of lovers she termed her "Golden Chain". This included the great man himself, Emperor Louis-Napoleon the Third. She was taken to Paris by her boss, the owner of the Argyle Rooms, a bawdy house in London where she had learned her trade. Cora stayed on when he went home and turned independent. Within months she had acquired the first in her chain, the Third Duc de Rivoli Victor Massena, who provided an apartment and allowed her to entertain only the wealthiest of clients while reserving the mid-week afternoons for himself.

She had marquisses, counts and dukes, then moved up a notch, attracting to her clientele Prince William of Orange, heir to the Dutch throne. She was never a woman of the streets, even in her early London days, but managed to pick up another of her Golden Chain when she went ice skating on the frozen lake

DEBT COLLECTING

Her huge clothing bills forced Cora's newest lover into a duel. She was exactly twice the age of seventeen year old Prince Achille Murat, a great nephew of Napoleon the First who challenged her accuser, a man sent to collect the debt who went too far in describing the lady. The prince won the sword fight and spared his opponent's life, but when he fell heavily into debt himself, courtesy of Cora, he was sent by Napoleon the Third to Africa.

of a Paris park. The Duc de Mornay was enchanted. He was a powerful figure in France, half-brother to the emperor, and moved her into a huge house overlooking that same park, paying her twelve thousand francs a month. This was only a retainer, enough to pay the household bills, for the lady could charge almost as much for just a few hours of her time.

Cora could not claim to be a beauty but her amazing figure captivated the men who saw her body in its natural form. She loved throwing lavish parties and playing practical jokes that she thought up herself. A general was surprised to receive an invitation to her house and even more surprised when he arrived to find he was apparently the sole guest. Upstairs, she undressed him slowly and when there was nothing more to remove the party got under way. Several of his friends had been hiding in the woman's wardrobes and now riotously emerged to join in the fun. On another occasion, there were several guests present at a dinner party but no sign of the hostess when everyone went in to sit down. She arrived in a huge tureen and rose naked from the platter when the lid was raised.

CAUGHT WITH A CROP

● ● ● ● ● ● ● ● ● ● ● ● ● ● ● ● ●

Cora herself fought a duel, with riding crops. Her opposite number was Marthe de Vere, and the subject of their argument was a handsome young prince from Yugoslavia. The ladies fought a draw and both were forced to remain at home for two weeks to allow the wounds on their faces to heal. Neither received a call from the embarrassed prince.

● ● ● ● ● ● ● ● ● ● ● ● ● ● ● ● ●

She was the only lady at another dinner party. Her maid apologized for her absence as the men arrived, "Madame is in the bath." Eventually all the men were shown into the dining room and there was Cora, taking her ablutions in a tub topped up with champagne, and she filled a glass for each of her admirers. The men were invited to sit where they pleased and under a silver platter on each of their plates, they found an under-garment – a stocking, a suspender belt, a corset, separate layers of petticoats, and taking their turn, they dried the hostess and helped her get dressed, cursing their luck if they had drawn one of the less intimate garments. Later, when the cognac was served, she announced, "Do you know, there is only one of you with whom I am still a virgin."

The lady had a spectacular lover who had no titles but as a millionaire, Alexandre Duval enjoyed spoiling her with wonderful presents, splendid pieces of jewellery and for a birthday, sent round a new carriage with a pair of black horses. When he gave her a book Cora threw it down in disgust but each page was actually a thousand franc note. In despair, Monsieur Duval shot himself in her house and managed to survive, but when she complained only of the blood stains on the carpets, the love affair was at an end.

So many of these ladies wrote their memoirs and most, including Cora, sent little notes of what to expect to former lovers and clients. It frequently attracted the desired response, a reply accompanied by cash. But the ploy had little effect on Cora's dwindling reserves. She was broke, lonely and very sad when an English newspaperman who had known her since the far-off days in London bumped into her in the South of France. Julian Arnold took Cora back to his hotel, promised to get her back to Paris and put her to bed for the night. She re-appeared in his suite naked and explained, "I found it impossible to rest until I had shown you that, if Cora Pearl has lost all else, she still retains that which made her famous."

She died soon afterwards, hard-up and living alone, aged fifty-one.

CHAPTER 5

PRINCES, PRESIDENTS, POPES AND POLITICIANS

✩ ✩

The Borgias

Looking back at how the world's various leaders have behaved over the centuries, it is difficult to know where to begin. Retreat five hundred years, and few can command greater fame for their sexual exploits than the Borgias. This Spanish family moved to Italy and dominated Rome around the same time Christopher Columbus was setting sail across the Atlantic to make his discoveries, and gave that city's already infamous orgies a new dimension. In that year of 1492, Rodrigo Borgia purchased the highest office in the Catholic church and became Pope Alexander VI and almost without drawing breath, committed a majestic act of nepotism, making his son first an archbishop and then a cardinal while he was still in his teens.

It was then not unknown in Europe for men of the cloth to enjoy the favours of the fairest members of their congregations. But Rodrigo had long since scandalized his calling and embarrassed the College of Cardinals where he was a leading member, by the enormous number of children sired on his way to the top. He was a handsome six-footer, very strong with dark, piercing eyes, who took prostitutes for casual sex but carefully targeted most of his early conquests, many of whom were young virgins or teenage brides. One of his long-lasting mistresses was Vannozza Catanei, who bore him several children including Cesare – the eventual teenage cardinal – Giovanni, and Lucrezia, who would follow very much in their father's footsteps.

He wore his church robes at his sponsored orgies, featuring naked and nubile dancers who shunned the privacy of the bedroom for their after-show enjoyment and entertainment. Their partners competed for a prize awarded by Rodrigo to the man who copulated most times in one night, not necessarily with the same woman, and the countdowns took place in public. A report on one of his banquets appeared in a Roman Diary, "Fifty whores supped with the Pope and danced with his guests, first in their robes then naked. The floor was lit with candles and strewn with chestnuts gathered by the women who wriggled and recovered the nuts ... but were not allowed to use their hands."

The Pope's private harem

FATHER & SON

These were free-wheeling times in Rome, and no sexual acts were out-of-bounds even for a man destined to become the Pope. For four centuries historians have debated whether one of Lucrezia's children was conceived as she bedded either her father Rodrigo or brother Cesare, a charge brought by the second of her three husbands. Incest was not uncommon, but when a nobleman asked for permission to sleep with his own sister, Pope Alexander extracted a penance of 24,000 gold pieces, and granted his wish.

When he became Pope at the age of sixty, he established a private harem, and Italian noblemen, anxious to please the Pontiff, sent gifts of beautiful young women to join his exclusive collection. When his own sons delivered their personal presents, father took a particular liking to Giovanni's offering, a magnificent girl transported from Spain. The jealous Cesare responded by his brother knifed and thrown in the River Tiber. The killing of his favourite son was soon forgiven, and Pope Alexander even found time to persuade Michaelangelo to carry out the rebuilding of St Peter's Church.

Cesare Borgia was totally unscrupulous. His brother-in-law Alfonso, the Duke of Bisceglie, who opposed his elevation within the church, was attacked on the steps of St Peter's, then strangled by one of Cesare's servants. Teenage brother Jofre wed Sancia, and within weeks of their returning from honeymoon, Cesare began an affair with the beautiful young bride, his sister-in-law. By now father realized the family's sexual excesses must be curtailed, and told Cesare it was time for him to marry and, perhaps, settle down. Some wheeling and dealing was done behind the papal palace and beneath the throne of King Louis XII of France, who was under pressure from a favourite mistress and wanted his own marriage annulled by the church. He promised to persuade Carlotta, daughter of the King of Naples, to wed Cesare but not surprisingly, with his record, she refused.

From Paris, King Louis offered a substitute, and Charlotte d'Albret was given away by her father the Duke of Gayenne at a spectacular ceremony on May 12, 1499. According to the records of that time, Charlotte and Cesare coupled eight times before the cock crowed the following morning, watched by her ladies-in-waiting through the keyhole of their bedroom. His only legitimate child, a girl named Luisa, was the product of that marriage but Cesare soon moved on to other bedchambers. In Florence he was introduced to Fiametta di Michelis, a voluptuous music teacher, but when he was captivated then spurned by Dorotea Caracciolo, he had the woman kidnapped and guarded by nuns in a convent where, for the next two years, she was visited and violated by the cardinal.

HORSE PLAY

As a diversion from the normal sexual entertainment during one religious festival, the Borgias introduced horses on to the central floor of the Pope's palace. There were two mares in season brought to readiness by a small pony, a "teaser" unable to complete the act. Then four stallions were led in, and the guests cheered as they fought for mounting rights with the pair of more than willing mares joining in the fray.

Through his teens and twenties Cesare had no need to resort to rape, but the syphilis he contracted along the way was beginning to show. In between his duties at the altar and officiating at orgies, Cesare was also a soldier and considered a clever strategist on the battlefield. Opposed by an army in Northern Italy led by a woman, Caterina Sforza, his forces overcame her stronghold at Forli and Cesare decided the spoils of war, his for the taking, were Caterina's favours. He raped her and later declared "the woman defended her fortress rather better than her virtue." When his father died, Cesare's own time was running out. In Italy he was twice captured and gaoled but managed to escape, then in 1507, in exile in the north of Portugal, the man rode into an ambush and to make quite sure this third time, his enemies ran him through with a lance twenty times. Cesare had crammed a lot of living and loving into his thirty-one years. Lucrezia lived on, but retreated from the orgies for which her family have remained infamous until she died at the age of thirty-nine.

Catherine, Empress of Russia

The Russian court in the mid-1700s was obsessed with sex, firstly from the frantic desire to protect and extend the Romanov dynasty, secondly because there was no natural heir to the throne, and thirdly because the woman selected to correct this anomaly became an out-and-out raver. Never mind about the pregnancy bit, when she discovered the joys of copulation the second Catherine the Great turned her palace at St Petersburg into a fornicatorium. New lovers were first given a medical test by a doctor, then a virility test by a lady-in-waiting and if they came up to scratch were introduced into the Royal bedchamber for a graduation ceremony few would ever forget. This arrangement lasted until the lady was well into her sixties though by then, some of the young partners were more interested in the "teaser" downstairs who had recommended them upstairs.

For a woman who spent the first seven years of her married life gaining stimulation from a pillow between her legs, Catherine more than made amends as she grew older. Lineage to the throne of Russia, like various monarchies in Europe, was highly complicated in the eighteenth century. The reigning Empress Elizabeth in St Petersburg was left childless when her husband died, so she brought a favourite nephew from West Germany and ordered him to produce heirs. She gave him a new name and married him off to a Prussian lass who was a granddaughter of an earlier Czar, Peter the Great. She was sixteen and a voluptuous looking virgin, her bridegroom a year older. He was also eccentric, neurotic, impotent and sterile, so the empress switched her attentions to young Catherine and told her in no uncertain terms to get herself laid by someone who could do the business.

By then the woman had reached twenty-three but was still a virgin. The

PONY TALES

• • • • • • • • • • • • • • • • • •

Catherine's reputation was well known, within the capital, across Russia and throughout Europe. A widespread rumour had it that she died attempting intercourse with a pony, but in fact she suffered a massive heart attack going about her normal business in the palace.

• • • • • • • • • • • • • • • • • •

grand seduction was planned for an island in the Baltic Sea, the seducer a young Russian nobleman and army officer named Sergei Saltykov. He came highly recommended and had imperious orders from Empress Elizabeth to keep trying until he succeeded. As it turned out that command was both unnecessary and unwarranted. Catherine was both a willing and very able accomplice. Morever, although conception was swift, the lady miscarried twice so the couple were still at it a year later.

Eventually and triumphantly, a son Paul was born and immediately snatched away by Elizabeth to be installed as heir to her throne. Catherine had found her true vocation and quickly became pregnant again. A different father produced the same result but Elizabeth was bitterly disappointed when the boy died. Now Catherine knew how though, more would soon be on the way. She selected a handsome colonel in the Horse Guards, Grigori Orlov, who fathered three more sons. Her husband Peter couldn't understand how his wife kept getting pregnant. She hid the early signs under her hooped skirts but the secret was rather difficult to maintain each time she went into labour.

Catherine was approaching thirty-three in 1762 and her son Paul was still an infant when her unpopular and insane husband succeeded Empress Elizabeth and became Peter the Third. The new Czar lasted six months. Orlov and his two brothers conspired with Catherine to oust him and kill him, a move welcomed by the Russian populace. The lady herself, dressed in the uniform of a captain of the Imperial Palace Guard, led the coup and installed herself as Empress. She had sworn to conserve the Romanov dynasty so refused to marry Grigori, but kept him on at the palace where he found rich pickings for amorous interludes above and below stairs. The colonel became a defaulter when he deflowered his thirteen-year-old cousin, and was sacked. Another Grigori took his place, the cavalry's Major Potemkin.

He was no great shaker on the mattress, but Potemkin was a shrewd mover on the political scene and during her thirty-four-year reign, he became an adroit statesman. He helped Catherine quell the power of the Russian Orthodox priests, put down the

WHERE THERE'S SMOKE...

The impotent Peter, who was originally Duke of Holstein-Gottorp, on the borders of Germany and Denmark, loved a good fire. Among his many eccentricities he was also a pyromaniac, so to divert attention from the birth of Catherine's third child, her manservant set fire to his own house and Peter watched in glee as it burned down, concealing the cries of his wife nearby.

massive Pugachov Rebellion, seize the Ukraine and altogether grab another 200,000 square miles of agricultural land beyond the country's borders to solve the food problem inside. However, it was his domestic policy that impressed his ruler. Realizing his own inadequacy, he set up the doctor and lady-in-waiting routine to provide an endless line of virile lovers for the Empress, mostly drawn from the ranks of her young Army officers.

She was never a lady for one-night stands but there were few men even half her age, who could keep up with Catherine's prodigious appetite for sex. They were examined, tried out and installed in a special apartment connected to the empirical boudoir immediately above by a private staircase. A day job around the palace was provided to keep up appearances, but the night job was far more important. They performed to her command and during a period of sixteen years she went through thirteen of these soldier-stallions who finally limped away with huge gifts of money, country dachas and estates, all paid for from the national exchequer.

KING OF THE POLES

● ● ● ● ● ● ● ● ● ● ● ● ● ● ● ● ● ●

Count Stanislaus Pontiakowski was welcomed into her bed and rewarded when Catherine made him King of Poland. He was a better lover than a ruler and unable to control the people, so his former mistress sacked Stanislaus and obliterated Poland from the map – annexing the major part into Russia and dividing the rest between Austria and her homeland Prussia.

● ● ● ● ● ● ● ● ● ● ● ● ● ● ● ● ● ●

As the lady said, "I shall be an autocrat, that's my trade; and the good Lord will forgive me, that's his." When these soldiers realized their manhood was on the wane, some tried to keep going with aphrodisiacs. This cost Lieutenant Aleksander Lanskoy his life, as he was left with insufficient strength to combat a bout of 'flu. Another young officer had enough stamina left over to put himself about among the young courtiers, and Anatole Dmitriev was allowed to marry a very pregnant lady-in-waiting. The empress was now into her fifties and more understanding, so when Captain Ivan Rimski-Korsakov, grandfather of the great composer, returned to Countess Bruce who had originally tried him out downstairs, the Empress forgave both of them.

For her sixtieth birthday, she decided to reward herself with yet another brand new lover and twenty-two year-old Platon Zubov from the Horse Guards passed all the tests with flying colours. He knew how to keep Her Highness happy, apparently spending no less time in her boudoir than any of his predecessors, and he occupied the apartment below for seven more years until she died in 1796.

King Henry VIII

The necessity of producing an heir for the throne of England was supposed to be the reason why Henry married six times, beheading and divorcing wives to leave him free to marry again. Infant deaths, miscarriages, still births and daughters followed in fairly rapid succession for Henry VIII first two wives, but his third queen gave him a son who later became king. She died and Henry, who by now had got into the swing of introducing a new woman to the royal bedchamber on a fairly permanent basis – apart from those on occasional visits – married three more times. He took England out of Catholic domination to make his first divorce possible but there was also the little matter of his lavish lifestyle.

The country was broke. Too much money had poured into the palace parties, which lasted days and weeks at a time. Funds were replenished when he ransacked the country's cathedrals and monasteries. The quest for a male heir sounded very noble but was rather more of a cover-up. His six wives are legendary and there is no doubt he got through a lot of feasting, jousting, wenching and lusting during his reign, but we must allow that the king's future, including the identity of his wife, was decided by guardians and advisors before Henry reached his teens.

A KING'S LUST

The king instituted his Bloody Statute when he was divorced from Catherine and the nation was removed from the Catholic church, and there were many dissenting clergymen, parliamentarians and noblemen – and a few of their wives – who went to the hangman's gallows or the axeman's block, and were subsequently disembowelled and dismembered. Some were even burned at the stake, and these years became known as the reign of terror. All to satisfy a king's lust.

Courting Catherine

Catherine of Aragon was his first wife, and the prince was only twelve when he virtually became engaged to the woman six years older who had been so recently widowed on the death of his brother. He married her at eighteen, six weeks after his coronation. The bride wore a splendid dress of white, proclaiming to the king, his courtiers and his people that she was indeed still a virgin. The same could not be said of the groom – he had been bedding the servant girls for the past couple of years. Indeed, the source of his venereal disease was never established but may well have arisen from these very early sexual forays. King Henry later suffered from syphilitic leg ulcers for several years.

Catherine was the daughter of King Ferdinand of Spain, slender and poised yet unable to converse easily in English. She quickly became pregnant but a daughter was stillborn then a son died only a few days old, followed by a premature birth Finally a healthy princess arrived. In eleven years she was pregnant seven times but only Mary, who would later sit on the throne, survived. Henry's eye wandered as the queen aged and came to rest on her young lady-in-waiting Elizabeth Blount, and the Queen was furious when her servant gave the King the son he desired. The boy could not be his heir and was given the title Duke of Richmond and smuggled quietly out of the palace. Henry was now determined to be rid of Catherine and petitioned the Pope for a divorce on the grounds that his eighteen-year marriage to his brother's widow was illegal.

STIFF NECKS

• • • • • • • • • • • • • • • • • • •

At their trials the verdict of guilty for anyone who dared to disagree with the king was a foregone conclusion. If a jury showed any sign that they were moved to acquit, Henry sent word that he would show them his "favourite remedy for stiff necks."

• • • • • • • • • • • • • • • • • • •

The truth is somewhat different. He was having an affair with Mary Boleyn, then switched his attentions to her sister Anne and told Cardinal Wolsey, "I have been discoursing with a young lady who has the wit of an angel and is worthy of a crown." That was the only way he was going to get this angel into bed, and the to-ings and fro-ings by churchmen and statesmen, between London and Rome, Paris and Madrid, Germany and the Netherlands, where Catherine had royal relatives, was astonishing. Anne held out for six years, while Henry was frustrated and in love. Eventually, he had his wicked way, with the Vatican and the young lady. Catherine became a divorcée and Miss Boleyn became Queen Anne.

The next five wives

As a brood mare, Anne was no better than her predecessor. One daughter, three miscarriages and a still birth later, Henry was on the lookout again.

With no time to cast around for support, no need to worry about the truth either, five men including her brother were all accused of having sex with the Queen and, along with the lady herself, they gave the executioner a busy morning. He had already dallied with another lady-in-waiting, Jane Seymour, and next day they were married. A son was soon born, on October 12, 1537 – at last! He was proclaimed instantly as Prince of Wales, Duke of Cornwall and Earl of Chester, but was better known as Edward VI, the boy who later assumed the throne aged nine. Twelve days after giving birth Jane died, and Henry was alone again.

Now Jane was no beauty but around the palace, Henry had been able to see for himself what the lady had to offer. He could not say the same for the next up to the altar so he sent the famed Hans Holbein over to paint her portrait. His canvas lied, the woman was tall, unfeminine, ungainly and entirely unremarkable, with a face badly pock-marked from childhood. The king was anxious to make protestant Germany his ally, so she sailed over and despite his shock on meeting her for the first time, Henry married Anne of Cleves, but that was as far as he went. There was no royal romance and she was relieved to relinquish her title and get out with her neck and her knickers intact.

That marriage was declared null and void on July 9, 1540, and on August 8, Catherine Howard appeared at court as the King's acknowledged escort. She was yet another lady-in-waiting, another teenager, and held to be the most beautiful of all his wives. Henry was fifty and showing signs of his dissolute life, but he was still a lusty monarch who expected to be obeyed so eighteen-year-old Catherine became his fifth wife and rapidly, his fifth ex-wife when he discovered she had previous and current lovers. Before the axe swung her way, she declared, "I die a queen, but I would rather die the wife of Thomas Culpeper." A nice thought, but rather irrelevant – Mr Culpeper was right behind her in line for the block.

Henry had finished with teenagers and virgins when he took his sixth and last wife. Katherine Parr was thirty-one, twice married and twice widowed, and in the four years she was at his side, she was more nurse than queen. Conscious to the last of his PR image, on his deathbed the king asked to be buried beside Jane Seymour, "the woman who died in order to give me a son."

John F. Kennedy

"John did for sex what his predecessor did for golf," said a commentator, referring to a pair of American Presidents. When John F. Kennedy was shot in Texas in 1963, the FBI agents who were also his bodyguards buried the file they had amassed on his carefree and constant sexual activities. Comedian Bob Hope joked when Dwight D Eisenhower stepped down after eight years in Washington's hot seat, "Would anyone like to buy four thousand golf stories?" That kind of aside on a presidential pastime was acceptable, but in the 1950s and 1960s the world's media looked the other way as heads of state misbehaved. In today's climate, President Kennedy would have been exposed as the enthusiastic profligate he undoubtedly was for nigh on twenty years.

Plagued by a weakness in his back and then injured in a ship-board fall serving in the US Navy during the First World War, John maintained he needed regular sex as a release. He told British Prime Minister Harold Macmillan, "without it I get bad headaches." But the frequent exercise did nothing for his back condition, in fact it did nothing at all, many of his women later described how he liked to remain horizontal and let them do all the work. He explained the back problem did not allow him to indulge in too much exertion. A friend and political aid, Senator George Smathers, had this to say about the man some years after the assassination, "No one was off-limits to John, not your wife, your sister or your mother. He had the most active libido of any man I've ever known and having two girls at the same time was one of his favourite pastimes."

It all began at the age of seventeen, when he was taken to a "safe brothel" in New York's Harlem by a school friend. At Harvard University, he was twice warned when he was caught with female undergrad-

IN THE GENES

His father provided the president with his sexy genes and his cavalier attitude to women. Joe, a self-made billionaire and firm ruler of the Kennedy clan, went from shipyard boss to government advisor and ultimately, America's ambassador in London. In the 1930s, leading film actress Gloria Swanson became his mistress and Joe took her on an Atlantic voyage to Europe along with his wife and sister, and later set up a production company to make her pictures. Twenty-five years later, Old Joe tried to date the rising young star Grace Kelly, telling her, "we Irish have to stick together."

uates in his room. He was free to play the field, making his way up the political ladder, and marriage at thirty-six to Jacquie Lee Bouvier did little to slow him down, neither did entry to the White House at forty-three, the youngest ever President of the United States and the first Catholic. He brushed aside threats to expose him and boldy ignored warnings to be more discreet. John was a ladies' man first, a statesman second.

F.B.I. surveillance began as soon as he arrived in Washington. As a young, wartime lieutenant in the navy, he had come to the bureau's attention through an affair with Inga Arvad, a Danish journalist based in America suspected of being a German spy. As a senator he kept two secretaries who agents coded as "Fiddle" and "Faddle", and having bugged his offices, the agents often listened to their dialogue with the boss –

BROTHERLY LOVE

• • • • • • • • • • • • • • • • • •

According to Marilyn Monroe, she copulated with the president at private homes, hotel suites, hurriedly in spare rooms at house-parties and on one occasion when she was smuggled aboard the presidential plane. John was happy to share her with brother Bobby, and a Monroe biographer claimed that on the night she made headlines by sexily singing "Happy Birthday" at the president's forty-fifth birthday party in Madison Square Garden, Bobby had already visited the star's dressing room. Her hairdresser said, "He left after fifteen minutes. Miss Monroe was red-faced, flustered and giggling when she called me back and asked me to help get herself together."

• • • • • • • • • • • • • • • • • •

which had nothing to do with business. When he became president, they were horrified when John began an affair with the dark-haired, sensuous Judith Campbell Exner, for she was having a parallel affair with Mafia boss Sam Giancana. Bureau chief J. Edgar Hoover suspected she may have been put in purposely to compromise the president, and cautioned him. In her memoirs published more recently, Judith said they were introduced by singer Frank Sinatra, and the one time she refused the President was the night he invited her to become the second lady in bed at his hotel.

John knew his wife was aware of his infidelity ut few knew the extent of his wild behaviour. He had women spirited into the White House when she was away, and sported with them naked in his private swimming pool before retiring to an ante-room. Photographs were shown to an aide revealing Kennedy leaving the home of a young woman recently hired to his staff, a magazine had copies, but when the boss was asked for his instructions, John merely laughed. The pictures were never published. The same thing happened years earlier, when a set of pictures showed him lying beside an undressed and over-endowed girl on a beach in Florida. Invited to comment Kennedy said, "Yeah, I remember her, she was great."

The President's Pimp

His brother-in-law actor Peter Lawford, married to Patricia – one of the five Kennedy sisters – was known around Hollywood as the "President's pimp", as he lined up aspiring starlets and more established actresses, reportedly Jayne Mansfield, Gene Tierney, Angie Dickinson, Lee Remick and finally Marylin Monroe. They met when she was still just married to baseball star Joe DiMaggio, continued a lengthy affair after that divorce, and went right on through her next marriage to playwright Arthur Miller. They met at hotels in New York and California, at Lawford's beach house and at Frank Sinatra's and Bing Crosby's homes in Palm Springs.

Monroe entertained ideas that she might be asked to marry him, "Imagine me as First Lady?" she said often, and not always in jest. But Kennedy had other fish to fry. "He was incredible, just like the rooster in a hen house," said a long-serving member of his staff. "Bam, bam, bam. At parties John would take a girl into the library, sit her on a desk, down with her panties, up with her dress, and five minutes later it was all over. The lady probably never knew how it all got started. Many a time I told him, "you forgot to zip up" as he got outside, looking around for someone else." Stripteaze artiste Blaze Starr claimed she made love to Kennedy in the middle of his presidential campaign, in 1960, "in a closet in a New Orelans hotel. My fiancé, the governor Earl Long, was hosting a party next door," she said.

His last long-term mistress was Mary Pinchot Meyer, a wealthy woman about town in Washington and recently divorced from senior C.I.A. official Cord Meyer. Mary shared his sense of adventure. She told friends they smoked marijuana together in a White House bedroom when Jackie was away or they met at her place in Georgetown. She carefully chronicled their affair in two diaries. Soon after Kennedy died, she was shot jogging beside the Potomac River. Her killer was never traced – and the diaries disappeared.

The Bonapartes of France

"Not Tonight Josephine"... a famous quip wearily muttered by the first Emperor of France, sweetly uttered by a million lovers all over the world, and a famous phrase used to launch a thousand advertising campaigns. How many of us realize those whispered words by Napoleon Bonaparte are based on his true life? Unlike his nephew, Napoleon the Third, who also ruled France and was a devoted sexual athlete, the man known two hundred years ago as Le Petit General pursued women to prove his dubious manhood. A favourite sister Pauline got the general's share – excessive sexual activity was diagnosed as a cause of her death. The nephew, who was called Louis-Napoleon when he became emperor, honoured his pillow-promises by despatching armies into battle. Many men lost their lives in the cause of his sexual conquests.

The first Napoleon advanced his career rapidly in the army. He was a brigadier-general at twenty-four, enjoying the by-products of fame and success with a series of ladies. But when he decided it was time to marry, he sought the safety of older, mature women after failing with a young beauty who went on to become Queen of Sweden. By now he was dabbling in politics and an adviser, anxious to dispose of his mistress, arranged for her to meet the gallant soldier who was instantly smitten and seduced. The lady became his first wife, Josephine de

MON PETIT GENERAL

"Mon Petit General," was indeed a fitting description for the former artillery officer, humbly born in Corsica, twice his country's ruler and twice exiled abroad. Following his defeat at Waterloo in 1815, he was imprisoned on the island of St. Helena in the South Atlantic, where he died six years later. Doctors were fascinated with the ailments which finally killed him – his pituitary, renal, thyroid and gonad glands were failing and shrinking his body. His height was reduced by several inches, his hands and feet by several sizes, and the autopsy revealed that Napoleon's penis had shrunk to only one inch, and his testicles were minuscule. The predatory Josephine mocked her husband's nocturnal performance, and soon after he became ruler of France another phrase, from her lips this time, was soon acclaimed in Paris. "Bon-a-parte est Bon-a-rien," she said – Bonaparte is good for nothing !

Beauharnais, a Creole courtesan already famed for her insatiable appetite and she outflanked, outfought and outwitted Napoleon in the Battles of the Boudoir. Exhausted by her demands, he fled the honeymoon bed after just two nights. During their fourteen years of marriage and his countless military campaigns across Europe, the lady made no secret of her lusty lifestyle and she found satisfaction at home with her own army of lovers.

Through an earlier marriage Napoleon fathered two children, and the general claimed Josephine was barren. In between military campaigns, their tempestuous couplings failed to produce an heir. Denying her accusations of impotence, he set about proving his manhood with a string of mistresses and he cuckolded loyal officers who served under him, rapidly seducing their wives after sending their husbands away to fight. The Emperor adored a "good set of buttocks" – not exclusively on the female form, it was claimed – and in Cairo, another of his officer's wives, Pauline Foures, pandered to his whim by wearing skin-tight white pantaloons below uniforms of gold-braided jackets and plumed hats.

> ### DIPLOMATIC AFFAIRS
> ● ● ● ● ● ● ● ● ● ● ● ● ● ● ● ● ●
> Unlike his predecessor, Napoleon III went public with his affairs, which brought a rebuke from a leading member of the government during a speech in the French Senate: "The emperor is not sufficiently careful in his intercourse with the fair sex and out of sheer consideration for the country, His Majesty ought not to place himself in the power of this or that adventuress." The emperor was not impressed. He was propositioned by the Italian Countess di Castiglioni, and was admitted to her bed on the guarantee that he would send an army to rid her country of its Austrian oppressors.
> ● ● ● ● ● ● ● ● ● ● ● ● ● ● ● ● ●

Revolutions and periods of unrest in France brought Napoleon to the throne as emperor in 1799, leading a military coup at the age of thirty. Ten years later, most of Europe was under his control or direct influence, and though he was too busy to conduct his own romances, his political aide-de-camp Duroc assumed the duties of the emperor's pimp. Napoleon would return from dealing with the affairs of state in Paris to his private apartments in the Tuileries to find unknown ladies ready and willing, waiting naked in his bed. He was very quick, but they were not allowed to complain about any feature of his performance. In public his sympathies, if not tendencies, were noted when he refused to introduce laws banning homosexuality, and several young officers he selected for his headquarters' staff were effeminate. But he kept up the hetero image.

While Napoleon's army straddled many countries in the early nineteenth century, Napoleon straddled many mistresses in Vienna, Warsaw, Madrid,

Geneva and Rome, frequently provided by sycophantic local politicians. Back home, yet another mistress brought him serious embarrassment – illustrations in an erotic book on sale in Paris identified his current consort Marguerite Weymer graphically performing with her lesbian lover. In between fornicating and fighting, Napoleon found time to write to many of his luscious companions and his love letters would make frequent promises like, "I kiss your lips, I kiss your breasts and lower down, much lower down, I kiss the little black forest…"

The Emperor's desperate quest to father a family – as much to refute his wife's charges as to produce an heir – may have prospered with one of Josephine's palace attendants Eleonore Denuelle, but the beautiful young lady-in-waiting could not be certain. He finally succeeded with Countess Marie Walewska, a "gift" from the Polish Government who needed France as an ally. On their first night together Napoleon became wildly aggressive and the nervous nineteen-year-old virgin fainted. Undeterred, the good general raped her but when she regained consciousness, Marie forgave him.

Later that year in 1809, the young countess gave him a son and the excuse he needed to annul the marriage to Josephine. Another son followed but born out of wedlock, neither was legally acceptable. A second Marie was introduced to his bedchamber, another teenage virgin. Political necessity forced him to the altar this time and within a year Empress Marie Louise presented him with Francois-Charles-Joseph. He assumed the honorary title of Napoleon the Second without ruling any country, and died aged only twenty-one. His son's arrival however, came just in time and the spurned Josephine may have had the last laugh. In 1811 Napoleon was officially and medically diagnosed as impotent.

Pauline

While Napoleon Bonaparte and Josephine achieved considerable acclaim with their love lives, neither were in quite the same class as Pauline Bonaparte, a favourite sister and one of his parents' thirteen children. Her fortunes followed her illustrious brother's, and she was a member of his household in Paris when her love life took off at the age of fifteen. She was only too anxious to surrender her virginity and caught the eye of forty-year-old Louis Freron, a member of the revolutionary government who gave her a taste of what she would soon adore. A classical beauty, modelling for artists and sculptors, Pauline Bonaparte became an unremitting nymphomaniac.

At the end of the eighteenth century she was firmly in the limelight of Parisian society. Pauline loved to fornicate and somewhere along the way found a partner who was extremely well endowed. From then on, only men strong on stamina and long on equipment could satisfy her. Napoleon intervened and, before the young woman reached twenty-three, had twice married her off, the second time to Count Camillo Borghese in Rome. Like his brother-in-law, the count was similarly poorly provisioned and now a Princess, Pauline declared, "I am wedded to a wealthy eunuch." Camillo's riches allowed her to wallow in luxury. Her carriage was drawn by six white horses, her wardrobes were filled with four hundred gowns, and she bathed daily in ten gallons of milk.

Her nymphomania was intense and returning to Paris she bedded a tall, muscular painter. Louis Philippe Forbin was massive, a better lover than an artist, and Pauline made him her Royal Chamberlain. Her word was his command and they copulated continuously. When she subsequently collapsed doctors diagnosed "acute vaginal distress", brought about by undue friction, and caused by her mating with Monsieur Forbin. The artist succumbed to pressure from the emperor's palace and enlisted in the army but Pauline was voracious and, recovering her health, she took off on a fifteen year long series of wild and passionate affairs. In Nice musician Felix Bhagini was hired to conduct her private orchestra, it had but one instrument. Rejoining her brother, she manoevred the more masculine members of his general staff into defenceless positions.

She collapsed again suffering from "inflammation of the uterus," her physician reported, "caused by the constant and habitual excitation of that organ." That was a recurring condition for the rest of her life. She was only forty-four when she died, officially from cancer, but doctors noted excessive sexual intercourse had again weakened her general state of health.

Louis Napoleon

Napoleon the First, who died in exile in 1821, was the better soldier. His nephew Louis Napoleon was the better politician, and unarguably the better swordsman. Two failed attempts to seize power in Paris eventually led him to the throne in 1848, and both before and after, he fathered an unaccountable number of children. He drew his genes and passions from his mother Hortense, the Queen of Holland, whose own affairs and infidelities had shamed society in the Hague. After his second failed coup, Louis Napoleon spent six years in a fortress in France where he successfully argued to be allowed conjugal visits. The military governor was not taking any chances and called for volunteers among the staff. Up stepped young laundress Alexandrine Vergeot who, on lying down, assumed the new job-description of "Bedmaker to State Prisoner No 1," and bore him two sons.

He was not ungrateful and when he assumed power arranged a pension for Alexandrine. At the same time he bestowed five million francs and the title Comtesse de Beauregard on a woman he lived with in exile after fleeing from prison. Elizabeth Howard was a beautiful English woman who was happy to hide the escapee in her London home, providing him with a far more acceptable form of incarceration until he was recalled to Paris. Five years later, in 1853, he selected an aristocratic young Spaniard to be his empress, Eugenie de Montijo, who quickly produced a son and heir and then banned him from her Royal chambers. Naturally the man continued with his affairs and like his uncle before him, Louis-Napoleon found foreign governments eager to grant him the favours of their womenfolk.

Closer to home he occasionally had to behave with more discretion, especially when he got lucky with the wife of his foreign minister. The politician was unaware of the liaison but the Empress Eugenie knew all about the affair. Angry and embarrassed by her husband's well-known forays she had set it up, for the minister's wife was a reliable friend. But when he spent some time at the chateau of another minister, a young lusty, busty countrywoman, Marguerite Bellanger, caught his eye. She was on the household staff and came to his rooms one night and the sixty-year-old emperor decided she should be re-deployed to Paris.

This time the Empress Eugenie stepped in, for seeing Marguerite for the first time she feared for her husband's stamina. Sexual exertions with this young lady might kill him she decided, and sent the girl away, possibly with his grateful collusion. The last Bonaparte provided his country with two decades of prosperity but failed when he took to the battlefield again in 1871. Losing the Franco-Prussian war, he was removed and the Third Republic was proclaimed. Exiled again in England, he died eighteen months later aged sixty-four.

Good Queen Bess

If you play slap-and-tickle with a teenage princess, watch out for your head when she becomes Queen. Lord Thomas Seymour, old enough to be her father, did the one but forgot the other when he romped in the bedroom with fourteen year old Elizabeth, daughter of the reigning king. Once on the throne, she had him beheaded when she discovered he was making plans to marry her and take over the palace. Queen Elizabeth I, whose sex life – or rather, the lack of it – was the number one topic of conversation in castles and palaces all through Europe, was a bad woman to trifle with. Not for nothing is she still considered one of England's greatest monarchs. Who will she marry was the hot question for two or three decades, but she died at sixty-nine as an old maid. Her other title was the Virgin Queen, and four hundred years of expert analysis have yet to fathom the absolute truth of that.

Amost certainly the queen had a medical condition which initially would have made sex very painful and very difficult. Her physician Dr Huick wrote of a "womanish infirmity" likely to make penetration impossible, while her principal advisor, the lawyer Lord Burghley, consulted a variety of doctors called to the palace and declared that Elizabeth was no different to many other young women and marital intercourse would cure all her problems. More modern speculation holds that she suffered a congenital defect, an exceptionally small vagina with a uterus which did not develop during puberty. A medical report from Sir James Neville has been unearthed, written when she was twenty-six and a year after she was crowned, revealing the queen had very irregular monthly cycles and, as a consequence, was showing signs of anaemia.

> ### VIRGIN STATE
>
> Sir Walter Raleigh, adventurer and Captain of the Queen's Guard, was a firm favourite of Elizabeth's. He may have been hinting at her sexual condition when he proclaimed one of America's original thirteen states should be named for her... Virginia !

That may be, but her tempers and tantrums and the treatment of some of the men in her life – Lord Seymour was not an isolated case – need some explanation. Elizabeth was an outrageous tease and as queen, one who could turn nasty. Having seen her own mother Anne Boleyn and her step-mother Catherine Howard beheaded at the direction of her father, following in his footsteps was easy. Men and women went to the executioner's block at her command.

She drew to the court, in various positions of authority, handome young studs from some of England's oldest and richest families and flirted with them publicly, encouraging their flattery and their natural reactions. It was important for her to know she could at least arouse men and had she not been queen, the young woman would probably have suffered a dozen attempted rapes. Foreplay for her, especially in the absence of any after-play, consisted of a projected exchange of words with perhaps the odd touch or stroke, and invariably had an audience.

> **THINKING OF ENGLAND**
>
> It would be a subsequent and equally influential monarch, Queen Victoria, who during her reign three hundred years later, would profess to "lie back and think of England," although this is probably unfairly attributed to her. Victoria's diaries were so intimate that her daughter had them burned after she died, to ensure they were never read in public.

Lord Robert Dudley proved he was one man who could play the game with Elizabeth but he had the benefit of being married, which should have gotten around any suspicion. Her ladies-in-waiting were surprised at his boldness and were frequently dismissed at his arrival. No apartment was too private for his meetings with the Queen, even her bedchamber. From time to time, rumours persisted in London and abroad that he had fathered "yet another bastard child by the Queen," and foreign ambassadors were continually requested by their governments and rulers at home, for news and information of the Queen's condition, but could the evidence of pregnancy and childbirth have been so easily concealed? There were other problems to surmount, too.

Divorce was not easy but had become almost the done-thing around the palace after Henry VIII showed the way. It was anticipated Lord Dudley would split from his wife and and would subsequently marry the Queen. But his wife Amy died suddenly and it looked a trifle too convenient to the public eye. Elizabeth valued her popularity and dared not proceed with Robert, her court favourite. Their affair or friendship lasted the best part of thirty years and whatever the rumours, she swore, "As God is my witness, nothing improper ever passed between us." When Dudley died, the Queen was inconsolable for weeks. She kept his last letter under her pillow for fifteen years, until she herself died.

Over the years, several European kings and princes viewed marriage to Elizabeth as ideal to ensure political union with a country growing in commercial and military influence. Perhaps they knew nothing of her small vagina – if they hoped for marital bliss they should have been grateful for her rejections. King Philip of Spain and Portugal had been married to her older sister Mary and he became a suitor, and King Charles of France followed him. There were archdukes from Germany, princes from Denmark, lesser noblemen from Sweden, France and the Netherlands, all with traces of royal blood, and all interested. At least, they sent emissaries to woo the Queen on their behalf, promising a personal follow-up if there was any response. However, they were all Catholics. The Queen was an avowed Protestant, and could easily turn them down without offence.

She kept their alliance and their country's trade and usually their friendship, though she was forced to send her navy to overcome the Spanish Armada when Philip turned nasty. Only the lady, herself struggling to maintain her looks with wigs and cosmetics and veils, will know the truth of her unofficial title, her physical and medical condition, and the genuine reasons why she remained unmarried and without any heirs. On her deathbed, she vowed James VI of Scotland should also take the English throne.

Benjamin Disraeli and William Gladstone

When politicians fall by the sexual wayside, it is usually because they are revealed as homosexuals with a particularly murky skeleton in the closet, or they are exposed as being wantonly unfaithful to an unknowing wife and electorate. Two of Britain's prime ministers in the last century, Benjamin Disraeli and William Gladstone, by no means conformed to this pattern. The first was an outrageous womanizer and did not bother to hide the fact, while the latter was more intent on saving than having women, and appeared very straight-laced. He was speechless when, after commenting that his political opponent "would probably die by the hangman's noose or a vile disease," the flamboyant Disraeli replied, "Sir, that depends upon whether I embrace your principles or your mistress."

The Liberal Party's William Ewart Gladstone had absolutely no experience of women until he was married at the age of twenty-nine, and within weeks his wife Catherine was pregnant. During the next fifteen years she was usually either pregnant or recovering from childbirth, and they had four sons and four daughters, remaining happily married for fifty-nine years. Away from home his pursuit of women was bizarre. When he went visiting among London's street-corner prostitutes it was to save them, not to offer them VIP business, and this charitable work brought him as much fame – and derision – as his high-profile political activities.

> **PAIN & PLEASURE**
>
> Among the entries in his diaries, Gladstone admitted he was a self-flagellant and posed the question, "Has it been sufficiently considered how far pain may become a ground for enjoyment?" While he was up at Oxford he was befriended by Richard Monckton-Milnes, a rich Conservative MP who was proud of his vast pornographic library, where young William spent hours fascinated by the collection of erotica.

In the second-half of the last century, he would walk around the dinghy streets of Soho, dimly lit by spluttering gas lamps at night and wait to be accosted, then spend hours talking to the woman, trying to reform her, beseeching her to leave this life, urging her to enter a home for reformed ladies of the night that he had founded. Women who had received and ignored his lectures would ignore him, and often avoid him. This was Queen Victoria's England and the morals of one of her premier statesmen were to all intents and purposes above reproach, but they were regarded with great suspicion by his colleages at Westminster and by the public at large.

They were probably right. After his death, biographers noted the number of hours he spent at the side of these young women, often at their own rooms, and suspected this may have been a form of voyeurism. They discovered he liked to read pornography, and they learned he loved flagellation. Throughout his life Gladstone maintained – even to his sons – his faithfullness to his wife Catherine, their mother, but always insisted on a strange form of words: "I have never been guilty of the act known as infidelity of the marriage bed." That covered intercourse, but still gave him plenty of scope, allowing for any number of sexual acts with another woman, short of penetration, which would not endear him to even the most understanding wife.

KEEPING IT IN THE FAMILY

Two years after his wife died, and just returned to Parliament for a second term as prime minister, Disraeli unaccountably fell for Lady Bradford, a faithfully and happily married grandmother. She ignored his pursuit and pleas that they should go to bed and in a bizarre twist, aimed at remaining close to this object of his desires, the man proposed marriage to Lady Chesterfield, her sister-in-law, who also turned him down.

His father was a wealthy Liverpool merchant who made the bulk of his fortune from the West Indian slave trade, and young William set his early sights on entering the church. Father decreed he should go to Oxford, and it was there, in the lovely old university city, that he began his work redeeming women who had chosen the oldest career in the world. His own career was set out by the family, study law and from there go into politics, which he did with resounding success, serving four terms as the prime minister – twice succeeding Disraeli – until he retired at the age of eighty-four. But William Gladstone, fervently religious and outwardly a great moralist, was seen as one of history's truly "dirty old men."

Benjamin Disraeli, on the other hand, made no secret of what he wanted from the women in his life – their bodies. A writer turned politician, his reputation in London through the years of his twenties cost him four election campaigns. He wore atrociously-coloured waistcoats, velvet trousers and lace-trimmed shirts, looking more like a dandy than a randy ladies' man, but he talked endlessly to women, listened to women, flattered them and portrayed quite a few in his books. He was only twenty-one when the older Mrs Sarah Austen fell in love with him, persuaded her husband to loan Benjamin enough money while he wrote a novel *Vivian Grey*, then laboriously rewrote his illegible manuscript in her own copperplate handwriting to present to a publisher.

Doctor's wife and dilettante Mrs Clara Bolton attracted his attention and provided several contacts in the literary and political world, and an entry to a unique sexual merry-go-round. The aspiring politician met Lady Henrietta Sykes, mother of four and more of a sexual athlete than even Disraeli. In fact, knowing his true ambition, she lay in wait for him at one of Clara's parties. Her husband Francis was away – regularly as it turned out – game-shooting in Yorkshire, and for the next four years the young man's elections vied with his erections, and where he failed miserably with the one, he was extremely successful with the other. Sir Francis became suspicious, then got caught with his own pants down, with none other than Clara, his wife's lover's former mistress. Blind eyes were turned, both affairs continued and Disraeli moved in with Lady Henrietta for a time, but she was too much. He was a man who needed his sleep and with Henrietta too often by his side, Benjamin's health began to fail.

At last he entered Parliament, and there came an opportunity to kill two birds with one stone. Lord Lyndhurst, a senior member of the Conservative Party, agreed to sponsor the young man's political career. In return his lordship, sought an introduction to Lady Henrietta leaving the new MP free to pursue pastures new. We know the noble lord kept his side of the bargain – Disraeli went on to become his country's premier – so we must assume Henrietta fulfilled the other side. Benjamin wed a widow twelve years older who inherited a fortune, paid his debts and organized his career so successfully he founded what we see today as Britain's Conservative Party. He had kept an eye for the women right up until his death at the age of seventy-six.

Maria Luisa and Mongkut

If birth control had been available a couple of hundred years ago, one hesitates to think of how royalty, the nobility and many of the world's upright leaders would have behaved when horizontal. They were bad enough without the comfort of avoiding pregnancy each and every time they copulated, though we must assume medical practitioners had enough knowledge and common sense to realize there were safer periods in a woman's life cycle. But whether that influenced these sexual athletes is open to doubt. If proof were required, we need look no further than Maria Luisa, the Queen of Spain who ravaged rather than screwed her men, and Mongkut, the King of Siam who had 3,000 concubines in his Bangkok harem.

No bluer blood flowed anywhere in Europe, or the rest of the world, than in the veins of Maria Luisa, who was married in 1765 at the age of fourteen to her cousin Charles, direct heir to the throne in Madrid. She was a member of the Royal Bourbon family by birth and marriage. Her mother was the eldest daughter of King Louis the Fifteenth of France, while King Charles the Third of Spain was both her uncle and father-in-law. None of this stopped the lady behaving badly. The Catholic morality of Spain could not contain her insatiable appetite for sex, and her only acknowledgment to public esteem was to build a separate back-staircase to her private palatial apartments. Like many others in a similar position, the pretty Princess Maria drew her long line of lovers from the ranks of the Royal bodyguards, though anything in breeches was fair game for this lusty lass.

MARIA'S MOLARS

• • • • • • • • • • • • • • • • • •

Habitual sexual exercise is not necessarily detrimental to general health, and it seemed to do Queen Maria Luisa a power of good. Continual pregnancy is another matter. Babies draw heavily on mother's Vitamin C, and gingivitis was, in those days, a natural result. By the age of thirty-seven, as she acceeded to the throne with her husband Charles IV, and with a dozen childbirths and several miscarriages behind her, the otherwise attractive and still very active Spanish Queen was toothless and forced to rely on false replacements.

• • • • • • • • • • • • • • • • • •

The grandees at the Court of Madrid soon realized what they were missing. There was the Duke of Abrantes and the Count of Teba, then Don Juan Pignatelli, a brilliant horseman who all came to call during the day, but the military enthusiasts had a clear field of fire at night and willingly climbed the steps of the secret staircase. The old king knew what was going on and limited Maria's activities, banishing her better-known escorts to foreign diplomatic posts and a few into exile. When he died in 1788, the princess now elevated to queen stood on her sexual accelerator, for she realized her peak had arrived and might not last long.

There were two brothers among her guardsman. Phillipe was good but Manuel de Godoy, sixteen years younger than herself, was much better and she moved him upstairs to be her personal assistant and chief adviser. Her husband was sounded out about his wife's lifestyle and commented, "If a queen feels tempted to sin and disobey the commandments, where would she find the kings or emperors to sin with?" The thought that any man without a title but with the necessary equipment could be a sinful substitute never occurred to Charles IV.

Manuel de Godoy was forced to serve a hectic four years beside and above Queen Maria Luisa to prepare him for a different position, that of Prime Minister. What dismayed people about him was not so much his lack of practice in high office, but the amount of time he would spend in it. The French ambassador wrote home to Napoleon, who was eyeing Spain for a likely takeover, "imagine a young man without any previous political experience being appointed to this most important ministry; a man for whom the Queen's love demands leave little time to devote to government affairs." Even worse, the Queen was not alone in making these love demands on Premier Godoy, who did nothing to dissuade any callers. Maria Luisa continued to put herself about as well, with advisers and visitors, with her guardsmen, and possibly even the king.

However, when push came to shove – in this case when Napoleon started his military campaign, captured the country and sent her into exile in Italy – she went with husband and lover, King Charles and Manuel. This happy *ménage-a-trois*, accompanied by several children – at least two of whom were Godoy's – soon became a *ménage-a-quatre* when the premier's regular mistress Pepita Tudo joined them with two more of Manuel's children. There they all lived, happily or otherwise, until Maria died in 1819, aged sixty seven, and the King followed her a month later.

Man may do much for his brothers, but to live in a monastery and endure celibacy for nearly twenty-seven years with a wife and two children at home was a selfless task for Mongkut, the man who inspired the smash-hit musical *The King and I*. When he left home to become a Bhuddist monk in 1825, the twenty year old prince was following a path many had trod before. The mystical traditions of the East demanded that the men destined to assume the throne of the country we now call Thailand needed time as a recluse to ponder their future responsibilities – but only a short time. Soon after the doors of the monastery closed behind Mongkut however, his father died and his older half-brother seized an the throne. To avoid family squabbles and any political argument, the rightful heir chose to stay put until the issue over the Royal ascendancy was decided. He waited a long time, until 1851, when his brother died and Mongkut left his monk's cell finally to become king.

> ## TRUNK ROADS
> • • • • • • • • • • • • • • • • •
> Mongkut proved to be a brilliant statesman, preserving his coutry's independence from European colonization, creating a buffer state between French Indo-China and the British Empire's Malaya and Burma. He was in regular correspondence with western leaders, but knew nothing of their countries – he offered to send elephants to President James Buchanan when he was told America was badly in need of development.
> • • • • • • • • • • • • • • • • •

The other side of the traditional scale in Siam, or Thailand, provides the Monarch with the biggest harem in the world. The Inner Palace in Bangkok had 3,000 shapely inmates when little brother arrived in April. Mongkut the Monk became King Phra Chom Klao, and he also went for the title King of Copulation as he set about making up for lost time. By August he had thirty wives. Children started appearing the following year, as they would throughout his seventeen-year reign.

No other men were allowed to enter the palace except for the occasional monk or priest – they were never a danger to matrimonial harmony – or a doctor. Even then, these male interlopers were accompanied by ladies of the Palace Guard. The King rapidly restored the old custom of entertaining ladies of the palace for two hours at midday; any other activity was considered overtime, and there were plenty of volunteers. Into his fifties and slowing down, the king decreed any of his concubines who so wished would be allowed to return to their parental homes or marry other men outside the palace. Only the mothers of his children would be obliged to stay. When he died a few days before his sixty-fourth birthday, Mongkut had sired eighty-two children at the palace plus the two he fathered in his twenties, and sixty-six of those, including a pair of babes-in-arms, survived him.

Eva Peron

The lady had much in common with her countrywomen. She knew what it was to be a peasant, to be dirt poor, barely able to read or write, hungry and prepared to earn a living any way she could and, like one in every four born in Argentina in the first quarter of the century, Maria Eva Duarte de Ibarguren was illegitimate. However her personality, her determination and her good looks were all put to good use and twenty five years after her death she was immortalized in the stage musical Evita. A child-prostitute at fourteen, she became a radio then a film actress and by the time she reached twenty-five, Eva Peron was married to her country's future president and dictator. She had put the arduous years of her start in life behind her and was now one of the most powerful figures in South America. Eva was a woman, and she had used a woman's ways to get there.

She was a blonde with sexy dark eyes and a slightly blown figure, giving her an extraordinary come-hither look. At fourteen she slept with singer Jose Armani in return for a lift to Buenos Aires, and fifteen when she met Colonel Juan Domingo Peron, recently widowed and lonely. The year was 1934 and exactly how they met has never become clear. Eva was attractive enough not to be forced on the streets but she was certainly a paid prostitute in Buenos Aires at the time.

ARI & EVA

• • • • • • • • • • • • • • • • • •

A year after she became the First Lady in Argentina, Eva Peron visited Europe, and the Greek shipping millionaire Aristotle Onassis did his diplomatic best to get an invite to a formal reception. He made another slightly less diplomatic but nonetheless successful approach, and was invited to her private holiday villa on the Italian Riviera. He was there for three hours and made love to Eva, who cooked lunch, and then Onassis gave the lady a cheque for $10,000 for her "favourite charity". Unabashed, she took the cheque and cashed it. Whether the charity benefited is not known, but the lady reportedly had healthy bank accounts in Switzerland.

• • • • • • • • • • • • • • • • • •

Years later, as champion of the poor, she tried to legalize the city's red light district and contain the women's activities inside that zone, to no avail. Many stories have surfaced since then – that she posed many times for pornographic pictures with men and with women, she was a live-in mistress to several wealthy men before Peron, and like Marilyn Monroe, had the reputation of being "good on her knees."

A rich publisher Emilio Karstulovic, set her up first, then theatre owner Rafael Firtuso took over and he not only kept her in small change, he put Eva on stage and changed her life forever. But she always found time for the army officer and the original loveless liaison began to change as her career moved up-market and he was promoted to the highest rank in the army. Eva had reached twenty-four when she went to live with him and two years later they wed. He was then a leading figure in an army coup and its success left him as Vice President of Argentina and Minister of War.

The following year, in June 1946, fifty-year-old General Peron was elected president and admitted "Eva is my constant advisor and inspiration." She was more than that, as she became sex procuress for him and for other officers in the Argentine Army and Navy, setting-up the Union for Secondary School Students, a flimsy disguise for a supply line of lissom and buxom – depending on preference – uniformed, young schoolgirls who gained better marks for their homework than they did in the classroom. It was supposedly bisexual, a voluntary union to provide political education for teenagers, but it was nothing of the sort.

MONSTROUS WHORE

The president's wife had a sense of humour and told this story against herself. The Italian Naval attache was by her side when a crowd recognized Eva and started jeering and cat-calling. "Do you hear, they're calling me a whore, that's monstrous," she said. "I know what you mean," replied the attaché, "I haven't been to sea for fifteen years yet people insist on calling me admiral."

There were branches all over the country and a very high percentage of members were pretty, willing girls. They had no formal training but were tested locally and if they showed any natural appreciation and ability for libidinous exercise, were sent to centralized "recreation centres" frequented by young officers attending lectures. Precious few political or military lecturers were on staff. There were plenty of nurses and doctors though, to take care of pregnancies and make sure the girls were clean. These government-sponsored centres were nothing more and nothing less than luxurious, high-class knocking shops, populated by keen amateurs.

Eva Peron was enigmatic and was virtually the country's Minister of Health and Labour at this time. Knowing her husband was off at his special apartment in the main recreation centre just outside Buenos Aires, the woman entertained at home and, developing her role abroad as Argentina's ambassador-at-large, Eva arranged her own clandestine meetings. However, her close aides believed her interest was in the power provided by sex rather than the sport itself. At home she was acting unpaid head of the trade union movement and while her husband's regime was sullied by graft and corruption on a grand scale, she made sure a bundle of money went on Argentina's welfare movement. She was loved and revered as a darling of the poor people, especially the women. Eva was probably sincere but it seemed very cynical, given her own immorality, that she introduced compulsory religious education into all Argentinian schools.

In 1951 when doctors told Eva she had terminal cancer, she persuaded the Peronista Party to nominate her for vice president but the army, whose officers she had served so well, forced her to withdraw. The following year, aged only thirty-four, she died of cancer of the uterus and the country went into national mourning. Three years later her husband was defeated in another coup and thrown into exile in Madrid, where he stayed until 1973. The Peronistas, back in power, recalled Peron as president and ironically, made his third wife Maria Estela their vice president this time. He died eight months later.

King Charles II

The Merry Monarch was the nickname his people gave their king, somewhat mild considering his antics outside the royal palaces. From the moment he returned from exile in 1660, the thirty year old King Charles the Second never went short, and he never went prepared either. As the Duke of Buckingham, himself more sinner than saint, aptly described the situation, "The king is supposed to be the father to his people. This king is certainly father to a good many of them." There are any number of earls, dukes, barons and various honourables who today can trace their lineage back to an ancestral grandmother who dallied with the randy King. He had legions of illegitimate children.

A governess, Mrs Eleanor Wyndham, is said to have seduced the prince when he was fifteen. A year later Civil War broke out in England, and at his father's insistence he fled into exile. Three years later, the king was beheaded. Those years roving around Europe did little to prepare him for the throne but a lot to ready him for life as a playboy – shooting, horse-racing, hunting, fishing and fornicating. He came home to a hero's welcome and a splendid coronation in 1660, and though he proved a fine statesman, the fast lane always beckoned. The bachelor king set about sewing his wild oats, along with brother James the Duke of York. Lucy Walters bore his children and he gave the eldest the title Duke of Monmouth.

> **THREE TIMES CHARLIE**
>
> • • • • • • • • • • • • • • • • •
>
> When Nell Gwynne became his mistress, she called him Charles III. "Because I have already had two lovers named Charles before you came along," she told him.
>
> • • • • • • • • • • • • • • • • •

The stunning and voluptuous Barbara Palmer, née Villiers, saw the monarch as a personal challenge. Where he had a healthy appetite, she was ravenous, and they indulged in some style. Children began to arrive looking nothing like Mr Palmer, so to keep her husband quiet the king made him Earl of Castlemayne.

Bad Barbara remained a favourite for some years and was good enough in bed to earn her own title, later advancing to Duchess of Cleveland. The diarist Samuel Pepys was moved to record, "My Lady Castlemayne rules him, who hath all the tricks of Aretin that are to be practised to give pleasure; in which he is too able, having a large prick." Parliament was dismayed and pressured the king to accept a wife, and King Louis XVI in France became matchmaker. Marriage to Caterina de Braganza, sister of the King of Portugal, was a shrewd political move.

They had never met, but she came with a huge dowry and seven days later they wed. Portugal promised £500,000, their settlements at Tangier in Morocco and Bombay in India, plus free trade with all their colonies. Caterina was well informed. She struck out the first name on a list of suggestions for the post of Lady of the Queen's Bedchamber. That was Lady Castlemayne but as it turned out, the marriage was a useful smokescreen for his wooing and screwing. Barbara moved into the court and over the years produced a small regiment of bastards. Ironically, the Queen appeared to be the one woman in his life who could not bear children and no rightful heir was ever produced.

He was strong and handsome, always charming, and as Pepys confirmed, reputed to be particularly well endowed with amazing nocturnal stamina. News of his barren wife was not slow to permeate through London and this only served to make the man even more attractive to titled and ambitious ladies. When coupling with the king, they did not mind becoming pregnant as they entertained the hope he might recognize their child as a descendant, might even suggest divorce and marriage. Not so long ago, Henry VIII had been through six wives in the quest for a son and heir, but Charles was content with granting a cash bequest or a pension, and a title for the offspring.

Parliament turned up the pressure again, palace aides advised temperance and the king turned on them. "How dare you level the mistresses of kings and princes with other lewd women? They ought to be looked on as above other men's wives." Around the court he was given the title "Old Rowley," the name of a great racehorse with a giant leap in steeplechase races, who became a famous stallion when he went to stud. He was angry when another mistress married and achieved the title Duchess of Richmond without his help, but the nobility

> **ROYAL EPITAPH**
>
> ● ● ● ● ● ● ● ● ● ● ● ● ● ● ● ● ●
>
> After the king, John Wilmot, the second Earl of Rochester, was probably the leading debaucher in court circles. He was a brilliant satirist and witty poet, forever in and out of royal favour, and before Charles died suggested this epitaph:
>
> Here lies a great and mighty king
> Whose promise none relies on;
> He never said a foolish thing,
> Nor ever did a wise one.
>
> The king replied, "This is very true; for the words are my own, and my actions are my ministers'."
>
> ● ● ● ● ● ● ● ● ● ● ● ● ● ● ● ● ●

was not the only source of pleasure. The London stage attracted the profligate monarch. Catherine Pegge and Moll Davies, it was claimed, had as many as a dozen children between them, all sired by the king.

In his forties he contented himself with only two permanent mistresses, one from either camp. The risqué actress Nell Gwynn represented the commoners, the elegant Louise de Keroualle the aristocracy, and they were the two main competitors for royal favours at this time. There were other women who remained casual consorts and he continued to excuse such behaviour saying, "I cannot think God would make a man miserable for taking a little pleasure on the way." There was no title for Pretty Witty Nell but he made their first son the Duke of St Albans, while Louise was rewarded as Duchess of Portsmouth.

King Charles loved the theatre and dramatists were urged to write playlets to be acted at court by the courtiers themselves, including the monarch. And if these included sexy scenes, so much the better. Parts were written in for youths to be played by young maidens, for the king liked to see the shape of a well-turned calf, a strong thigh or a pair of firm buttocks trapped in tight-fitting trousers instead of hiding beneath voluminous, hooped skirts and layers of petticoats. He held that sex was no sudden activity to be indulged quickly and forgotten, and he loved the foreplay to begin some hours before the ultimate coupling.

ROYAL RHYME

● ● ● ● ● ● ● ● ● ● ● ● ● ● ● ● ● ●

The Earl of Rochester's best remembered lines referring to the king are these:

Nor are his high desires above
  his strength
His sceptre and his prick are of a
  length
And she that plays with one, may
  sway the other

● ● ● ● ● ● ● ● ● ● ● ● ● ● ● ● ● ●

King Charles lived only to the age of fifty-five, and on his death-bed had two important messages for his brother James, the Duke of York, who would succeed him to the throne. "I have been an unconscionable time dying; I hope the people of England will excuse that?" and famously, "Let not poor Nelly starve." James saw to it that his brother's favourite had ample funds.

Hitler and Mussolini

Corporal Schicklgruber made rapid promotion when he turned to politics and, as Germany's Chancellor, he became the most powerful soldier and the most dangerous man in the world, declaring war on Europe in 1939. There has never been a dictator to equal the infamous Fuhrer Adolph Hitler, a military conqueror and wholesale slaughterer. Part of his historical background which is less well known concerns the strange circumstances surrounding the deaths of several women who attracted his attention. Benito Mussolini, who ruled Italy and became Hitler's ally at the outbreak of World War Two, was a poor military imitation of the Fuhrer, and took his women rapidly, on the floor, on desks and on windowsills, and rarely bothered to remove his clothes – not even his trousers.

Little is known of Hitler's love life, for the very simple reason that few women who shared his bed lived to tell the tale. His mistresses died mysteriously, in unusual fatal accidents and more often by their own hand. At least, their deaths were made to look like suicide. The early rumours that he was either impotent or a latent homosexual seem untrue, though in the 1930s at political rallies when he stiffened his arms and wrung his hands fiercely before him, opponents said he was "hiding the last unemployed member of the Third Reich." Women said he was a masochist, and known to be keen on pornography, adding to the collection with his own pencil sketches and photographs, including nudes of Eva Braun, his long term mistress and the woman who

ALL BALLS

Rumours of Adolf's fifty percent defficiency in the testicle department spread far and wide during the Second World War. British and American soldiers used to sing this ditty about Hitler and his military leaders, the head of the Luftwaffe air force, the hated S.S. chief and his propoganda master. To the tune of Colonel Bogey, it went:

Hitler.......has only got one ball
Goering's....are very, very small
Himmler's....are something similar
While poor old Goebels..has no balls..at all !

In 1945, at the fall of Berlin, Russian doctors who conducted a post mortem on the body that was believed to be Hitler's confirmed this fact.

married him hours before his death in a Berlin bunker.

Hitler's first mistress was Geli Raubal, the twenty-one-year-old daughter of his half-sister and housekeeper in Munich. He was just making a name for himself in Germany, installing the girl nearly half his age in an adjacent bedroom. Two years later, after telling student girlfriends, "My uncle is a monster, you wouldn't believe the things he makes me do," Geli shot herself with Hitler's personal weapon. This does appear to have been a genuine suicide but soon afterwards, Renate Muller, a blue-eyed and blonde-haired beauty who had just reached the top as a film actress, jumped 40 feet from her apartment in Berlin to her death. But did she jump or was she pushed? This was in 1937, and Nazi intelligence officers had discovered Renate was sharing Hitler with a Jewish lover.

INFECTED AND MAD

Two of the strongest theories used to explain Hitler's fanatical hatred of the Jews are that he was infected by a Viennese Jewish prostitute at the age of nineteen – if true, that might explain his madness in later years – and that his paternal grandmother was seduced by her Jewish employer's son. His father Alois was illegitimate.

Suzy Liptauer hanged herself after being driven home from dining with Adolph. Maria Reiter took an overdose after holidaying with him, but managed to survive. Unity Mitford adored him, one of six English sisters who all achieved fame for different reasons, and on the eve of war, shot herself in the head in Munich. Taken home, she lived like a vegetable until 1948. Above all else, Hitler's reputation was zealously guarded. Eva Braun, his last mistress, was quite different but their affair was not without fatal overtones. Eva had a very small vagina, too small for normal intercourse, and had a series of painful operations to correct this. Her gynaecologist declared the treatment successful, and days later he died in a mysterious car crash.

Eva pandered to Hitler's whims, wandering around the house, the garden and the pool in the nude. She adopted some unusual poses for his camera and some unusual positions for his pleasure. On their last day on earth she took cyanide moments before he shot himself.

Benito Mussolini, popularly known in Italy as Il Duce, spent time as a schoolteacher and a journalist before he became a political activist and then the first Facist dictator in Europe, preceding both Hitler in Germany and Franco in Spain. His love life began among the whores of Milan at sixteen, but he put his money away and had a wild time in his late teens with the young women in the nationalist movement and various political associations he infiltrated as a "spy". Angelica Balabanoff, thirty-five and Russian, taught him a few tricks but his premature ejaculations left her frustrated and she gave up. He seduced a cousin, several of her school friends and then as a young teacher, he laid some of his own students.

At the same time he was bedding his landlady Anita Luigia, who is believed to have given him syphillis, and a fellow teacher Ida Dalser, who bore him a son. She started using his name so to spite her, during the school holidays Benito seduced a young barmaid in his father's tavern and married the girl, named Rachele Guidi. She remained his wife and as he rose in power she chose to ignore the outside affairs. As prime minister he frequently agreed to see women who wanted to air their grievances personally, and at these meetings both knew full well how each side could be satisfied.

These couplings in his office provided Il Duce with his wham-bam reputation, as the corpulent dictator un-zipped and, depending on the lady's size and disposition, took them sitting or standing or occasionally, lying down. The business was all over before these ladies could complain of their discomfort. In his political prime as well as his wife, Benito had two long-lasting mistresses, French writer Magda Fontange and the young and luscious raven-haired Clara Petacci. She was assassinated with him in 1945 after a ten minute trial in a village near Lake Como, by Italian communist partisans. That was ten days before the end of World War Two.

UPSIDE DOWN

Mussolini's last mistress Clara Petacci, despised by the Italian peasantry, chose to die and is reputed to have thrown herself in front of his body when the first shots were fired by the execution squad. Their bodies were taken to Milan and hung upside down in the Piazzale Loreto, where the ladies of the street regularly touted for business – the spot where Benito's love life had begun forty-six years earlier.

Cleopatra

She may have been the first "femme fatale" in history, though going back to pre-Christian times it becomes difficult to separate fact from fable. Any woman who was not particularly good looking yet was able to seduce both Julius Caesar and Mark Anthony, even if she was the Queen of Egypt, must have had something going for her. Cleopatra was enough of a get up and goer to be immortalized by William Shakespeare, and to require that the lovely Elizabeth Taylor take the eponymous role when, two thousand years later, the lavish film production of her life story came along. Her love affairs cost thousands of men their lives and caused two years of battles between Roman legions and Egyptian forces.

The Greeks had a name for her, *Meriochane* – "she who gapes wide for ten thousand men" – which may have been something of an exaggeration, but Cleopatra was said to have fellated one hundred Roman noblemen at a famous orgy one night, and her promiscuity on her knees, among the tribunes at court and her lovers in her palace, was reputedly renowned throughout the Middle East. For weeks on end she arranged nightly orgies to entertain the leaders in Rome and she was not above taking a full part and enjoying herself as well. Rome would not see anything like it for fifteen hundred years, until the Borgias came to town.

GREEK GODDESS

• • • • • • • • • • • • • • • • • •

Cleopatra is regarded conventionally as Egyptian, but her looks are European. She was really a Greek from Macedonia. Her family dynasty had ruled from Cairo since Alexander the Great had swept through Asia three hundred years earlier. She studied the Greek Goddesses and their ways of love before adding a few of her own refinements.

• • • • • • • • • • • • • • • • • •

Cleopatra was born in 69 BC, and became ruler of Egypt at eighteen. Tradition decreed she should marry her younger brothers Ptolemy XIII and XIV – the first one died young – because she needed a male consort to reign as queen, though consummation was not necessarily a requirement. When a power struggle ensued involving her sisters as well, Cleopatra left them to it and presented herself to Julius Caesar, who was resting beside the Mediterranean at Alexandria. She had heard all about the Roman dictator. He was a dedicated ladies' man o she fluttered her eye-lashes, lifted her skirt and after he ascertained the lady was for real, he took his legions down the road to Cairo and re-installed Cleopatra on the throne.

Caesar was already married but that didn't matter in Egypt, and a local ceremony was performed to legally unite the couple and give their son Caesarion legitimacy. Ceaser took Cleopatra home, doing as thousands more have done ever since and setting up the lady in an apartment near his palace. He did not bother to hide her from public view – in fact all of Rome was to witness her influence when he erected her statue in the Temple of Venus. Roman concern was the possibility of a part-Egyptian heir to the throne, for Caesar had no legitimate sons. But he was captivated by Cleopatra, thirty years younger, and they had four good years together, partying and orgying, until he was murdered.

The stories of her scandalous love life made Cleopatra an easy target, and she hurried home to Cairo to plot another seduction. She knew of another Roman hero regarded as heir-apparent to Caesar, one Mark Anthony, who was currently leading his troops to battle in Turkey. Cleopatra set off in a splendid barge which had, according to Shakespeare, purple sails, oars of silver and a deck of gold, and teams of a hundred oarsman powered the vessel to Tarsus. She delayed his return to Rome long enough to present him with twins. Ignoring his wife at home, Mark Anthony went back to Egypt with Cleopatra instead, and this presented a serious complication.Most of Asia and parts of Europe were under the Roman yoke, divided up between Mark Anthony and Octavian who were at the same time partners and rivals. Mark Anthony was married to Octavia, his partner's sister, and having fallen under Cleopatra's spell, neither wife nor brother-in-law were pleased. In Shakespeare's view, he was "The triple pillar of the world transform'd into a strumpet's fool."

This overlooks the fact that the lady threw extremely good parties. All of Rome was incensed that yet another of their leading lads would rather fornicate than fight, at least where Cleopatra was concerned. It took the best part of ten years, during which time another second-marriage, again for Cleopatra's convenience, was performed in Egypt, before Octavia challenged Cleopatra.

Battles broke out between the armies and lasted for two years until finally the rival fleets met on the high seas, Cleopatra by her lover's side, opposed by Octavia's lieutenant, Agrippa. She panicked and fled to the Egyptian shore, Mark Anthony foolishly followed her and the Romans won. A little propoganda then came into play. A message was rushed to Mark Anthony to say his Queen had died and having failed him, she had taken her own life. In grief, he plunged a knife into his chest only to learn that she was very much alive. Mortally wounded, Mark Anthony was taken to her and expired in Cleopatra's arms. The rest is history, as they say, and the vanquished Queen of Egypt actually did take her own life.

Louis XIV and XV

As the king and commander-in-chief, he was not so much concerned about the risk of disease to his military forces or their comfort and relaxation, when he specified a unique punishment for any prostitute found consorting with his soldiers within a five mile radius of Versailles. He had built a sumptuous home there, away from the smells of Paris, and ordered that these women should have their ears and noses cut off. Not surprisingly the soldiers went short, and while that was one way of maintaining the character of the surrounding neighbourhood, it was also a very perverse order in 1674 from the French King Louis XIV, whose own moral standards lowered the profile of the entire nation. His great-grandson who succeeded him was not much better, with such a terrific sex drive that his "official mistress", the delicious Marquise de Pompadour, felt she had to keep pace, living on an aphrodisiac diet of her own design – vanilla, truffles and celery.

Both of these kings came to the throne at the age of five and between them, ruled France for a total of 131 years, from 1643 to 1774, through countless wars, broken international treaties and internal strife. Their own lives were surrounded in splendour, they gave their names to architectural building and interior design styles, and while the nobility never had it so good, the rest of the country suffered to pay for these extravagances. When Louis XIV finished building the palace at Versailles, he filled the apartments with scores of high-born women and hosted never-ending parties attended by counts and barons and dukes who assumed the royal invitation was tantamount to a command. So did the women. Some were married, most were single, but all were willing.

WHAT A SURPRISE

Conflicting stories over the birth of a coloured baby to Queen Marie Theresa circulated in the court of the older King Louis. She is said to have been given a black dwarf by an African prince – this is in the late 1600s remember – and while the queen acknowledged the birth, she claimed she was pregnant when the dwarf surprised her and the shock caused the baby to be born black.

There was nothing surreptitious about the court he overlorded at the turn of the seventeenth century. The noblemen of France had become rebellious. He bought their co-operation in time-honoured fashion – he laid on the ladies. The men were also offered new titles, positions at court, country estates, fortunes in cash, and the ladies were not forgotten in these Royal hand-outs. The king was extremely generous with tax-payers' money. This was seduction on a grand scale.

For eighteen years he ruled under a consort until 1661, and the Cardinal Mazarin could never claim he had done a good job preparing young Louis. He was propositioned at fifteen by a young tapestry worker, who ogled the monarch and made her intentions clear by stripping off and sitting on his lap. When the cardinal found out, he introduced his pretty young niece and Marie Mancini thought she was heading for the throne, but he married another lass, Marie Therese, daughter of the King of Spain – a political necessity. Louis was not above putting the affairs of state before affairs of the heart but the new queen was plain, religious, dull and though she went through six pregnancies – only one son survived infancy – not at all sexy.

The king overcame this problem by establishing official Royal mistresses, quietly acknowledged by the queen. While that par-

> **UNDERHANDED**
>
> • • • • • • • • • • • • • • • • • •
> When he secretly wed Madam de Maintenon, a commoner previously married to the dramatist Paul Scarron, Louis XIV gave her his left hand instead of his right one. That allowed her to be his wife without becoming queen or having any claim to the inheritances or riches which usually went with the title.
> • • • • • • • • • • • • • • • • • •

ticular *Maitresse en Titre* ruled the royal bedchamber, she was forbidden territory for any other man, including her husband if she happened to be married. But a little mischief on the side, with perhaps a servant girl after lunch, was all part of the King's life at Versailles. Quite apart from his largesse, he was an excellent host, amusing and charming with an abundance of energy which he used to good effect. This is how he ruled France as an adult for more than fifty years. The cultural centre of Europe was a rollicking, frolicking, knocking-shop, and the king had countless women. Any off-spring were declared legitimate and given a title. Louis held that he was the "Visible Divinity", and could do what he liked. At times there were upwards of two hundred ladies, enthusiastic amateurs, fornicating with the noble guests, all in the loyal service of the king.

Three woman stood out among the rest through this period, the gorgeous Louise de la Valliere, and the shrewd Maquise de Montespan, both married, and the widow Francoise de Maintenon. The Maquise was around when Louis was in his prime and she relied on lucky charms and love potions to keep up with his demands. Francoise was more fortunate, coming on the scene in his declining years, and though the infidelities continued, she was still there when he died at seventy-seven.

Louis XV was nowhere near as dynamic as his great grandfather, succeeding him in 1715, but he was every bit as randy. The boy king was fifteen when his ministers married him off to twenty-three-year-old Maria Leszczynska, daughter of the former King of Poland. They were worried about his lack of sexual awareness and hung pornographic drawings in his rooms to show him the theory. But Louis had a better idea. He persuaded a married courtier, Madame de Falari, to teach him the practicals. She must have been good, for on his wedding night Louis made love to his bride seven times and the tired but grateful Maria bore him ten children in the next thirteen years, then locked the bedroom door.

> ## FORGET YOUR AGE
>
> • • • • • • • • • • • • • • • • • •
> The leading churchman in France, Cardinal Richelieu, asked Louis XV why he still kept a mistress. The Comtesse du Barry was the daughter of a monk, and as enthusiastic about sex as the king had been in his prime. "Because she makes me forget I will soon be 60," he told the cardinal.
> • • • • • • • • • • • • • • • • • •

He had enjoyed numerous affairs during her many pregnancies, so the lack of home comforts did not trouble Louis and he found splendid sexual accommodation with a succession of four Mailly-Nesle sisters. This Louis was a very laid-back monarch, king in name for almost sixty years, but the country was ruled by his ministers and they were often influenced by the current mistress. The king believed in keeping the ladies happy, in and out of bed. He was thirty-five when he met the superb Maquise de Pompadour the lady who for many years maintained her influence and horizontal attractions with her own aphrodisiac diet. She was not good enough to satisfy his virility and to save time and avoid fuss, Louis decided to invest his valet Lebel with an extra task, that of King's Pimp.

A small love-nest was established at Parc aus Cerfs, outside Versailles, where woman were kept on tap for his majesty. Many were artists' models, most were young prostitutes, and they often had no idea who was in bed with them. They knew how the nobility behaved. As he started to slow down, facing bankruptcy, he gave up the love-nest and at the age of fifty-eight Louis appointed his last mistress, the beautiful, bosomy Comtesse du Barry who was there when he died of smallpox six years later.

King Carol of Rumania

The sexual antics of Europe's royalty down through the ages were the cause of much wanton behaviour in and around the palaces. Were parents proud of their offsprings' performances, kings, and possibly queens, standing back to admire such 'chip off the old block' conduct? If so, King Carol the Second of Rumania would not have been a disappointment, running off with his country's defence budget in the face of war to be with mistress. His father, King Ferdinand, had a string of women, abdicating in order to live with a commoner before returning to the throne in time for a state wedding. His mother was marginally worse, still having the wanderlust at the age of fifty-seven. She staged a public row when her soldier lover was deliberately posted away from Bucharest.

Carol was the first of his country's rulers who was actually born in Rumania, and unlike some of his predecessors he could even speak their language. Unfortunately, he was anything but loyal to his people. As the opposing forces in the Second World War rumbled across Eastern Europe, he was unable to decide between the German Nazis, the Soviet armies or his own Iron Guards, so he grabbed the funds for the planned Rumanian Air Force, badly needed to defend his territory, and fled into exile for the second time. He had twice been married, but the woman the forty-seven year-old king took with him this time was his publically-hated mistress, Magda Lupescu.

King Carol spent his early life vacillating between the women he wanted and those who were more the royal type. He was attracted to dominant women – his mother Queen Marie set that pattern, picking out his girl-friends to maintain

> **THE NAKED KING**
>
> • • • • • • • • • • • • • • • •
>
> When he returned to Bucharest to claim the throne in 1930, the girl-friend went too. She moved into the palace and, like King Carol's other women, Magda Lupescu ruled his life. She often slapped him and remonstrated with him in public as well as in their private apartments. She was once seen chasing the naked king through palace corridors, brandishing a pistol and screaming, "I'm going to kill you."
>
> • • • • • • • • • • • • • • • •

maternal control. Encouraged by her, he used them and abused them until one of her maids, Zizi Lambrino, enticed him. They carried on a secret liaison until he asked Marie's permission to marry her. The young Crown Prince was enrolled into the army and immediately posted off to make him forget the girl. But Zizi was a knockout. She had learned a few tricks to keep Carol in tow, and he deserted his regiment to elope with her. His parents knew a few tricks as well and gave him a choice, either to face court martial for desertion or agree to an annulment. Zizi came second, but had her wicked way with the troubled prince again and in 1920 bore him a son.

Queen Marie was just as determined and the following year she selected Princess Helen, daughter of King Constantine of Greece, as an admirable match for Carol who conceded and took Helen's hand. He was willing to do anything to keep his parents quiet and after getting Helen pregnant, he returned to Zizi's side. A son Michael was born, but Carol never went near Helen again – a private agreement between them prior to the wedding – and she stayed home while the handsome prince galivanted around the European flesh-pots. Zizi also had a child to raise rather than objections, and became the bitten biter as he began a series of well-publicized affairs.

In later years Zizi was forced to sue Carol for maintenance, losing her case at home and in the French courts, so she revealed the background to palace life in Bucharest. Far from being enraged at his scandalous life, when the king and queen realized the romantic Rumanians loved their boy and were lapping up the stories of his many lady-friends, they fed the publicity machine and massaged his image. According to Zizi and, later still, a third wife's biography, Carol was not the stud in bed he was made out to be. Fairly average would be a closer description.

The Queen cunningly retained some sort of control, setting up Carol with a succession of palace aides all drawn from the military, selected and briefed by her. This went disastrously wrong in 1923, when the Navy's Captain Tautu, who had his own reputation as a playboy, took his boss to a party and introduced Carol to Magda Lupescu. She was a red-head, a Jewess and a divorcee, none of which brought the blessing of Queen Marie. Magda was also a manhunter, a strikingly attractive woman whose looks spelled sex and trouble, and she knew what would happen while first resisting the 30-year-old prince. Both king and queen recognized her as a threat to their existence and to the monarchy, and set her up with a story that if she exercised any influence over the Crown Prince, the strong anti-Semite faction in Rumania was getting ready for a wholesale slaughter of the country's large Jewish pop-

ılation. They were just a few years ahead of their time, though the reasons
vere somewhat different.

Magda was paid off and fled to France without telling her boy-friend, but
within a few months he went after her and, in 1926, renounced all claim to
he Rumanian throne. The couple settled down together in exile in Paris, a
:ity that had seen many European monarchs in a similar position grace its
»eautiful boulevardes and its nightspots. Carol and Magda did not disappoint
he Parisiens. Of course, he still had a wife back home, and the Greeks were
»y no means keen on the way she was being treated. But Princess Helen rec-
»gnized the inevitable and began a suit for divorce.

Then King Ferdinand upped and died, throwing everything into wild con-
ùsion around Bucharest. His will denied any chance for Carol, whose son by
Helen, the seven-year-old Michael, rapidly advanced from Crown Prince to
Prince Regent, ready to assume the monarchy when he came of age.
Although his love life was pretty hot-stuff, Carol mostly stayed on the
traight and narrow with his mistresses, if not his wives. Magda was there to
»ressure him once again in 1930, when a *coup d'etat* at home threw out the
uling regency and invited him back to become king. The deal was supposed
o leave Magda behind, at least for a couple of years, but within weeks he
»rought her home to Bucharest.

For ten years he wore the crown while she wore the trousers. At her bid-
ling in 1937, Carol proclaimed himself dictator but time was running out.
The politicians had allied themselves with the elite army force, the Iron
Guards, and Magda was on their death list if and when they got the chance.
n 1940 the couple grabbed the money and ran, commanding the driver of
he royal train to run a blockade on the border, preferring capture by German
roops to their own forces. They were allowed to continue the journey, across
Europe to Spain, then across the Atlantic to New York and all over South
America, and eventually to Portugal, where they were finally married in
947. They lived in permanent exile in the holiday resort of Estoril until
Carol died aged sixty in 1953 and Magda survived him until 1974.

The Princes
of Wales

Three heirs to the throne in Britain have had more in common with each other than the mere title Prince of Wales. Their love lives and infidelities, reaching well into the realms of promiscuity for the first, have continued to shock their subjects for a hundred and fifty years. Many of the women they loved and took to their beds – courtesans and actresses, debutantes and divorcees, even ladies who were married to their friends – became as well known as the princes themselves. These same friends often provided alibis and country homes where the lovers could meet in secret. The kings and queens they were destined to follow were horrified, royal advisers were ignored, but these men refused to be dominated. And the story is not over yet.

Traditionally, the next in line for the throne may bear many titles, but until he becomes king he is always, first and foremost, the Prince of Wales. Edward VII was not crowned until he was sixty, the eldest son of Queen Victoria, and has was known as Bertie. Born in 1841, the prince started life as the austere queen directed, at school, then university and the army. His fellow officers serving alongside him in Ireland, had other ideas. He was inexperienced in the ways of the world, so they made sure he had a worthwhile campaign medal when he returned to London and they carried out a military exercise without parallel. They sneaked actress Nellie Clifden into the prince's room at the barracks, then retreated while the hand-to-hand combat began and one or other was overcome.

Back home, his natural instincts were soon recognized. The queen held that his irresponsible attitude was partially the cause of his father's untimely death later that year. Bertie was the most conscientious hedonist alive in his day – at the faintest scent of entertainment in any form, he was off. If the entertainer wore a dress, so much the better. The Queen came to the conclusion that at twenty-two, it was time to find her son a bride.

Unfortunately, marrying the Danish Princess Alexandra brought little change in his life-style. He smoked big, fat cigars and preferred his meals to be multi-course affairs. In the winter when he wasn't out hunting, he was shooting on his own or a friend's country estate. He adored horse racing, particularly the classic affairs at Royal Ascot or at Epsom, where three of his horses were Derby winners. He gambled at casinos, and reasoned one didn't have to be a bachelor to go on "bachelor outings", one just left one's wife at home. So he went off with his bachelor pals for weekends and holidays to Deauville, Paris and Monte Carlo, to the spas in Bavaria, to Vienna and Venice. Life was one, big, jolly party.

Within a few weeks of the wedding in 1863, Alexandra was pregnant, and again and again, producing five children in six years. Home and away, Bertie kept himself sexually busy. In England there were always private houses he could use for his assignations, but abroad he didn't care and took his mistresses to hotels. His behaviour was outrageous and possible only because the limited media of that era could not bring itself to publish such salacious gossip. The well known actress Lillie Langtry was his first love at home for a time, and equally renowned Sarah Bernhardt was the same in Paris. By all accounts he was rated a first class lover, but with their backgrounds, both these girls could show the prince a thing or two.

> **QUICK DRESSER**
>
> • • • • • • • • • • • • • • • • • •
>
> Bertie was always properly attired and exceptionally smart. He led fashion in his day, and his name was given to a distinctive pattern, the Prince of Wales check. His married mistresses said of Bertie, "He dresses very well – and if necessary, very quickly!"
>
> • • • • • • • • • • • • • • • • • •

Police officers from the Sureté in Paris reported details of his lusty trail to their counterparts at Scotland Yard in London which were quietly fed to royal aides at Buckingham Palace. Imagine their horror when reports showed the Prince of Wales was now a regular at La Chabannais, a famous Paris brothel, where he was always escorted by a friend who settled both their accounts at the end of the evening. Bertie was virile enough to run up fairly large bills at this establishment.

It was reported he was the target for the courtesan Cora Pearl, who had herself served stark naked beneath a huge silver tureen at a private dinner party. The prince was certainly at the dinner, and just as certainly one of her lovers. Another of his courtesan conquests, though it was probably more like a surrender, was La Belle Otero, who laid just about every duke, prince, king and emperor in Europe during the years she spent on her back.

Madame Barucci wrote promising the prince a surprise when they were due to meet the following week at a Monte Carlo ball. She called herself

"The World's Greatest Whore," and lived up to the title when confronting Bertie. She allowed her gown to slide gently to the floor, revealing her naked figure. "I am sure you have more tricks than that to show," said the smiling prince but what happened later no one knows for sure. There were more actresses and dancers in Paris, including Louise Weber, leader of the can-can line-up at the Moulin Rouge. Back home again his lady friends often displayed no sign of jealousy, knowing they would gain his gratitude as they introduced him to more friends, who hitched up their skirts to curtsy, and hitched them up again somewhat higher when the formal greetings were at an end.

From time to time he went off the rails and seduced a young unmarried girl but rapidly returned to the safety of the married bed. Any married bed would do as long as it wasn't his own. The prince's preferred daily schedule was to call on the newest of his married partners while her husband was out for the afternoon, spend the evening with his current mistress and leave to meet an actress when she finished at the theatre, to stay the night with her. This was a sexual athlete at the top of his form. The Queen forbade him any diplomatic posts. She would only allow Bertie to meet and greet foreign royals and dignitaries in London.

Daisy, the Duchess of Warwick, supplanted Miss Langtry in his favours when her husband threatened to name the prince as correspondent in his forthcoming divorce suit. The man was dissuaded, and Bertie had hardly overcome that scandal when Lady Harriet Mordaunt gave birth to a blind boy and confessed to her husband, "it was the curse of God for what I have done with the Prince of Wales." In court the man she did it with, the prince himself, swore he had not been her lover. His reputation left few in doubt of the truth.

> ### ROYAL CUCKOLDER
>
> Marlborough House off Pall Mall was Bertie's home for forty years, and the young blades and fast-spending bachelors he drew around him as a young prince were known as the Marlborough House Set. They remained members as they grew older then married and many, apparently, were content to be cuckolded by the Prince of Wales if he took a fancy to their wives. The ladies were more than content to be bedded by such a notable performer, and he was soon to be their king!

Alexandra had a fair idea of the extent of his infidelities. She befriended "Jersey Lily" Langtry and the Duchess of Warwick. She knew what Bertie was like, and knew that the women posed no threat to her. But the duchess posed a real threat to the prince – she was twenty years younger and every bit as voracious as he – and Bertie had to give up his other women to keep her satisfied. When she moved on after seven years as his recognized mistress, an even younger woman took over. Mrs Alice Keppel was thirty years Bertie's junior, and for a dozen years acted the part of second wife, received by the Queen when the family were away at Windsor Castle or on the royal estates at Sandringham in Norfolk.

Mrs Keppel was the current mistress when the prince finally made it to the throne in 1901, dropping the name Albert in favour of his second name Edward. She was even invited to see him shortly before he died, less than nine years after the coronation, from bronchitis, at the age of sixty-nine. He was a rogue prince, and the British people loved him for it.

The conduct of the next amorous Prince of Wales was by no means in the same league. When he abdicated less than a year after taking the throne as Edward VIII so that he could marry the American divorcee Mrs Wallis Simpson he left an indelible mark on history. Christened Edward Albert Christian George Andrew Patrick David Windsor, he was Prince of Wales for twenty-five years, looked upon as the world's most eligible bachelor. It was still the done thing to marry royalty, but he showed little interest in the blue-blooded beauties of Europe. He was twenty-one when he fell for Lady Coke, who was thirty-three and living with Lord Coke, and she continued to do so, despite being deluged with flowers and letters from her royal admirer. No one admitted the depth of that affair, or perhaps friendship.

Towards the end of the First World War, he took shelter from German bombs and met Mrs Frieda Ward, another older and married woman – the wife of an MP, no less – and their dalliance lasted sixteen years. It overlapped with Lady Furness, whose marriage of convenience to Marmaduke, the shipping magnate, left her free to bestow her favours elsewhere. Besides, she had once been Thelma Vanderbilt, one of the fabulously wealthy, wild and beautiful American twin sisters. They had a passionate five year affair but she complained – later making her objections slightly more public – that the prince suffered permanently from premature ejaculation. On top of that, a man who might have become a relative by marriage confessed, "To put it bluntly, the man has the smallest pecker I ever saw."

He showed his continued preference for married women when Wallis Simpson came on the scene, and she was still in the throes of her second marriage when they met in 1931. His love for her caused a constitutional crisis after his coronation in 1936 and he abdicated in the same year to take the title Duke of Windsor. The entire episode was still a hot topic when he died, living in exile in Paris, aged seventy-seven with Wallis still by his side. That was in 1972.

The present Prince of Wales, the heir to Queen Elizabeth's throne, has lived an altogether different life, continually under the glare of television cameras and the scrutiny of newspapers and magazines. Prince Charles has by no means led a blameless life, wed to Diana and then divorced not for either of their admitted adulteries but due to the irretrievable breakdown of their marriage. Compared to Bertie a hundred and fifty years earlier, he is still a boy but nonetheless, he has created an extraordinary period in the annals of royalty.

The story is not over yet. It is a story as old as the hills, a story that will continue as long as men have the strength and determination to make illicit love, and as long as there are women who have the energy and desire to partner them. Few of these characters could have realized they would leave such a mark on history yet – as Prince Charles has shown with his frank and remarkable interview on television and his tacit admission of adultery to an audience of millions – that aspect has never troubled anyone, certainly not the Princes of Wales.